MJ Magazine

VOLUME I • ISSUE 1

The Magazine Created by Authors for Authors

Fran Lewis, Founder

PUBLISHED BY FIDELI PUBLISHING INC..

ISBN: 978-1-60414-762-9

Fideli Publishing Inc.
119 W. Morgan St.
Martinsville, IN 46151

www.FideliPublishing.com

TABLE OF CONTENTS

DEDICATION

To My Precious Sister Marcia:

You filled my life with meaning and joy. You were and still are the one person who understood me and helped guide us both through the good times and the bad. Your smile and unique hello lit up a room and warmed the hearts of everyone that you met. As you go on your next journey remember that you are not alone. Let the memories and fond recollections of our life together keep you strong and safe. Let there be memories that you will carry with you of all of your loved ones and let them remain near in spirit. Knowing that you will receive a tender, surprising, heartwarming and welcome to the afterworld and your spirit and love will live on for eternity. May the memories of those who loved and adored you surround you always and bring you comfort.

You are a beacon of hope and joy for our family. Whenever I get stuck I will stop, think and remember: To figure it out!

I love you now and forever

Your sister, best pal and best friend,
Frani

About My Sister Marcia Joyce

Self-acceptance means accepting yourself fully for the person that you are. True acceptance comes from accepting the things about yourself that you like and those that you don't like. It is an active process that you do consciously and is a willingness to accept emotions, feelings and experience them without denial or evasion. But that is not the only kind of acceptance.

INTRODUCTION

Fran Lewis

When companies merge into one the members of both need to work together and accept each other for the betterment of the company. When two families merge each new member must learn to understand and accept the newer members and embrace them making this new family even stronger and one.

My sister embraced everyone she met equally. It did not matter whether you were in her family or her extended one, everyone was loved the same way and treated with respect and Marcia's brand of love and caring.

Marcia learned to accept the reality of situations whether she liked them or not. She realized that a problem was a problem and never ran away from them but tried to solve them in her own special and methodical way. But, in doing so, she put the feelings and needs of others way ahead of her own. The burdens that she carried were only known to her and often masked by her smile, her sunny personality and her compassion for others.

Marcia felt that she was not really accepted for who she was by everyone. She felt that she always had to prove herself in order for people to know that she was truly a brilliant, intelligent and amazing person. Marcia: Those that did not appreciate you and cherish you for who you are missed out on a lot and it's their loss. You enriched so many lives, especially mine, your children's and your brothers with your calm, cool and even-tempered personality that always knew how to defuse problems before they got worse. You taught me when to step back and tack a deep breath. I could not fix what was wrong with you and for that I am truly sorry, but I can put the pieces of the puzzle together that still need to fit and then I will have fixed what needs to be done for you.

Our family might be missing you but your picture will always be in our frame and in our hearts.

I would like to introduce you to our inaugural issue of *MJ Real Magazine*, a publication dedicated to authors and the art of writing. We will provide information, writing tips, book reviews, author interviews and more all written by fellow authors *in their own words* to help motivate and educate authors everywhere. If there are typos or other, I please excuse them — we're new at this and want to get the information to you quickly. I hope you enjoy this issue and want to continue to read it monthly.

Since this is an e-magazine, we will make it available in all ebook formats and it will be available for $2.99 every other month from most major e-retailers, including Amazon, Barnes & Noble, Smashwords, iBook store, Sony's ebook store, Kobo.com and Diesel-ebooks.com.

I hope you enjoy reading, and we encourage comments and contributors.

Turn the page and start reading …

FEATURED AUTHORS

"The latest in Jon Land's electrifying series is another fast-paced, intensely absorbing thriller . . . Intricate, intelligent plot development and realistic characterization are Land's trademark tools and he wields them with an expertly deft hand in Strong Rain Falling."

—FreshFiction

"A superb thriller which I devoured and thought was an incredible page-turner. With Strong Rain Falling Land, a thriller author who is writing at the highest level, has outdone himself."

—Strand Magazine

"Few men can 'write' women. They're usually a parody, what a guy wants. But Caitlin Strong is a real woman; tough, present, and caring."

—Jacquelyn Mitchard, New York Times bestselling author of The Deep End of the Ocean

STRONG RAIN FALLING

Page Count: 368
ISBN: 978-0765331502
Formats: Hardcover, ebook

The buzz is already building for critically acclaimed, bestselling author Jon Land's latest book: *Strong rain Falling* (A Forge Hardcover; $25.99; August 13, 2013), a modern day thriller that is an exhilarating mix of action, adventure, and contemporary hot-button issues.

Fellow authors and literary heavyweights, including Nelson DeMille, Richard North Patterson, and Jacqueline Mitchard, have high praise for Land's talent as a writer and his ability to build tension from his opening page to his climatic last. They're also huge fans of Caitlin Strong, a fifth-generation Texas Ranger and the star of Land's adrenaline-charged series, calling her a terrific character — at once gutsy, resourceful, flawed, and vulnerable.

Land is also renowned for his ability to undertake new challenges in his writing, and has a penchant for pushing the envelope. He frequently tackles current events in his thrillers, and *Strong Rain Falling* is no exception. This time around, Land uses the very real fear of terrorists blacking out large segments of the U.S.'s power grid, and once again centers his story on Caitlin Strong who gets caught up in a terrifying plot that reaches into every home and threatens the very core of America.

Mexico, 1919: The birth of the Mexican drug trade begins with opium being smuggled across the U.S. border, igniting an all-out battle with American law enforcement in general and the Texas Rangers in particular.

The Present: Fifth-Generation Texas Ranger Caitlin Strong and her lover Cort Wesley Masters both survive terrifying gun battles. But this time, it turns out, the actual targets weren't them, but Masters' teenage sons.

That sets Caitlin and Cort Wesley off on a trail winding through the past and present with nothing less than the future of the United States hanging in the balance. Along the way, they will confront terrible truths dating all the way back to the Mexican Revolution and the dogged battle Caitlin's own grandfather and great-grandfather fought against the first generation of Mexican drug dealers.

At the heart of the storm soon to sweep away America as we know it, lies a mastermind whose abundant power is equaled only by her thirst for vengeance. Ana Callas Guajardo, the last surviving member of the family that founded the Mexican drug trade, has dedicated all of her vast resources to a plot aimed at the U.S.'s technological heart.

Sabotage proves to be as deadly a weapon as bombs in a battle Caitlin must win in cyberspace as well. Her only chance to prevail is to short-circuit a complex plan based as much on microchips as bullets. Because there's a strong rain coming and only Caitlin and Cort Wesley can stop the fall before it's too late.

Jon Land is the critically acclaimed author of thirty novels, including the bestselling series featuring female Texas Ranger Caitlin Strong: Strong Enough to Die, Strong Justice, Strong at the Break, Strong Vengeance, and Strong Rain Falling. In addition, Land is the author of the nonfiction bestseller, Betrayal, which was named Best True Crime Book of 2012 by Suspense magazine and was recently announced the winner in the True Crime category for the 2013 USA International Book Awards. Land graduated from Brown University in 1979 Phi Beta Kappa and Magna cum Laude and continues his association with Brown as an alumni advisor.

Land often bases his novels and scripts on extensive travel and research as well as a 25-year career in martial arts. He is an associate member of the US Special Forces and frequently volunteers in schools to help young people learn to enjoy the process of writing.

He currently lives in Providence, Rhode Island. To learn more about Jon Land and his work, visit www.jonlandbooks.com.

REVIEW: *STRONG RAIN FALLING*

Strong Rain or a heavy downpour can create a flash flood, overflow highways and destroy property. Falling with a strong intensity in excess of 0.30 inches per hour great damage can be done. The intensity of some situations, the fear of death and the result death can create the same effect as the strongest rainstorm, the most devastating earthquake or even a tornado. Imagine a group of killers whose prime target is boys. Imagine finding ways to butcher these innocent children because of something that happened in the past that these persons want to settle it in the present.

Imagine a small child walking out of the desert alone without anyone to protect him. Picture an environment without any vegetation, a town that has been destroyed and a life filled with drug dealers, cartels, smugglers, death and human trafficking. One young man will be the link to what will spill over into the present. As he walks out and finds himself dealing with two Texas Rangers, his silence is overwhelming. He's unkempt and has fear in his eyes as he forms one word that will start a chain of events taking readers into the present and then back to where it all began in 1919 when this young man meets William Ray and Earl strong. Danger permeates the air and the boy's awareness of the events that transpired are vivid. He relates the events to both men. Hoping to stop these dangerous men would be coming up against people that not only wanted money but also were prepared to go up against anyone that would place any barriers to stop them. Whether Rangers or anyone from any branch of law enforcement, these men dared to defy them and cross any road in order to get what they want.

Willow Creek in the past becomes the same in the present as we hear the voice of Ana Callas Guajardo soothing the fears of five young children taken from their school while trying to lead them to safety. What does she show them and what causes them fear? What are *esos Demonios* and are they real? The screams are deafening. Her real purpose will terrify more than these innocent boys and the result will make you cringe, shiver, shake and bring tears to your eyes. The vivid descriptions that follow will create images in your mind that will make you wonder just what kind of demons there are in the world that would take the lives of the innocent who cannot defend themselves.

Caitlin Strong is at Brown University College along with Dylan Torres, who is like a son to her. They spend the day together talking about his future. Learning about his thoughts, finding out what he plans to do, Caitlin is not happy that he wants to become a member of a frat and tries to explain the dangers. While walking with him, in the town Providence, Rhode Island, two figures catch her eye, but when she focuses on them they are gone. They reappear when she and Dylan are about to go to dinner at Paragon. The events that follow change everything as Caitlin's skills as a Texas Ranger and her own radar save more than just Dylan. Caitlin Strong is related to William and Earl Strong and her abilities are quite prominent and her morals quite high.

Cort Masters is a feared man who was released from a Mexican prison before his sentence was completed. Cort has two sons, Dylan and Luke. He and Luke are spending the day at Great Flags when something happens that puts them both in danger.

When Caitlin, his colleague Cort Masters, and Cort's two sons survive a gun battle with what seems to be a new generation of smugglers, the Rangers gather information that is tied to the past. This time, the smugglers are not after law enforcement, they're targeting Cort Masters' boys. Five men try to take them both out, but Cort, with some help from a close friend, proves that strength is not always in numbers but in skill. With the men killed, Cort is questioned as is Caitlin, and the pieces still do not fit together. Who was behind the hit? The reason seems obvious to many as Caitlin takes a trip back in time as she views the crime scene of the five murdered boys. What does the date April 24, 1919 have to do with present? Why is what happened in Willow Creek in 1919 being repeated in the present? The author allows readers to understand what the Texas Rangers endured in the past has resurfaced in a more violent and potent way in the present.

Getting to know Ana Guarjardo, you begin to understand why the President of Mexico is more than on guard, how he got elected and the corruption in his government. The drug traffic is high, cartels rule and most of all their hate for the United States is more violent and powerful than the venom of the most poisonous snakebite. Guarjardo is out to destroy our country. Her hate and true feelings are more than expressed and the end result for this President isn't good. Decisions are made, threats meted out and no checkmate is in sight. Re-enter Caitlin and D.W. Pepper, her superior, as she relates what she witnessed in Willow Creek today, sees the photos of one young teen killed and the link to the drug cartels becomes more evident.

Author Jon Land's research is extensive as he introduces readers to Esteban Cantu, a real historical figure, who ran the drug trade into Mexico starting in 1916 with the blessing of the Mexican President. When the past becomes the present and a country's fate is on the line, what will these rangers do to stop esos Demonios this time? The author also includes a few pages of history about the Mexican drug trade.

Issues from the past are related including information about the Mexican Revolution and how it played its part. When the drug cartel's leaders come face to face with the Rangers just what will happen? So, are the boys the primary targets? Why kill five? What message were they sending to the one man who was trying to stop them? Opium was smuggled into Mexico and provided great revenue to fund the revolution.

Revenge is the name of someone's game added in with a variety of other resourceful games created by a team this person enlisted to do more than just wage a war against the U.S. As the pieces of the puzzle and the past start to filter into the present and the clouds are lifted, the dusty trail becomes a clear. Soon something will happen that will change more than just the playing field.

Guillermo Paz is devoted to Caitlin Strong, yet at times they are on opposite sites. A man named Jones who seems to be at the center of this investigation is bent on sending more than just obstacles in her path. As Paz sits in college classes and often puts the professors more than on the spot for their lack of knowledge related to what is being taught, there are some who would do anything to take him and Caitlin down. Opium, marijuana and more are grown on many farms and those involved seemed to be able to skirt the law. Esteban Cantu did most certainly run the first major drug smuggling ring in Mexico with the help of many others. What part does the man working in Homeland Security play and why was his son killed along with the other four? Just where did this begin and why involve Cort Masters? Sandoval and several men who run drug cartels lost their sons at the hand of one person, but why? Just how far will this plot go and what happens when another boy is kidnapped?

Caitlin's grandfather and great-grandfather fought back in 1919, along with Emiliano Zapata. They took out all of the early drug lords. But, when you read what happened and you learn about the betrayals, who was responsible and the crimes committed, you will be surprised. Throughout the novel the author shares with us information and history about the Texas Rangers, and includes short passages before each chapter that hint at what will come next.

As we get to know Ana Callas Guajardo better, we find that she seeks understanding for why she is so bent on getting her revenge. Readers will also learn what her connection to Cort Masters is and her primary goal. When face to face with Caitlin which one will finally stand down?

As we hear the voices of the Strong Raiders in 1919 and we meet Pancho Villa, the Mexican revolutionary leader, who according to history "advocated for the poor and wanted agrarian reform." We also learn that he was "a killer, bandit, revolutionary leader, and many remember him as a folk hero." Pancho Villa was also responsible for a raid on Columbus, New Mexico, in 1916, which was the first attack on U.S. soil since 1812."

What part did he play with his men in working with the Strongs? Who betrayed Villa? What happens when William Ray faces off with them? What is their primary goal and what really happened in 1919 that reset these events and caused them to spiral out of control in the present?

The remnants of that powerful criminal lineage are out for vengeance against Zapata's remaining relatives. This book provides a powerful ending, and reveals a plan so diabolical that Caitlin and Cort Masters risk it all to save more than just the U.S. from what Ana has planned. When face to face and truths, lies, betrayals and disloyalties, who will come out the victor and who will be plunged into darkness?

Strong Rain Falling: Do you want to be there when the storm hits? Author Jon Land really raises the bar this time with strong characters that handle difficult situations in a way that is not only resourceful and unique but also quite powerful. What's next for these two if they survive? What about the spirits that guide them? Will they continue to hover over them? Cort and Caitlin: Just when will they get there?

Other books by this author include: *Strong Justice, Strong at the Break,* and *Strong Enough to Die.*

RECOMMENDED READING

BY R.J. ELLORY

In mid-November, 1959, Truman Capote, renowned author of *Other Voices, Other Rooms* and *Breakfast at Tiffany's* was struck by a newspaper article that appeared in the *New York Times*. Little more than a brief squib, it outlined the brutal shotgun slaying of a farmer, his wife, and their two children. It reported that in the small village of Holcomb, Kansas, Herb Clutter, his wife Bonnie, and their two teenage children, Nancy and Kenyon, had been found bound and murdered, the mother and daughter in their beds, the father and the son in the basement of the home.

Capote, at the time a staff writer for the *New Yorker* magazine, decided that this was the story he next wanted to write about. He left for Kansas almost immediately, taking with him as his "researcher and bodyguard" Nelle Harper Lee, author of *To Kill A Mockingbird* and lifelong friend of Capote's. As children they had grown up beside one another, and even in *Mockingbird*, the characters of Dill was supposed to have been based on Capote.

So began one of the most famous and fascinating partnerships in literary history — the diminutive, effete, homosexual Capote, and the methodical and pragmatic Lee.

But the story of how *In Cold Blood* came to be written is not really the subject of this little article. That story has been covered in two recent films — "Capote" (with a deserved Oscar-winning performance from Philip Seymour Hoffman, and "Infamous" starring Toby Jones). The book itself is the issue at hand, and there are two very simple reasons I have chosen this book above all others. I am of the belief that non-fiction possesses as its primary purpose the conveyance of information, whereas fiction is there not to entertain (as we are so often told), but to evoke an emotion. Those books that continue to stay with me, regardless of how long ago I read them, are those that somehow connected and impinged on an emotional level. I remember being quarantined at boarding school with chicken pox, aged thirteen and sleeping alone in a locked room. Through the porthole window in the door all I could see was a black and white chequerboard-floored corridor, and what did I read while I was there? *The Shining* of all things. Half of it I didn't understand, the other half scared me witless. That was emotional impingement.

So we have these two elements — non-fiction conveying information, fiction evoking an emotion — and in *In Cold Blood* Capote does both brilliantly.

Even before you begin the book you know that the Clutter family are dead. This is a matter of public record. It is a fact. And yet we begin the book with them alive. A human, real, honest, hardworking, religiously minded family, helping one another, helping their fellow townsfolk, the bright and talented Nancy, the father — a rock, a pillar of the earth. Capote leads us down a road, a brilliantly constructed road, and as we travel he shows us everything we need to see to become so emotionally involved with this family, this town, these events.

The ending is inevitable, terrible and brutal.

And his protagonists — Hickock and Smith, the brief and breathtaking events of the night of November 15, 1959, and the subsequent years they spent on Death Row. The way that Capote draws it out, the way he shares their viewpoint with us, the way he opens up this world and shows us all the inhabitants.

A truly remarkable work.

And that doesn't even begin to touch on the edges of the longstanding and unresolved question: Who wrote *In Cold Blood*? Was it Capote? Was it Lee? Did they write it together? And who wrote *To Kill A Mockingbird*? Again, was it Capote, was it Lee, or did they conspire to produce two of the most remarkable books in modern American literature? *To Kill A Mockingbird* was the only book Harper Lee ever published. We do not know whether it is the only book she ever wrote. It spawned a film that won an Oscar for Gregory Peck. *In Cold Blood* made Capote one of the most respected and influential authors in American literary history, and yet he spent the subsequent twenty years drinking himself to death and never really published another word. Norman Mailer wrote an article about this very issue, and he raised the question: Were they individual authors in their own right as far as these two seminal works were concerned, or did they create them together, and then keep that truth from the world?

Who knows? I believe we will never know. I just know that *In Cold Blood,* certainly for any crime author, is perhaps one of the most necessary books to read — it is written in an inimitable style, and constructed so well. A work of genius.

Though it is utterly impossible to say, "This is my favourite book," I believe that if I was destined to be marooned on a faraway island and could take one book and one book only, then In *Cold Blood* would very likely be first on the list.

R.J. Ellory is the author of *Three Days in Chicagoland,* which focuses on the brutal murder of a young girl in Chicago in 1956, as told from three different viewpoints: The Sister, The Cop and The Killer. His other books are *Candlemoth, Ghostheart, A Quiet Vendetta, City of Lies, A Quiet Belief in Angels, A Simple Act of Violence, The Anniversary Man, Saints of New York, Bad Signs, A Dark and Broken Heart, The Devil and the River.*

BY JOHN LAND

WHAT MAKES A THRILLER?

Bookstores and libraries love to categorize. Generally "crime" gets its own spot, whereas a "thriller" will get placed within the 'general fiction'. So what separates "crime" from a "thriller" and when do the bookstores and libraries get it wrong?

That's actually my absolute favorite question in the world. Could take a whole book to answer, but let me try to give you the gist of things here.

First off, some background: For much too long, thrillers were the bastard stepchildren of the publishing industry. Denied a firm placement of their own, they have struggled to carve out an identity and definition separate from mysteries and crime stories. Sure, there's some overlap, quite a bit sometimes, but for our purposes today, let's review the primary criteria that define what makes a thriller distinct.

1) **STAKES:** In his first book, *Killing Floor*, the great Lee Child introduces his iconic Jack Reacher character stopping over in a town where his brother, coincidentally, was just murdered. Now if Reacher was concerned only with finding his brother's killer, we'd have a mystery. Along the way, though, he uncovers a massive counterfeiting plot that his brother had been investigating. So the book isn't just about investigating a murder, it's about seeking revenge on the perpetrators and bringing down their crime ring in the process. That's a perfect example of how a book's stakes figure into defining what that book is. Think back to James Bond's cinematic debut in *Dr. No* and the great line where Bond, lighting a cigarette, responds flippantly after the evil genius villain has just sketched out his plan, "World domination … Same old plan." Maybe so, but stakes as high as that are what help make a thriller a thriller.

2) **A HERO IN JEOPARDY:** Another key element in distinguishing a mystery or crime novel from a thriller is the plight of the hero. In a mystery, we follow the investigation through the eyes of the hero who is chasing the perpetrator while not always being threatened by that perpetrator or larger forces surrounding him. But a thriller

places the life of the hero at risk, in danger. In order to survive, he or she must get to the bottom of what's going on. The villains must not just be caught; they must be stopped. See, thrillers are at their heart quest stories in the grandest tradition and for that reason they are often intensely personal. Remember the great Hitchcock film, "The Man who Knew Too Much"? Jimmy Stewart's son is kidnapped to stop him telling the authorities what he knows, so the only way to get the boy back is to stop the bad guys himself. The ultimate quest with the lives of his entire family hanging in the balance as he gets to the root of an assassination conspiracy.

3) **AN OUNCE OF PREVENTION:** Jumping off a bit from the point above, thrillers are almost invariably about stopping something really bad from happening, not just investigating something that already has happened. It's not a mystery, so much as a puzzle where the hero must fit all the pieces together in order to preempt a truly evil plot sure to harm lots of people. In that sense, the thriller form is interactive, asking the reader to play along with the hero in assembling all the clues. The villain, in turn, is determined to stop the hero's efforts, which creates the kind of nail-biting suspense that lies not only in wondering whether the hero will survive, but also whether he or she will succeed in preventing the "Really Bad Thing" from happening.

4) **SETTING:** Thrillers, for the most part, are defined by their rapid-fire pace. And that kind of pacing tends to move the heroes around a lot as they embark on their quest to stop the Really Bad Thing. The great tales of James Rollins and Steve Berry take us all over the world, any number of countries per book. While there are plenty of exceptions to this, Lee Child's books foremost among them, the nature of the thriller has long been defined by characters shifting about settings both dark, mundane and exotic in a staccato-like fashion. Like a treasure hunt, where each clue leads to another that takes the hero somewhere else. This is in stark contrast to mysteries or crime tales which normally take place in a single city or, even, town.

5) **HOLDING UP THE MIRROR:** Mysteries and crime tales are seldom motivated or defined by societal concerns. Contrast that with the modern evolution of the thriller. The great paranoid conspiracy books by Robert Ludlum, like *The Holcroft Covenant* and *The Matarese Circle,* were spawned by the Watergate era where government became the enemy. Ronald Reagan restored trust to government but also reignited the Cold War, giving birth to the likes of Tom Clancy and a whole spate of thrillers more interested in machines than men. The end of the Cold War that accompanied the collapse of the Soviet Union in the early 1990s pretty much killed the thriller form for a while. Sales plummeted, as thriller writers sought a new identity, a new enemy. We got both on 9/11. Suddenly a whole new generation of bad guys were born in Islamic terrorists, obviously capable of doing the "Really Bad Thing" thought to be only the product of fiction until that fateful, redefining day. The post 9/11 era, that birthed the likes of Vince Flynn, Brad Thor, Daniel Silva, and Alex Berenson, reinvigorated the thriller form and planted the seeds for the explosion of the genre's popularity today. All of a sudden, we needed heroes again, and characters such as Mitch Rapp, Gabriel Allon and Scott Harvath more than fit the bill. If we couldn't kill the boogeyman in real life, at least we could kill him in fiction, and the new wave of heroes was more than up to that task. But thriller writers are also ahead of the curve as

well. Before he created Hannibal Lecter, Thomas Harris foresaw 9/11 in *Black Sunday,* his brilliant book about a terrorist attack on the Super Bowl. The "Really Bad Thing" in Ian Fleming's 1961 Bond novel *Thunderball* was nuclear terrorism. Who could have known?

I could go on with this forever, but any writer needs to know when to stop, when enough is enough. There are no absolutes in this business and exceptions surely to every rule. Thrillers are as broad as our imaginations, elegantly encapsulating what the great John D. McDonald defines as a story: "Stuff happens to someone you care about." To that, let me add "lots of stuff" and someone you care about "who's in danger." Now, that's a thriller!

Jon Land is the bestselling author over 25 novels. Some of Jon's books include *Strong Vengeance, Betrayal, Strong at the Break, Strong Justice, and Strong Enough to Die.* Ebooks include *Vortex, The Vengeance of the Tau, The Valhalla Testament,* and *The Omicron Legion*, as well as many others. Books may be purchased from his website, www.JonLandBooks.com, bookstores and online retailers.

A WRITER'S LIFE

A writer's life is often considered to be a life of ease. Apparently there was a survey last year of the British public, and following on from 'professional footballer' as the most favoured profession, writer came second. I think somewhere there must be a viewpoint that a writer rises late (he would have to following the quantity of alcohol consumed at last night's lavish launch party, surrounded by adoring fellow celebrities, the red carpet rolled out, assistants and attendants on hand to cater to every whim), and while fielding telephone calls from Hollywood producers vying for movie rights, both Alan Yentob and Melvyn Bragg offering ever-increasing quantities of money to feature in a prime-time documentary, our writer would breakfast on scallops and quail's eggs, smoke a packet of Lucky Strikes, down three cups of Blue Mountain hand-ground coffee, and then type a handful of words on his battered Underwood or Remington before retiring to the club for an afternoon of witty repartee and fine cigars with the likes of Sebastian Faulks and Ian McEwan.

Sorry to have to let you down, but a writer's life is not quite this way.

I think it was Gideon Flowers who said, "Writing is easy … all you have to do is stare at a blank page until drops of blood form on your forehead."

Leo Rosten said, "The only reason for being a professional writer is that you just can't help it."

As Bennett Cerf so astutely observed: "Coleridge was a drug addict. Poe was an alcoholic. Marlowe was killed by a man whom he was treacherously trying to stab. Pope took money to keep a woman's name out of a satire, and then wrote a piece so that she could still be recognized anyhow. Chatterton killed himself. Byron was accused of incest. Do you still want to a writer — and if so, why?"

Of course, once you attain that lofty position of having been published at all, it then becomes a full-time job to stay there. Writing is a competitive business, to say the least. Apparently only two percent of books published are bestsellers. Over eighty percent of books published in the UK sell less than five hundred copies. The average working writer in the UK draws a salary from his writing of less than seven thousand pounds. This, my friends, is not the level of independent income that will provide scallops and quail's eggs for breakfast.

So why do people do it?

Russell Baker said, "The only thing I was fit for was to be a writer, and this notion rested solely on my suspicion that I would never be fit for real work, and that writing didn't require any." A nice idea, but — frankly — utterly untrue. Writing is a job of work, and for those few that generate enough income from their writing that they can survive without extra-curricular activity (like a full-time job), then the discipline necessary to get out of bed and write three thousand words a day can test even the hardiest literary animals.

Terry Pratchett said, "There's no such thing as writer's block. That was invented by people in California who couldn't write." So no excuses there, I'm afraid.

Hemingway added, "It's none of their business that you have to learn to write. Let them think you were born that way," which implies that continuing to write requires a degree of study, continual self-education, the willingness to listen to editors and critics and see where your own work could be improved.

Which, as a necessary aside, brings us neatly to critics…

You've worked like a dog for a year. You've sweated blood through your fingertips onto the keys of the typewriter. You've written and re-written, self-edited, edited once more, and then with a huge rush of accomplishment and self-satisfaction you release your child of a book into the world … and you are met by the critics.

"I picked up this book and from front cover to back cover I couldn't stop laughing. One day I might even read it." (That was from Groucho Marx, but you get the point, right?)

C.N. Bovee commented, "There is probably no hell for authors in the next world — they suffer so much from critics and publishers in this," while Christopher Hampton was astute enough to observe, "Asking a working writer what he thinks about critics is like asking a lamppost how it feels about dogs."

Though I am nowhere near as vehement or vitriolic in my dislike of critics (and I have found, routinely, that they have actually been extraordinarily kind), it does nevertheless raise a question about criticism. I think it is safe to say that there is criticism and there is review, and they are entirely different subjects.

Somerset Maugham was quick to point out, "There are three rules for writing. Unfortunately, no one can agree what they are," which explains why one book is loved, and another hated. Criticism, even review, is utterly subjective. By its nature, by its perspective, it can never be anything other. In an attempt to edify a potential reader regarding the "likes" of a book, a fair reviewer or critic is bound by the nature of the task to illuminate also the "dislikes." Sometimes a critic might be an unpublished author. Here we sometimes encounter an attitude influenced by sour grapes. An author — dented and disillusioned by critical slant — might be well served to appreciate Sibelius' comment when he said, "Pay no attention to what the critics say; no statue has ever been erected to a critic." Also Jean Kerr who advised that when confronted by an absolutely infuriating review it is sometimes helpful for the victim to do a little personal research on the critic. Is there any truth to the rumor that he had no formal education beyond the age of eleven? In any event, is he able to construct a simple English sentence? Do his participles dangle? When moved to lyricism does he write, "I had a fun time"? Was he ever arrested for burglary?

It is true that writing is one of the only professions where no one considers you ridiculous if you earn no money. But that does not mean it is an ignoble or ill-advised profession. A philosopher once said that a culture was only as great as its dreams, and its dreams were dreamed by artists.

Telling stories is as old as speech, and no less important. Telling stories is a tradition, a heritage, a legacy … it is the past making its way toward the future in an effort to show us those things we have failed to learn by our own experience.

Telling stories is a hope that magic can be restored to an age that has almost forgotten.

I consider myself exceptionally fortunate to be a working writer.

I consider it a privilege to be able to spend my time in the business of writing, and now I have accomplished at least some small degree of success I believe it is my duty to work as hard as possible to maintain the relationship I have established with my readers. I believe that a reader and writer have a contract. It is very simple. A reader is asked for a small financial contribution, and then a larger contribution of time to read the book he or she has bought. The writer's clause dictates that he provide entertainment, perhaps education, some degree of enlightenment, but most of all that he convey the reader to some world, some universe, some reality that the reader would otherwise never experience. If the writer fails to do this then he is in violation of the terms of his unspoken contract. Readers are forgiving, but only for so long. Violate that contract two times, perhaps three, and your reader will find another writer who works harder to maintain his end of the bargain.

So, aside from the work itself, aside from the reviews, the criticisms, the spats that one has with one's editor when he smiles, nods resignedly, and says, "Perhaps it needs a little more work, eh?"... aside from all the extraneous additions to this trade, there is only one important factor to be taken into consideration: the reader.

We write for ourselves, yes, but really we write for our readers.

We write because we don't have the nerve to rob banks, of course, but truthfully we write for our readers.

So buy books — buy as many as you can — and then read them. Not only will it entertain you, enlighten you, enchant and edify you, it will also keep writers off the streets.

Roger Jon Ellory was born in Birmingham, England, June 20, 1965, at Sorento Hospital. The hospital has now been demolished. There is no direct evidence that the two events were linked. His father having already left before Roger was born, he was then orphaned at the age of seven. His mother, Carole — an actress and dancer — died as a result of a pneumonia epidemic that claimed more than a dozen victims in the early 1970s. In 1973, Roger was swiftly dispatched to a boarding school and stayed there until he was sixteen. Upon leaving school, he returned to Birmingham to live with his maternal grandmother. His grandfather had already drowned off the Gower Peninsula in the south of Wales in 1957. In April of 1982, Roger's grandmother died following a number of heart attacks.

At seventeen years of age, he was arrested for poaching. He was charged, tried, and sentenced to a jail term, which he served without causing too much trouble. Upon his release he vanished quietly into relative obscurity to pursue interests in graphic design, photography and music. As a guitar player in a band called 'The Manta Rays' he was partly responsible for their reputation as the loudest band south of Manchester and north of London. Following the untimely death of their drummer, Roger quit the music scene and devoted himself to studying obscure philosophies and reading. Through the complete works of Conan Doyle, Michael Moorcock, JRR Tolkien, numerous books by Stephen King and many others, his interest in fiction steadily grew, not only from the viewpoint of a reader, but a burgeoning interest as a writer.

Ellory's most recent books include *The Devil and the River*, and an ebook exclusive trilogy of novellas titled *Three Days in Chicagoland*, which focuses on the brutal murder of a young girl in Chicago in 1956, as told from three different viewpoints: The Sister, The Cop and The Killer. His other books, in order of publication are: *Candlemoth* (2003), *Ghostheart* (2004), *A Quiet Vendetta* (2005), *City of Lies* (2006), *A Quiet Belief in Angels* (2007), *A Simple Act of Violence* (2008), *The Anniversary Man* (2009), *Saints of New York* (2010), *Bad Signs* (2011), *A Dark and Broken Heart* (2012), *The Devil and the River* (2013). Visit his website: www.RJEllory.com

WHY CRIME FICTION

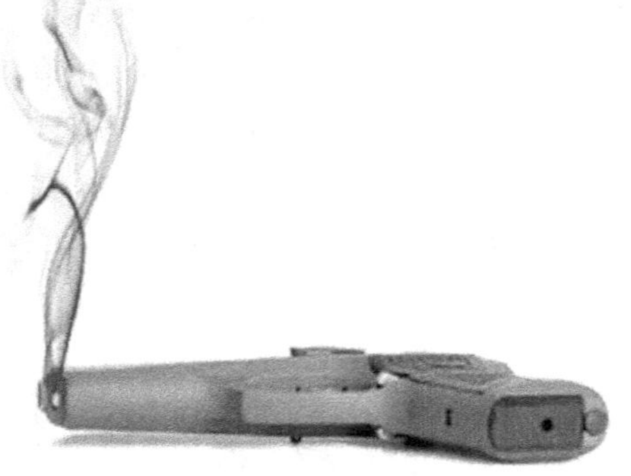

I'm occasionally asked why I write crime-thriller novels. Sometimes, I think the answer is easy: I love to read them, so I write them, too.

But the range of human emotions and experiences can be tapped in virtually any genre, so what about crime novels is so attractive?

I suppose in part, it's because these things could actually occur—they could really happen to people like you and me. The chance you'll encounter a ghost, be transported to another planet, or have some paranormal experience is pretty remote. Those sci-fi novels truck in pure fantasy, which is fine, but basically, these events can't really happen.

However, you could very well be the victim if some thug's violent intentions, or end of being the target of extortion or threats. You could unwittingly run afoul of the law, or become embroiled in some criminal enterprise.

In other words, crime novels tap into the prospect of the possible, which makes them ever more compelling and frightening. These things could actually occur. But more than fear drives these novels. Greed, lust, avarice, revenge, cowardice, nobility — all run rampant in crime novels. Yet, it's vicarious, so the tension, anxiety, and outright fear occur to someone else—not to you or me. You can live it through a character's experiences, not your own. That makes it tolerable—even enjoyable. You can pull back anytime you want.

Of course, there's the page-turning, heart-racing element of suspense. Will this brilliant and bold bad guy (who we admire, despite his crimes) really get away, or be brought to justice? Will this flawed detective or FBI agent prevail, despite his or her shortcomings?

Many characters in crime fiction are larger-than-life. If they're well-developed, they draw the reader inexorably into their spheres. You are "there" amidst the danger, pulse-pounding exploits, or the nerve-racking chase.

Think of the power of Vito Corleone in *The Godfather*, the tenaciousness of Harry Bosch in Michael Connelly's novels, or the daring exploits Ben and Chon in Don Winslow's novel *Savages*. Consider the stealth of Barry Eisler's John Rain, a master assassin; or the characters in *Get Shorty*, by Elmore Leonard, or those in *Mystic River*, by Dennis Lehane (which was also a great Clint Eastwood-directed movie). How about the cunning brilliance of Thomas Harris' Hannibal Lecter (He's even in Wikipedia). You can't help but love some, and hate others. The best have become American icons.

Maybe it all boils down to basics—the good versus evil dichotomy of human existence.

I just love good crime thrillers. I love reading them and writing them.

Mark Rubinstein was born in Brooklyn, New York. He graduated from New York University with a degree in business administration. He then served in the army and ended up as a field medic tending to paratroopers of the 82nd Airborne Division. He was so taken with these experiences that after his discharge, he re-entered NYU as a premed student. e entered medical school at the State University of New York's Downstate Medical Center. As a medical student, he developed an interest in psychiatry, discovering in that specialty the same thing he realized in reading fiction: every patient has a compelling story to tell. He became a board-certified psychiatrist practicing in New York City.

In addition to running his private practice he developed an interest in forensic psychiatry because the drama and conflict of the cases and courtrooms tapped into his personality style. He also taught psychiatric residents, interns, psychologists, and social workers at New York Presbyterian Hospital and became a clinical assistant professor at Cornell University's medical school.

Before turning to fiction, Rubinstein coauthored five medical self-help books: *The First Encounter: The Beginnings in Psychotherapy*, *The Complete Book of Cosmetic Facial Surgery*, *New Choices: the Latest Options in Treating Breast Cancer*, *Heartplan: A Complete Program for Total Fitness of Heart & Mind*, and *The Growing Years: A Guide to Your Child's Emotional Development from Birth to Adolescence*.

Rubinstein lives in Connecticut with his wife and as many dogs as she will allow in the house. He still practices psychiatry and is busily writing more novels. *Mad Dog House*, his first novel, was named a Finalist for the 2012 ForeWord Reviews Book of the Year Award (Thriller & Suspense). His second novel, *Love Gone Mad*, coming out this September, is available for preorder through Mark's website, www.MarkRubinstein-Author.com

VALUABLE MARKETING TIPS FOR AUTHORS

Marketing Tips for Nonfiction Authors:

Establish yourself as an expert in the field that you write about. Join associations, give talks, blog, and write articles, opinion pieces, and columns in your area of expertise. Look for national news stories about your field, comment on, give your opinion, and become a resource and reliable source.

- Search out speaking engagements for groups that are interested in your topic.
- Make your website a resource for reliable information on your topic.
- Network with other experts in your field.
- Find book reviewers that write and review books in your genre.
- Learn good interview skills for TV, radio and print.

Marketing Tips for Fiction Authors:

- Know your audience so all marketing efforts will be targeted to that demographic.
- Find book reviewers that write and review books in your genre.
- Offer incentives and giveaways on social media sites.
- Give book talks and signings at book stores.
- Investigate virtual book tours. Make sure you have the time and money for this (time consuming and costly).
- Write blogs in your character voice.
- Get a book trailer for website.

Most authors are busy and have difficulty finding time to market their books. Hiring a publicist is recommended by book publishers and marketing companies for authors who wish to develop a wider audience for their books.

Diane Dennis is a publicist who has provided PR services to bestselling authors including Harville Hendrix, bestselling author of *Getting the Love You Want*, and *Imago International* through her PR Firm Inspired Media Communications. Inspired Media Communications is a resource for authors, speakers and organizations. Visit www.InspiredMC.com for more information and like them on Facebook at www.facebook.com/InspiredMediaCommunications

TO CATCH A STORYLINE

Every author at some point is asked the very same question: How do you plot a book? In fact, entire books have been written about how to plot books. I'm sure there has even been a book about how to write a book about how to plot books. So I'm not going to write one here or tell you every little detail about all the ins and outs necessary to construct the storyline of your next (or first) novel. This is a blog, not a library. But I will attempt to offer a summation of the basic principles that guide plot creation and how to envision the entire book before you write it.

By the way, this is something I wish I'd known before I wrote my first book, Absolute Authority. Had I known then what I know now, it probably would not have taken ten freakin' years to write it! Here goes…

Pardon me if I employ an over-used analogy, but I can think of no better comparison for plotting a book than a road trip. I frequently drive the twelve long hours from St. Louis to Hickory, NC, and have become fairly familiar with pretty much every landmark along the way. (Even ate at the original Cracker Barrel in Lebanon, TN.) Somewhere along the way, as I was staring at yellow hash marks zipping by my car in the middle of an incredibly boring stretch of Interstate 40, the description of a book plot as a road trip began to gel inside my gray matter. I thought, mapping out a book is like mapping out a trip: you have a starting point, an ending point (or at least an idea of where you want to stop), and a whole series of individual landmarks along the way that you must pass to get where you want to go.

But how do you break down a road trip/book plot into individual chapters? And what do you do with said strips of boring highway that will surely lose the reader along the way? Well, how do you stay awake and alert when you drive that far? You make it interesting, right? So do the same thing for your readers. The beauty of writing fiction is you get to make stuff up. So what if it's not real? Who cares? It's a novel, for cryin' out loud!

So here's how you take a road trip and turn into a story line.

First, understand where you're starting and where it'll end. No, you don't have to have to the final sentence in your head already, but you do need to have a general idea of how you want the story to play out. I didn't have that when I wrote my book, and it caused me much consternation when I hit the 70,000-word mark and froze. I had four different plot lines that all had to miraculously tie together in the end. And it took exactly that: a miracle. Had I followed my own advice, divine intervention would not have been necessary. Now I know. And so you do. Start with the end in mind, at least generally. This gives you the, ahem, bookends of your story and provides a framework for everything else you're going to write.

Now on to Chapter One. But don't write it yet. Think of each chapter as a landmark along the way. For instance, if I start in St. Louis and head to

Hickory, the first thing that happens is I drive past Busch Stadium, whiz past the Gateway Arch, cross the Mississippi River, and I'm in Illinois. Stage One complete. That could be the first chapter.

Each subsequent chapter would simply be the next landmark along the way. For instance, I always stop at the Phillips 66 gas station in Mt. Vernon, Illinois, right after I change from I-64 to I-57 on my way south. But what about all the distance between downtown St. Louis and Mt. Vernon. Do I include that in my plot? Is it necessary? It's mostly boring, flat farmland. Interesting? Not really. (You ought to see it in the dead of winter. Talk about dull!) Would someone think it is? Probably, but not enough readers would care for me to put it in the story. So I would leave it out and move along to the next landmark: Chapter Two.

And so it would go for the rest of the trip. Each landmark and the space between it would be a chapter or section of the bigger plot that would all come together to form the story. Filling in details is where it gets fun … and separates good writers from, well, not so good writers.

For instance, did you see the size of that deer carcass lying beneath the billboard for the adult superstore? Yuck! Times two! Think readers might find those details amusing? You'll probably want to leave them in. Unless you're writing a YA novel, in which case the adult superstore may need to become a Stuckey's truck stop.

But you get the point. Plotting is the road map for your book. You have to know your destination to know where to go and what's important along the way. Filling in the details makes the journey more interesting.

Follow this simple framework and watch your next novel flow freely from your fingers onto the screen.

David Workman's debut novel, *Absolute Authority,* hit the shelves in early 2012 to roaring acclaim. A native St. Louisan, he was recently named by local television station KMOV as one of St. Louis' Top 5 New Authors. Along with writing novels, David has spent most of his 20-year writing career hammering out advertising and marketing copy for companies large and small, including his current gig as the lead contest specialist for a major athletic shoe company. His second novel, a sequel, is scheduled for a winter 2013 release. Find him on Facebook.

TO OUTLINE OR NOT TO OUTLINE ... THAT IS THE QUESTION

I am often asked whether or not I write an outline or a synopsis for the novels I write. To date, the answer has always been, "No, no outline, no synopsis," and I think that will always be the answer. Writing a novel — for me — seems to be a spontaneous and organic thing, constantly changing, constantly in flux, and in this way I seem to be able to surprise myself with the twists and turns that a plot can take, even as I write it. I can change my mind. I can change the ending. The guilty party in *A Quiet Belief In Angels* became someone else entirely merely fifteen pages from the end of the book.

However, there are two constants for me; two things I always establish before I begin a novel. The time and place, just as one concept, is vitally important. A Depression era-set serial killer novel is going to be an entirely different novel from a Washington-based contemporary political conspiracy. So the era and locale is vital. But, even more important for me, is the mood and atmosphere with which I want to imbue a story. How do I want the reader to feel when they are reading the book? How do I want them to remember the book long after they have finished it?

With *Saints of New York* I wanted to create a very definite feeling: a sense of bleak desperation, a feeling of darkness, a sense of constant and imminent foreboding. I remembered films from the seventies — "Klute," "Serpico," "The French Connection," and then more recent releases such as "8mm," "The Pledge," "The Flock" and "Seven," and it was that kind of depth, that kind of disillusioned and defeated realism that I wanted to convey. Of course, I didn't wish to depress the reader, but merely to take a step away from conventional plots, to leave behind central characters who seem to always get it right, to make guesses and giant leaps of assumption, and always be vindicated in their hunches. The world is flawed. The people who inhabit the world are also flawed — both criminals and cops. They make mistakes, they screw things up, they get it wrong. It does not always work out well for the protagonist; the antagonist does not always get his comeuppance. This is what I wanted the book to be about — the simple truth, the simple reality, the frustration of real police work.

In the early part of 2008, just a couple of days after Obama had been inaugurated; I had the good fortune to go to Washington with the BBC to make a feature piece about *A Simple Act of Violence. Simple Act* is a tough book about a tough subject — the covert ops activities of the CIA during the war in Nicaragua, the illegal trafficking of cocaine out of Managua into Miami in CIA-chartered aircraft, those same aircraft piloted by known criminals who had been given carte blanche and exemption from prosecution by the US intelligence community, all this set against the backdrop of a contemporary Washington serial killing spree that spirals beyond anything the lead investigator, Detective Robert Miller, can envision. During that Washington trip, I had the great fortune to spend time with people from the FBI, the *Washington Post*, and even the lead detective on the Washington sniper case, June Boyle. I spent four hours in a snow-covered children's' playground in Fairfax County, Virginia, and here she spoke of her life, her experiences, and her vocation as a detective.

Towards the end of our discussion I asked her — if she could — to summarize her lifestyle, her work, her vocation — in some sound bites. She was pensive for a while, and then said, "No two victims are created equal. If you come from one side of the city, well your murder might be investigated by five or six detectives. However, if you come from another side of the city, your murder could be one of five or six I am investigating alone." She said it was a view that had been shared by herself and the Fire Chief. The Fire Chief said he had never put out a fire in a rich white guy's house. Secondly she said something that sent a chill up my spine. "I have a work cellphone," she told me, "and when it rings … well, every time it rings there's a dead person at the end of it. It could be a domestic, it could be a twelve-year-old in pieces in a dumpster, it could be a serial killing victim or a hit-and-run. Whoever it is, and whatever the reason for their death, my day starts when their day ends."

I thought about that for a long time. I considered the kind of effect such a job would have on your life. Could you keep a marriage together? Could you raise kids? Could you go out and enjoy a ballgame, a barbecue, or a weekend in the country with that kind of shadow hanging over you all the time? Perhaps, perhaps not.

After I returned from Washington, I started to think about forgotten victims. I looked at the fact that something in the region of 850,000 Missing Persons Reports are filed each year in the USA alone. I considered the fact that 93% of abduction victims are dead within three hours … dead before anyone even knows they're missing. I thought about the ones that were never found, the bodies never located, the parents never knowing what really happened to their son or daughter. I imagined what that would do to your life. Would you ever be able to let go, to get over it, to carry on? I didn't believe so.

That was where Frank Parrish came from for Saints of *New York*. That simple meeting in Virginia was where 'Saints of New York' was born — as an idea, a vague fleeting image, a feeling of the kind of story I would like to write that dealt with the obsession of one policeman to learn the truth of what had really happened to a young victim. Why? Because if he didn't, no one else would. The victim — a teenage girl — was a nobody, someone who had fallen through the net, someone about whom no one really cared. Until Parrish decided to care. Until he decided to learn the truth of her fate, no matter what it took.

And so I started writing, and — as with all books — it became consuming, something I thought about all the time, something I worked at furiously. "Driven," my wife calls me, and perhaps I am. It became an important story to tell, not out of any high-minded and pretentious view that I had "something important to say." Quite the opposite. I was humbled by it in a strange kind of way. Writing about someone like Parrish made me all too aware of the fact that there are thousands of people who spend their lives in the service of others, who sacrifice personal security, stability, family, vacations — all the things we take for granted — in an effort to help others less fortunate. "Forgotten victims" was the phrase that came to mind time and again, but as I wrote the book I started to consider the "forgotten saviours" even more. These were the real "Saints of New York," the real saints of any city, any neighbourhood, where such work is undertaken by self-effacing and anonymous people, people often criticized and harassed, people viewed as corrupt or self-serving, when — in reality — they were quite the opposite.

Saints of New York is not an easy read. I didn't want it to be, never intended it to be anything other than brutal and harsh. All I wished was that it would convey some small part of the emotional effect I had experienced when I spent time in Washington with June Boyle from Homicide, with Brad Garrett from the FBI. I wanted to present some small part of the reality of their lives, to get under the reader's skin, to make them feel how I felt when I stood by the edge of an industrial lake and listened to Brad tell me of the one case that still kept him awake at night: the discovery of a 30-gallon trash can that had floated to the surface of that same lake, the lid wired shut, and within it the dead and drowned body of a young mother and her baby boy tied together inside. Twenty-five years of homicides, 25 years of seeing the very worst that human beings were capable of doing to one another, the only FBI agent to ever track a terrorist assassin out of the US into the Middle East, to bring him back, to see him charged, arraigned, tried, convicted and executed for the gun killing of two CIA agents on US soil, the agent who was assigned to the Starbucks employee murders in Georgetown … and the case that still gave him nightmares was the seemingly senseless death of a baby.

That was what I wanted to do, to tell that story, to share that viewpoint of humanity.

And I hope that is what I have achieved.

Truth be told, I care little whether people remember my name, even the name of the book, but yet — when reminded of that book six months after having read it — I would consider it the highest compliment if they were still able to recall how it made them feel. That's what I like about the books I read, and that's what I am still trying to accomplish with every book I write.

So, for me, there will never be outlines or plotcharts or synopses. For me there will be a basic idea, a time and a place, and a feeling that I am trying to evoke in the reader. That is all.

R.J. Ellory is the author of *Three Days in Chicagoland*, which focuses on the brutal murder of a young girl in Chicago in 1956, as told from three different viewpoints: The Sister, The Cop and The Killer. His other books are *Candlemoth, Ghostheart, A Quiet Vendetta, City of Lies, A Quiet Belief in Angels, A Simple Act of Violence, The Anniversary Man, Saints of New York, Bad Signs, A Dark and Broken Heart, The Devil and the River.* Visit his website: *www.RJEllory.com*

THOUGHTS FOR THE NEW WRITER

So many words of advice, perhaps too many: Beginning writers are inundated. Don't use the passive voice. Show; don't tell. Sentences shouldn't begin with conjunctions. Vary sentence and paragraph length. Don't use the same word too often. Be sure you use all the senses. Adverbs are the enemy. Always use said when attributing quotes — after, never before the character's speech. Beware of fragments. No big words.

The advice flows and flows. Much of it is helpful once you're actually writing; but it is devastating to those first efforts. Until you know who you are as a writer, what your style is, you have no business worrying about all that advice. Forget about it and get to grinding out the pages of that great new novel, the one that will take the world by storm.

Seriously, if you don't write, you'll never learn how. Experience is the best teacher; and unlike most other endeavors, the worst that can happen when you try writing on your own is that you'll waste paper and of course some ego. Not to worry, if you're fated—or doomed—to be a writer, the ego will grow back; and paper does literally grow on trees.

There will be time later to hone your skills. There will be time to agonize over each word. There will be time to read each page aloud over and over until you have perfected it just enough to throw it into the overflowing wastebasket, an essential tool for this craft. There will even be time to argue with your editor over the grammar that you learned in eighth grade only to find that it holds you back when there is an actual story to be told.

There will be time. But first you must write! Let those words flow. Of course, they won't; they never do. They come in pumps and bursts as water from a long unused pipe. Specks of rust and debris and then the air blocks and finally a clean flow. "Wonderful," you will think just before the spigot somehow gets jammed again.

Not to worry. Keep writing. If necessary the same word over and over until the next one forces itself from your pen. In the end it will be okay because — just as your mother hung those crayon masterpieces on the refrigerator when you were a child — you will write that book you desire; or perhaps you will be lucky enough to take up sculpting or playing the clarinet instead.

Life itches and torments Kenneth Weene like pesky flies. Annoyed, he picks up a pile of paper to slap at the buzzing and often whacks himself on the head. Each whack is another story. At least having half-blinded himself, he has learned to not wave the pencil about. Ken will, however, write on until the last gray cell has retreated and there are no longer these strange ideas demanding his feeble efforts. So many poems, stories, novels; and more to come.

Learn more about Ken at http://www.kennethweene.com You can find Ken's novels in print, e-format, and audio.

WRITING TIPS FROM AUTHOR CLAYTON BYE

I think a great story depends on a wicked Hook, something that settles the reader into the book almost immediately. The hook need not be recognizable as such, but it must be there. Following the hook comes the Problem: every story has some problem that must be solved by the main character or characters. If there's no problem, there's nothing to hold the reader in a state of suspended disbelief (the goal of all good fiction). The middle of the story or the Development is when the character and whatever challenges him do battle — sometimes to the point of what seems like a hopeless situation. Following Development comes the Resolution or Dénouement. This is when the author has his character(s) solve the Problem. If this is not done with finesse and great imagination, then the reader will experience disappointment instead of excitement. And, finally, a nice ending always helps to clear up loose ends and to slowly bring the reader back to the here and now, something I call Emergence from the Dream.

So Story = Hook + Problem + Development +
Resolution + Emergence.

And I would say this to aspiring authors: Why not begin to put these structural components in place in your stories consciously rather than instinctively?

I believe all fiction writing comes from our experience or is extrapolated therefrom. One of my major influencers, Damon Knight, stated that a person should not be allowed to write (for the consumption of others) until the age of forty. He explained that until this age a writer didn't have the personal experiences from which to draw. Now, this doesn't mean that everything must be gleaned directly; no, book learning, movies, even the development of your own imagination is acceptable. The point being that age and experience enhances the ability to draw rich and useful imagery from your mind.

I have no fear. I will go anywhere my stories demand, and genres be damned.

I was surprised that while writing was very difficult one could make it a habit like anything else in this life. That's what I have, you know—a writing habit. That's what makes someone a writer.

I celebrate all the way through. For example, if I solve a particularly difficult dialogue problem, I might go out and treat myself to ice cream. But, of course, the big celebration is when something is published. Not written, published. It's then I pull out a fine single malt scotch and have a "wee dram."

Yes. I sit down in front of a blank screen and stay there for at least an hour. Once I get writing, there's no preset time limit. I work until tired or until the outer world intrudes.

Yes. I have a huge selection of music on my laptop, mostly soft rock and folk music from the 50s forward. Oh yes, Doris Day show tunes and lots of Billie Holiday!

Dealing with other editors.

Damon Knight, Stephen King, John D. McDonald and a slew of others.

The Fountainhead by Ayn Rand. *The Wolf's Hour* by Robert McCammon. All of John D. MacDonald's books. All of Louis L'Amours Westerns. Everything by Stephen King. *Fear* by L. Ron Hubbard. *The Man in the Tree* by Damon Knight. All of Alistair MacLean's books. All of Desmond Bagley's books. *The Rowan* by Anne McCaffrey. *The Foundation* series by Isaac Asimov. *See You at The Top* by Zig Ziglar. The complete works of Robert Frost.

Other writers.

They all think I'm pretty weird. That being said, my family has supported me completely in anything I've decided to do.

What advice would you give an aspiring author?

Write! If you don't write and do some marketing every day, then you'll stay an aspiring writer

---

Clayton Bye is a writer, editor and publisher. The author of 9 books and a varied collection of short stories, poems, articles and hundreds of reviews, he has also published 2 anthologies of excellent short stories by some great talents from around the world. The first book featured general fiction, while the current offering is horror, through and through. *The Speed of Dark*, Clayton's most recent effort, is available online from his websites www.ClaytonBye.com and Shop.ClaytonBye.com

FROM COP TO AGENT TO AUTHOR

On my first day of patrol after graduating from the police academy, I got dressed in my freshly pressed uniform at home. I did not know what to expect when I reported to my sub-station in the Washington DC suburb, Fairfax County. Would I even have a locker, or would the new rookie be relegated to the bathroom stall?

Barely out of college, with little money, my ten-year old used car was beaten up just enough to look like an unmarked anti-crime car. Dark and rainy, I drove slowly on the highway, half out of driver prudence, half out of a mind distracted by what was to come. On my left, I noticed a car speeding up. As the car passed me, I noticed the woman passenger look at me — mostly my uniform and then quickly turn to the male driver. I saw her mouth out the words, "It's a cop, slow down." Their brakes light went on. I had to laugh. If they only knew that I was much more nervous than they. That proved a great day. I made my first arrest. I wore that uniform proudly. Yes, I had arrived.

After two years of patrol, despite liking my squad-mates and having made some exciting arrests, I was ready to try something new. When an opening came to be the first full-time hostage negotiator on the Special Weapons and Tactics Team, I jumped on it. I went to the interview with no knowledge of hostage negotiations. I was selected and received a promotion to senior officer and got one stripe on my sleeve.

When we were not SWATing, we were in plain clothes, doing anti-crime work. Even those cars were newer and in better shape than the car I drove on my first day. Shortly after being assigned to this team, I was thrust into the spotlight when I negotiated the take-over of what was unofficially known as the "Libyan Embassy." My last arrest with this team was that of a serial rapist, who had eluded a long and intense manhunt. From the evidence we found at the time, we knew we had just stopped another rape, though we later had to question some of the decisions we made. The complexities and emotions of that investigation inspired the backdrop of my crime novel, Midnight Sin.

I was enjoying that assignment and all the members of my team, but after one year, I found myself leaving the police department on to my next challenge — heading off to the FBI. My mindset was never satisfied once a challenge was faced. Young and ambitious, the FBI seemed like the next logical step in my career. On my last day my captain sat me down for a final discussion. He offered me assurances of a great career in the police department, but acknowledged that he did not expect to change my mind. He told me that one day I would learn to "stop and smell the roses." Now retired, I understand his message, but I have not stopped looking for the next mountain to climb.

The FBI was much different from the police department; more than anyone could imagine. During the Academy, we were conducting a practical exercise. My partner was also a former cop, though ex-cops were not that common. During the exercise, we decided to affect an arrest and started placing the handcuffs on the "actor" who was an Academy staff member. The instructor quickly stopped the exercise.

"Did you get permission to make the arrest?" he shouted to my partner and me.

"Hah, permission to make an arrest! That's a good one." We laughed at that obvious joke - except, he was not joking. The idea of requesting permission to make an arrest was almost an oxymoron to a cop. Split second decision making kept a cop alive.

I spent approximately ten years on the street as a field agent. My most memorable years were spent on an FBI-NYPD Organized Crime/Drug Enforcement Task Force. This was in the late 1980s and early 1990's in Jackson Heights in Queens, NY. We were targeting Colombian cocaine trafficking and money laundering. We did it all - surveillance, wiretaps, undercover operations and drug raids. I even executed a sneak-and-peek search warrant, 15 years before that became a controversial aspect of the PATRIOT Act. Not only were the cases exciting, but so were the dynamics of FBI Agents and NYPD Detectives working so closely together. We were different beasts. Despite the strong personalities, long hours and dangerous situations, we had fun. My experiences on this task force served as the inspiration for my recent crime novel, Bad Intent.

I eventually left that task force to enter management for the remainder of my 24-year career with the FBI. By the time I reached Special Agent in Charge, I had held numerous positions, served in several field offices and was involved in the inner-workings of the FBI; I had seen the best and the worst of the FBI. The public would be surprised by not only what the FBI could do, but also what it could not do. A highly accomplished agency, the FBI is made up of people — imperfect, as we all are. Office politics, big egos and petty conflicts were as prevalent in the FBI as in any organization — government or private industry. But through it all, we took on spies, mobsters, white-collar criminals and corrupt politicians. And just like any police department, we could not wipe out crime and corruption, but maintained enough control to keep our country safe and secure. After 9/11, the FBI undertook some deep introspection. The FBI quickly recognized that the face of the enemy had changed and needed to change with it. The FBI continues to evolve hoping to stay a step ahead the next impending threat.

When I retired six years ago, I was home decompressing and reconnecting — I had lived away from home the last four years of my career. I thought about all my experiences — from fistfights as a patrol officer to management decisions to media appearances. Most of those memories made me laugh and I thought there were some life lessons to be learned. I put those thoughts into writing with my first book, *Walking the Corporate Beat: Police School for Business People*. Only after giving several successful presentations on business risk, based on the book, did I find the confidence to publish it. I continue to give business presentations, most notably, "The Stranger" using those concepts to teach executives how to deter and detect hidden operational risks.

My crime novels, Midnight Sin and Bad Intent are hardboiled and gritty and take you to the dark side of the cop world. Law and Order Producer Peter Giuliano described Midnight Sin, "Michael captured his heart and soul as a cop. My heart was pounding. This is a powerful story, no matter which side of the law you happen to be on."

People always ask if I miss the action. They are surprised when I say no. I enjoyed being a street cop in uniform and in plain clothes, being a field FBI Agent and an FBI executive. Every position and experience was challenging and fun in its own way. Yet, there is always a time to move on.

I nearly failed creative writing in high school. Even my written reports in the FBI were returned by my superiors for being too pithy and lacking "fluff."

In my presentations and in my books, I tell a story within my story. I hope to leave you thinking and wondering.

Michael Tabman was born and raised in New York City. After serving as a police officer for three years with the Fairfax County VA Police Department on patrol, in plain clothes and as a hostage negotiator, he joined the FBI.

A 24-year FBI veteran, Michael investigated crimes ranging from white collar to bank robberies, organized crime, drug trafficking and money laundering. While stationed in New York City, he was the case agent investigating one of the country's largest drug money laundering operations. He rose through the ranks reaching the level of Special Agent in Charge. Michael commanded the investigation of the Red Lake High School Massacre. His professional travels took him to Israel, Russia, Ukraine, Vietnam, Singapore, Malaysia and Thailand.

An author, keynote speaker and security consultant, Michael is also a frequent commentator on local news stations. Visit his website at www.MichaelTabman.com

OF INTEREST

IN THESE TRYING TIMES ...

Here are some interesting industry statistics. I know these figures are a good few years old, but they still tell a fascinating story.

1. Of the 200,000 books published worldwide each year only 2% become bestsellers.
2. 84% of the bestsellers are published by the 5 largest New York publishers.
3. 2 out of 10 books published make a profit for the publisher.
4. In 2004, 950,000 titles out of the 1.2 million tracked by Nielsen Bookscan sold fewer than 99 copies. Another 200,000 sold fewer than 1,000 copies, which means that 1,150,000 books made an average of £10,000 ($15,358) for the publisher before any production, marketing, advertising and distribution costs were deducted. This translates to approximately £900 ($1,382.22) for the author.
5. Only 25,000 books sold more than 5,000 copies.
6. The average book in America sells about 500 copies. In the UK it is significantly less.
7. Only 10 books a year sell more than a million copies.
8. Fewer than 500 books sell more than 100,000.
9. The magic number for a book to be considered successful is 10,000, which makes an average of £100,000 ($153,580) for the publisher before all production costs are deducted, and approximately £9,000 ($13,822.20) for the author.
10. The average income of a published author is in the region of £7,000 ($10,750.60) per year.
11. In excess of 90% of published authors do not make enough money to live on with this as their sole income.
    - You only have to sell 5,000 to be in the top 2% of bestselling books, but despite this statistic you'd still only be making something in the region of £4,500 ($6,911.10) per year.
    - Royalties on books usually start at 10% — and unless you have a major publisher, they are now based on wholesale price and not retail — and the reserve against returns is

15-25%. So the odds on making your fortune from a book alone are slim.

- The book business is like every business. People who have made it usually build their readership slowly over time, and ultimately gain a wider following after years and years of hard work. It is necessary to continue to produce better and better books, to do whatever is necessary to stay in good favour with your publishing company, and do any and all promotion you can yourself. Go to libraries, do signings, readings, whatever you can, and in this way you will hopefully sell enough books to make enough money for the publishing company so they can continue to justify further publishing contracts.
- The harsh truth is that the publishing industry — just like the movies, just like the theatre, the opera, the ballet, the art gallery — is a business. If money is not made it will not survive, and as an author you have a responsibility to give your reader the very best work that you can, and at the same time work towards assisting your publisher in their very difficult task of making the world take notice of what you are doing. To take you on in the first place means that your publisher must have a very definite and passionate belief in what you are doing, and to do anything other than contribute in every way possible to what they are doing will only serve to let you down.
- Being temperamental, over-demanding, acting like a prima donna, will accomplish worse than nothing. It will make your publisher unwilling to work with you. There is an abundance of talent in the world. Many, many tens of thousands of manuscripts are received by the main UK publishers every year, and this figure is growing. The bulk of them find their way into the slush pile, never to be seen again. To have located a publisher who believes in your work sufficiently to put many, many thousands of pounds behind all that it takes to bring a book to a store shelf is a miracle in itself. To then waste that serendipitous and tremendously fortunate opportunity — that chance of a lifetime — by being "artistically difficult," is actually artistic suicide.
- The world needs great novels, and thus it needs great authors. Greatness possesses, inherent in its composition, not only skill and brilliance, but also compassion, empathy, patience, understanding, tolerance, and — above all — humility. Humility is the very essence of review, for without humility one considers one's own viewpoint important above all others, which is all very well and good until one considers the possibility of what it would take to publish your book alone.
- **This is perhaps where self-publishing falls on its face, and though I have no problem with self-publishing, I know that the first draft (which is, almost invariably, the draft that a self-publishing author releases) is not the one that is ready for reading. Someone else needs to look at it, to view it, not from a writer's perspective, but from a reader's, and that — in my opinion — is what shows up the plot-holes and inconsistencies that you can park a truck in.**

- The book industry is going through one of its toughest and most demanding times. Fewer authors are being taken on, more authors are finding themselves "between contracts." I do not think that any author would be badly-served by being as hard-working, dedicated, co-operative and accommodating as they can possibly be right now, all the while maintaining their creative integrity, and really writing what they feel they should be writing.
- As I have always said, the very worst book that you could write is the one that you believe others will enjoy reading. The very best book is the one that you yourself believe you would enjoy.
- It is a fine balance to maintain — the production of viable works against the demands of internally established and maintained creative integrity — but it can be done, now more so than ever.

R.J. Ellory is the author of *Three Days in Chicagoland,* which focuses on the brutal murder of a young girl in Chicago in 1956, as told from three different viewpoints: The Sister, The Cop and The Killer. His other books are *Candlemoth, Ghostheart, A Quiet Vendetta, City of Lies, A Quiet Belief in Angels, A Simple Act of Violence, The Anniversary Man, Saints of New York, Bad Signs, A Dark and Broken Heart, The Devil and the River.* Visit his website: www.RJEllory.com

AUTHOR IS FINALIST IN READERS' FAVORITE 2013 INTERNATIONAL AWARD CONTEST

Clayton Bye, writer, editor and publisher is a finalist in the Readers' Favorite 2013 International Award Contest in the anthology category for his book, *The Speed of Dark*.

Bye is author of 9 books and a varied collection of short stories, poems, articles and hundreds of reviews, he has also published 2 anthologies of excellent short stories by some great talents from around the world. The first book featured general fiction, while the current offering is horror, through and through. *The Speed of Dark*, Clayton's most recent effort, is available online from his websites ClaytonBye.com and Shop.ClaytonBye.com

REVIEWS & INTERVIEWS

A QUIET VENDETTA

Author: R.J. Ellory

Page Count: 496

Star Rating: 

REVIEW BY FRAN LEWIS

Enter the world of a Medical Examiner as he takes you through the process of discovering a corpse, placing it on the table, seeing where it was found and the work needed to identify the person in order to show respect for who he/she was. The car is unique, the smell is overwhelming and the case will prove to be unusual as one man finally comes forward after seeing a lone car sitting for three days, peers inside the window and what he finds would probably make anyone lose their lunch and a lot more.

Police on the scene, one detective called out of a deep sleep, the evidence limited the mutilation of the body horrific and the work begins to find out why anyone would surgically remove this man's heart and then place it back in his chest cavity. According the ME it signifies revenge. New Orleans is the place and the author describes the areas, the people, the scenes so graphically that you witness the events first hand and feel a part of the story. The medical examiner's terminology, the police investigation and the body are so vividly described that the squeamish might close their eyes when reading this book but the more hardy and interested as this reviewer is will not stop reading the book or the events until the answers to the questions you might ask if you went along with the police are answered and the killer is caught. But, there is much more that has not unfolded as I review A Quiet Vendetta by bestselling author R.J. Ellory.

Review

John Verlaine is the detective assigned to the case. This would prove anything but an ordinary investigation as he seeks the help of one man to try and understand the circumstances surrounding the murder, the way the victim was killed and the graphics on the victim's back of the constellation Gemini. The man whose help he seeks instructs him to walk away and dismiss the case from his mind. The next thing he knows, the FBI takes it over. We learn the victim is an ex-marine who was guarding the daughter of the Governor of Louisiana. The daughter, who is supposed to be spending time with her mother, never shows up.

Catherine Ducane has been kidnapped. Now, the mystery begins.

The FBI has taken over the case and they cannot seem to find any leads or direct links to the man killed or the kidnapping. One phone call to the agent in charge changes it all as the voice on the phone assures the agent that Catherine is okay but he wants something in exchange for her safe return. Just what that is has not been revealed.

Ray Hartmann holds the future of Catherine in his hands as the kidnapper calls the FBI and demands his return to New Orleans for a one-on-one, face to face explanation of why this happened and where the girl might be. Ray is in law enforcement and has a highly volatile personality that cost him his family's confidence and caused his present state of living alone.

Expert at dealing with the mafia, lone-sharking, fraud and other related crimes, he readily joins the House Judiciary Subcommittee to assist the District Attorney and others with cases involving organized crime. Used as the catalyst to bring this kidnapper in, he agrees to speak with him to help bring Catherine home. One word spoken in a phone call to the police "ALWAYS" just might be the key to another person's involvement.

John Verlaine knows what that means as he relates it to Hartmann in a private conversation — the man who told him to walk away and never look back ... Feraud. How he might be connected has not been revealed. As the kidnapper is about to appear, Ernesto Perez will take control.

Detective John Verlaine of the New Orleans Police department sets the wheels in motion when investigating the murder of Catherine's bodyguard. Enter one man who wants to tell his story at all costs, even to himself. The history he recounts will bring chills to the reader's spine and put fear their hearts for the kidnap victim.

The deal made is for Ernesto Perez to tell his story, one which allows the reader to get an insight into a man who wants the attention which surrounded others in the past focused on him in the present. Je tells of living with a father who was violent and entering a world that would turn him into not only a psychopathic killer but a hit man, too.

As the inner thoughts of Ernesto Perez are revealed, you begin to understand the rationale behind his ramblings and his need for attention. Comparing himself to Castro through many memories of the man and how he created his dictatorship and his reign over the people in his country, you learn that his motivation is not to help them learn where Catherine is, but to unburden himself of his past wrong deeds and let the world know that at one time he was no better than his father who killing his mother. An act that he retaliated in his own brutal way.

Starting with the murder of a salesman and going on after that with no remorse, Perez tells how he loves the rush of the kill. As he continues to tell his life story, the FBI, police and Ray become frustrated and hope of finding Catherine fades. Readers eventually see how her father fits into the picture, as well as the link he has to those involved. His reasons for choosing Hartmann are unbelievable and the result will definitely haunt you at night and bring chills down your spine.

Author R.J. Ellory takes the reader on a psychological journey inside the mind of a killer who thinks murder is the only way to survive. Hartmann is a drunk and buries himself in his job to the exclusion of his wife and daughter. He even has the violent tendency that mirrors Ernesto. Could this be the hidden link? The frustration of listening to this man talk about himself and justify who he is and what he has turned into even though someone's life is hanging in the balance adds to the suspense and the outstanding craftsmanship of this book.

As you hear Ernesto's story and learn more about his background, you begin to see the dark shadows in his life as he tries to create parallels between him and Ray. Deaths he's caused and brags about and the violence that he justifies makes it seem like this confession is a cleansing of his soul and he hopes to be absolved at the end. When the police lose patience, they enlist Ray to make a deal with him and the result is more than horrific. Ray and John visit Feraud and there is a backlash you won't believe.

You will have to learn what really happened to Catherine for youself. You will also learn where Ernesto winds up and what the truth behind the kidnapping. Once again, author R.J. Ellory has penned a story filled with history, twists, turns and an ending so dramatic and so filled with surprises that you won't want the story to ever end. You'll also hope that you might meet Ray Hartmann again. One dramatic ending that will send chills down your spine one outstanding author. *A Quiet Vendetta*: Much more than silent, I would have to say.

WITHIN MY GRASP

Page Count: 224

Star Rating: ★★★★★

REVIEW BY FRAN LEWIS

An Unforgettable Memori. Every story has its own beginning, middle and end. Life does, too. Some start out by being born to two great parents, going to school, graduating college and hopefully engaging in a career that is fulfilling and rewarding. But, not every story has a happy ending and some stories change midstream when the main character encounters an obstacle, roadblock or villain and needs to find a way to overcome these with the help of minor characters or his/her sheer will to succeed and forge ahead. This story begins with a man who loved life, flying planes, taking risks and enjoyed the fun of the open air, competitions, racing cars, and exploring new avenues.

One morning, you get up and you text a message to your wife, you wash the dishes to surprise her and you take her car to the car wash to get it cleaned. You wave at your neighbor, you flag down a cab to take you back home while you not only get the car washed but detailed too. You make a simple phone call on your cell phone. You unlock you car door with the remote and you enter your house with a simple key. That was today and then there is tomorrow.

Deciding to enter a car race, Mike Pinkest never thought that his life would change. His car crashed on the Salt Flats and the rest was like a nuclear blast that had a fallout with tragic results. Imagine waking up in a hospital and hearing the voices of the doctors but not being able to respond. Induced coma or sleep helped his injuries heal, but the whole time he was comatose, he could hear every word that was said around him. He spent time trying to figure out how to respond and wanting to know what was being done to him and why.

Yesterday he could race a car, fly a plane and make simple phone call, then in flash he could not. Both of his hands were gone — so badly injured they had to be amputated. He also had a traumatic brain injury compounding things and making his recovery questionable. As you read Mike's incredible true story, in his own words, you feel his frustrations and applaud his successes. He never gave up on himself. This is a story that will appeal to adult readers, young children, teens and seniors and will help everyone realize that you, too, can attain your goals and live every day "within your own grasp" if you have the drive and will to succeed.

As we take a trip back in time along with Mike, he reflects on his childhood we learn about his passion for planes. His parents encouraged him to be curious and learn about planes, then share the information with his teachers and friends. He created his own planes and called his bedroom "The

Airplane Factory." This is the prologue of the story, but there is much more.

Mike had drive, and airplanes were just one of his passions; playing baseball was the next. With the help of his father, he managed to become a pitcher. Mikem till this day does not take "No" for an answer and strives to succeed at everything he does. He never considers his limitations a drawback.

The '50s and '60s were an exciting time for him as he played ball, drove race cars, hot rods, and the tons of girls that came and went. Through it all, his strong desire and will to become an airline pilot remained. Spending time at many airports, going through numerous training programs and finally enlisting in the Marines when he could not get a job with a major airline, Mike did it all. He put in the time and went through the training in the Marines, followed by Officers Candidate School and then enrolled in an Aviation Scholarship Program. Throughout the chapter titled Nuclear Weapons and Napalm he reveals his world at that time. He tells of the many flights and training and we join him as he weaves his way through skies and gets his wings. Imagine his feelings when, after all is said and done, he can no longer fly.

Mike makes trips to the Philippines, is part of the West Pac Tour and getting discharged from the Marines in 1975. His life had just begun. His next step was fighting fires from the air as he became a flight instructor and then became hooked on the fire fighting industry. This brought him into dangerous situations, and he met some great people and made many new friends.

Chapter Four is exciting, as he relates his training, becoming a fire fighter pilot and the loss of a great friend. Next, he takes several trips to South America and flying with the fire bombers. The descriptions are so vivid you feel as if you are in the air with him. The Department of the Interior Contract funded the South American Research Project and what he describes is exciting, and flying a Corsair is his ultimate dream.

The story really comes alive when you see the amazing photos that Marti Smiley Childs includes in the book. Also included are stories of when he landed a job with Air Cal and his introduction to Aerobatics. But, the real story is how he fought so hard to get his pilot's license back after the accident, the hard road he walked, the steps he took, the support of his wife Mary Ann Harr and the many missteps that came before and after.

Not everything in this story is the way you would hope it would be and when the main character faces a villain or a conflict he/she has to find a way to beat the odds, win at all costs and hope for a great ending. When the harsh reality of what happened to him finally set in, Mike had several avenues he could travel.

One marriage that dissolved, and another that would take him to new heights and make him realize true loyalty. He found someone with as much drive within her to help him prevail and succeed as he had.

Chapter 9 brings it all into perspective as he describes the crash and the result of having both hands amputated. Atrophy and other obstacles are described in Chapter 10, as the author shares his innermost fears, thoughts and his life spent in the University of Utah Medical Center. He tells of the work they did to bring him to the point of being released and going to the University of California Davis Medical Center. The road to recovery was not smooth. He had to first learn how to deal with daily life and then decide whether to have hooks attached to his stumps or push the doctors for a prescription for myolelectic body powered prosthetics.

His never lost his desire to fly and it propelled him to succeed. New hands, learning to use them and becoming more independent took time, determination and definitely patience on the part of his wife, Mary Ann. Describing the difficulty of performing simple tasks Chapter 11 reminds readers that carrying a tray, brushing your teeth or even drinking from a glass should not be taken for granted.

The inventive ways Mike used to change a print cartridge, drive a car, get his license and go through every test, trial and course to get a reissuance of his third class FAA certificate and his private pilot's license lets you know that he is a fighter. Flying is in his blood and he would not stop until he was back in the air. Winning the battle, he decided to have someone build him a custom plane and become more involved in aerobatics once again.

After all the tests and trials, he regained his license and then joined a program called the Touch Of Understanding. This decision was made after going to Hope School and seeing the disabled children there. They made an impact on him and he was in spired by how they managed to smile despite their disabilities. The trip to this school and his trip to Africa would start him on a road that he would never veer from. His voice became and still is powerful in his enthusiastic discussions with the children. They enjoy his sense of humor and the impact he made in their lives. *(As an educator who taught students with learning disabilities, I always reminded them that you will succeed and can if you set your mind to it and never give up. This program is not only valuable, but should be worldwide.)*

This daredevil who lost his hands but not his spirit. He regained his license, became a spokesperson for Touch of Understanding, and learned about Canine Companions for Independence and the many dogs that needed homes and how they would help him. Mike's unwavering tenacity, persistence and love of life comes through on every page.

Within My Grasp tells us that everything is within your grasp if you don't give up and decide that, "You can Do it! Never take 'no' for an answer," and understand that just because you might not be able to do everything you want does not mean you cannot do what's meaningful to you. So, how does this story end? It does not! Mike relates in the Epilogue what he is doing now, what he has learned and summarizes his life and what he invisions for his future. We meet Magy, Joyce and Taylor who play a great part in his life. If you want to know who they are and how he met them, you are going to have to read this outstanding memoir. Told in the first person, you hear Mike's voice on every page and every step of the way. His last sentence sums it up perfectly, "Life is Good." You are so right.

Let's dedicate this to all those children out there that might be different on the outside but will learn that we are the same on the inside and never give up. To my cousin Dr. Mark Swerdloff, a double amputee (Lost both legs) one of the top oral surgeons in the world. I dedicate this to you.

Let's dedicate this to all those children out there that might be different on the outside but will learn that we are the same on the inside and never give up. To my cousin Dr. Mark Swerdloff, a double amputee (Lost both legs) one of the top oral surgeons in the world. I dedicate this to you. — Fran

ACTS OF SURRENDER

Page Count: 218

Star Rating: ★★★★★

One reads a biography or an autobiography to find out more about a public figure or politician, celebrity or writer. What if the above person was someone you consider a friend … someone you met using social media?

On Facebook you get snippets of peoples lives but when a person you have come to know takes the courage to lay himself bare on paper. Gone are the superficial things you know as you find out what lies beneath.

In deciding to read *Acts of Surrender*, I wanted to know a couple of things about the writer. What lead him to leave Canada and pursue a life in the southwestern states? Why does he love to be called Mark David?

I found this out through his writing and spiritual calling. There were also a few other revelations along the way that had me asking more questions as I read the book.

All I can say is, what a journey! There were times I felt like I was riding shotgun on his many road trips to either find his true calling as a writer and a metaphysical spiritualist. I am not sure if the latter is a real term, but let's just go with that.

We met Mark David in Montreal in the '70s where circumstances of his life are revealed to him. Things he thought he knew to be true but weren't. This gives him something to think about and shapes who he is called to become in later years.

He moves a lot, and he takes his reader with him through each move. He reveals tense times when he is living on his last dollar and moves on to find miraculous windfalls.

We see him struggle with personal aspects of his life and triumph with him when he finds love and experiences parenthood when he didn't ever think he would.

Like I said, I felt as if I was right there with him as I read this story. *Acts of Surrender* is one of those books that challenges the reader and makes them ask questions about themselves as they read it. It was hard to put down, but at times I needed to take a break just to absorb its contents. Some of the quotes at the start of each chapter really spoke to me as well. I would advise having tissues handy as you read.

Over all, I thought it was a powerful read and full of insight and learning. I would recommend it to lovers of autobiographies and give it 5 stars.

REVIEW BY KAREN VAUGHN

WHY SHE LEFT US

Page Count: 432

Star Rating: ★★★★★

Semi-finalist in the 2013
Kindle Book Review Awards

REVIEW BY FRAN LEWIS

It was the summer of 1985, and she was young and inexperienced, but longing to love and to be loved in return, when he entered her life. At the same time, while she was desperately seeking the love and approval of a mother who never wanted her in the first place, events totally beyond her control claimed her as their victim, leaving those she left behind unable to cope with the enormity of her absence.

Why She Left Us is written as a series of diary entries, the events seen through the eyes of several different people. But at its center is a love story chronicling a romance that transforms the lives of two people who, for too brief a period of time, experienced the greatest happiness they had ever known

Review

Why She Left Us by David Dennis a compelling tale about three sisters and their muddled love lives. Their mother, an amorously restless and seemingly selfish and disinterested woman, and their aunt, who is unhappy and single, have little influence on them. Not surprisingly, it is two young men who drive the plot forward. The girls' rivalries over the two and between the two men make for interesting reading. On a deeper level, the book deals brilliantly with the issues of self-worth and the desire to be loved.

Told by various separate narratives, the book allows great insight into the motifs and the thoughts of the five characters in the story. Although this had me a little confused about the plot at times, it allows the reader to feel intensely the pain, confusion and desires of those characters. It also works incredibly well for the unfolding the story and revealing some of the twists and surprises to come. A lot is implied but not said until much later, keeping suspense and interest high. What distinguished this book from coming of age and superficial teenage literature and makes it so precious is the non-stereotypical characterization, the clever plotting and the raw insights the author provides into his characters' psyches. This is an intense and emotional read; one that is hard to forget. It should do well in literary circles.

About the author: David Dennis taught English to seventh-grade students for 28 years, retiring in June 1999. In addition to the novel *Why She Left Us*, he has published nine books in the Brett Cornell comedy-mysteries. These novels are deliberately written in a tongue-in-cheek style and feature a crass, wise-cracking private detective who's something of an anti-hero. They're meant to be breezy, lightweight entertainment — not to be taken seriously.

The idea for *Why She Left Us* originated as a sub-plot in a huge family saga that David was writing during his college years.

Excerpts from my interview with David on my blog

"Decades later, I decided to develop this sub-plot into a stand-alone piece of writing, prompted mainly by the personalities of the characters involved, as well as the dramatic and even tragic possibilities that the story-line entailed. Since all of my other writings were created in a fairly traditional and conventional manner, I wanted to try something different with this work. Hence, the idea arose to utilize multiple narratives and a timeline that bounced back and forth from the past to the present. The main message of the book deals with the idea that the loss of an individual can often have a profound effect upon those who are left behind, often in such a way that one doesn't realize right away that such a thing is actually happening to them. For example, one of my characters mentions that, even while attending the funeral of the recently deceased person involved, she couldn't think of a real reason why she should be grieving at all. Later on, as the reader finds out, the death of that person has drastic repercussions for her own life — perhaps even more so than many of the other characters in the book.

I'd advise new writers to try to exercise patience in not rushing to see their books in print, without their writing having undergone some serious editing and, most of all, some serious contemplation. After finishing a book, it's usually a good idea to literally stay away from it for about 2 weeks, then go back and re-read it and analyze the sort of impression it's making on you."

TRAILS IN THE SAND

Page Count: 408

Star Rating: 

Semi-finalist in the 2013
Kindle Book Review Awards

REVIEW BY CHRISTOP FISCHER

A Family Saga Filled with Love Triangles, Sea Turtles, and an Oil Spill. When environmental writer Caroline Carlisle sets off to report on endangered sea turtles during the Deepwater Horizon oil spill, the last thing she expects is to uncover secrets — secrets that threaten to destroy her family, unless she can heal the hurts from a lifetime of lies. To make matters worse, Caroline's love for her late sister's husband, Simon, creates an uproar in a southern family already set on a collision course with its past.

Using real-life events as the backdrop, Trails in the Sand explores the fight to restore balance and peace, in nature and in a family, as both spiral toward disaster. Through it all, the ancient sea turtle serves a reminder that life moves forward despite the best efforts to destroy it.

Review

Trails In The Sand by P.C. Zick is an emotional read about family secrets and making peace with the past. After her sister dies, Caroline reconnects with her family and with Simon, the man that her sister stole from her and married. Said widower Simon has an adopted daughter that needs to come to terms with her status and with the new relationship between her aunt and her father. Thrown into the mix are a few more family issues such as a drowning in 1956, and more revelations that come from diaries. There are a lot of issues to be resolved in this family, making it an emotionally charged story.

Zick uses several separate narratives to bring different perspectives into the book and also includes several subplots making for a rich reading experience.

There is an important plotline which concerns the 2010 Deepwater Oil Spillage in the Mexican Gulf, a metaphor for hidden or covered-up tragedies and wrong-doings that ultimately force their way to the surface and spill onto the shore. Caroline being a writer and journalist that concerns herself with environmental issues — not just the oil spill — describes the horrific damage to the wildlife and the coast. She also writes also about a coal mining disaster in Virginia, which helps to take the focus off just one or the other oversight or cover-up, making it a more global theme. The family is under severe stress from both external and internal forces and as they unite to save sea turtles and work together on the present, they let go of the past and begin to forgive and to heal.

The writing in this novel is immaculate and tight; for example, the Prologue begins in 1956 with the drowning of Alex, Caroline's uncle, and the story ends in the same spot, a beautifully chosen way to complete the circle. The dialogue and the weaving together of the various plots and narratives works well to let the story unfold smoothly and make this an interesting read. The characters are well composed and believable and make for an engaging and convincing portrayal of their inner struggles.

Zick writes with much empathy and insight into her characters, showing a very caring and committed attitude towards the environment and the human beings in it. The interplay between the story lines, private lives and newspaper stories that are woven into the narrative adds much depth to the book.

Interview with the author

I've always known I was a writer deep down, but I didn't admit it until I decided to leave my career as a high school English teacher. I lost my passion for teaching and was scared I would become one of those old, mean teachers who hate their job. I thought about what else I did well, and I kept coming back to writing. I'd dabbled with a novel; I liked writing Letters to the Editor; I was known as the "writing teacher" among my peers. Probably the biggest motivator was the praise I always received when I wrote something and published it.

I wrote an essay about my mother's hands after she died in 1998. I read it at my writer's group, and they said, "Get that published." I took it to the editor of the local paper and asked if they wanted a column. They did. So many people told me my piece helped them heal after the death of a parent that this thing called writing hooked me. During the next summer break, I pulled out the novel that had been languishing for ten years in a file cabinet drawer, and I finished the darn thing. I sent it to ten publishers and the tenth one — a small publisher — picked it up. The local paper started hiring me to do freelance, and that's when I decided it was time to give up teaching and go into writing. As a journalist, I've written news reports, feature articles, editorials, and columns. As a freelance writer, I've written two nonfiction books, biographies for an encyclopedia, and reports. However, writing fiction heads the list of my passions.

I write contemporary fiction with an environmental theme. Redemption is a common thread running through most of my novels. I hope readers walk away from reading my novels knowing it's never too late to change for the better.

Some of it comes naturally, or perhaps I learned it as a teacher. As a journalist, I learned to research. I took many more notes than I actually needed. In the beginning of working on a novel, I usually have far too much material and sometimes I may be familiar with a topic and give too little information. My beta readers help me with this problem. They tell me when I've gone on too much and when I haven't provided enough information.

BEYOND VINYL

Page Count: 254

Star Rating: ★★★★★

REVIEW BY FRAN LEWIS

Let's Take A Trip Back In Time! Head for the vintage store and check out the fashions. Make sure that you find a great pair of bell bottoms, colorful shirt and even a few pairs of capezios, baby dolls and even some Oxford ties. Add in my favorite those great mini skirts and some chunky high heels and you are definitely ready to take a trip back to an era when music really popped, and the sounds were unique and the artists were filled with Soul. There are details about a time when the world was dealing with the Vietnam War, Woodstock, hippies and where 1963 started off a decade filled with sounds and music by artists who began in the previous decade and continued to soar.

Included are Elvis, Ray Charles, Dion and the Everly Brothers and the Beatles, as well as the social causes, the music related to the war, sit-ins, Kennedy and Martin Luther King's assassinations and much more. These all influenced what was popular, setting the stage for the eclectic music of today. The British invasion with the Beatles, the Civil Rights Movement plus Motown, R&B, Fold and much more were just some of the fires that lit up this colorful decade. Joseph Rabinowitz takes readers back to this time period along with author Donald Riggio and relates the history, and brings us the music, the wars, the deceits, the betrayals and the love that brought his family back together as he shares the next chapter of his story.

Beginning with his daughter, Danielle, we learn about her relationship with her parents and how she tries to be more independent. Listening to Joseph talk, we take the first journey back in time to 1969, when Janet and Joseph reignite their love and decide to restart their lives together. We meet him at the Majestic Theater after the Du-kanes' reunion performance, setting off a chain of events that would bring them back into the limelight.

Teaming with his former partner Leo Klein, Jacob Miliewski and many more, a decision was made to book more concerts for this group. The author then flashes to Janet's life and history, including Ian Markham, who is her daughter's father. In Chapter 2 we meet the Du-Kanes — Kenny, Jimmy and Bobby, as well as their families. They then take their own journeys down memory lane with readers.

In 1964, we meet Janet, a naïve photographer who just wanted to take some shots for her new book, *Priory*. Enlisting the help of Ian Markham, she thought would expedite matters. However, their business arrangement turned personal and when Janet learned she was having baby Danielle, Ian's attitude was anything but supportive.

Turning to drugs, liquor and other women was his solution to living his life large.

When Janet learns the truth about him, she immediately changes the course of her life. The Have-Nots was his group and their popularity was on the rise, but like the Grateful Dead they spent much of their time in front of a judge or magistrate. Using her for his own purposes, he thought she would write a song for him to use for his group and send them up to number one on the charts. You have to learn for yourself how she reacted to this idea.

Next, we learn about the man that started Chanticleer Records, how he was discovered, the part he played and his relationship with Teddy Boyette. This is one book chocked full of history, solid research and so much music you can hear it on every page. So, before you put those hot dancing shoes on, get out that old stereo, find those 45s (make sure you have the round piece that goes in the middle), and let's party.

From learning about the Fonz, to finding out that Boyette had a son and a stolen guitar, Joseph Rabinowitz shares many stories with readers as well as continuing with Danielle's discovery. Let's not forget the history the author shares about the Nixon era, Watergate and, of course, we have to remember the Baby Boomers. Many young people who fought in many wars returned home to the U.S. and needed jobs. Some used their G.I Bills to go back to school and others hoped for employment. But, it was not easy. There were more changes as both kids and adults not only listened to the radio but with many more shows on television they were doubling hooked.

Elvis, Jerry Lee Lewis and Roy Orbison were the rage and they created the Sun Record Company. Learning the truth behind TJ's birth, finding out about his mother, Dee, led Joseph on a quest to learn more. What did Danielle discover? You just won't believe it as Joseph, Dani and Janet hear Teddy Elvis singing on some rare tapes found hidden in his basement.

The author shares the truth about Elvis, his addiction to drugs and other meds and what happened on the day he passed away. He talks about the disco scene, Bobby Vitale and the places he frequented. Castle Hill Diner, The Thruway Diner and Jo&Jo's bring back great memories. Imagine learning more about the Pixies and their star performer, add in when the King died plus Danielle's scheme to get into TJ Russell's show and what she did when she tricked the manager into letting her and her two friends backstage and you have one interesting story. Priceless!

Demolition Night and Radiation brought in great crowds when the Chicago White Sox were taking the field. Disco music might have been on the decline, but disc jockey Steve Dahl's campaign to revive it soared. Imagine detonating explosives and watching pieces of vinyl permeate throughout the air. The end result not what they expected.

Next, Janet and Danielle visit Israel. Janet is creating a new coffee table book. Going on a guided tour with Danielle and Janet, we see many of the sites, learn a lot about the young people and the security needed.

On November 4, 1979, a mob of "over 300 militant students stormed the US Embassy in Tehran chanting that the building housed a den of spies." More than 60 military and civilian men and women were taken hostage and the event became embedded in our minds forever. The friendships gained in Israel, Dani bonding with the translator and going home with a special gift really made this chapter even more special.

The mafia does come into play in this book, as they had plans of their own for their record company. Using a man named Max Seiderman who was an accountant who "cooked" the books. Add in TJ Russell, who decided to leave the group Amadeus, and many thought it for the best. The hostage situation and what was not being done about it was the topic on everyone's minds.

Of course what would any book about this era be without including Ronald Reagan, the advent of Monday Night Football and the murder of John Lennon. In the story, things are about to change. One member of Joseph's team lost his life and Danielle celebrated being 16. *(On page 171 the author really brings to light the neighborhood where I did tons of shopping, the best bakeries, pizza and more Morris Park in the Bronx and it is still there and better than ever.)* Jimmy Stannic was part of their team and we cannot forget the information included about him working on the subway and trying to better his life. Next, comes the CD and Danielle's time in High School. An incident in school might have gotten her in trouble but a date with her heartthrob definitely worth it if you ask Danielle.

What would this era be without the icon of the late fifties: "American Bandstand" and Dick Clark? *(The $10,000 Pyramid was one of my mom's favorite shows and Dick Clark filled every living room on New Years Eve.)* So, why wouldn't Danielle want to be there to meet Dick Clark? An encounter that evening with TJ Russell is quite enlightening and allows readers to know this young lady was force in her own right.

Author Donald Riggio keeps readers and this reviewer glued to the disco label, printed page, the time period and the record companies until the very last page. The dramatic, surprise ending is great.

From Michael Jackson to Motown and Don K. Reed, Alan Freed and of course Cousin Brucie this book has it all. Fatal shots fired at Louis Pizzeria, which is still there a few doors down from the Interboro theater where the Du-Kanes were performing, really sets the tone for what is about to happen to The Seracinos, Liebermanns and Bobby Vitale, who were in this restaurant at the time of the shooting. Just who did the shooting? The reason for it will surprise you! Why would anyone emulate the Son of Sam? Who died? You will have to learn for yourself.

There is much more as TJ asks Joseph for help and has to reveal information that would betray others. Racketeering, corruption, organized crime and much more marked this time period. Loyalties, betrayals, lies, changing relationships, family tension and a volatile time period and an ending that changes many lives and provides new directions — great reading. Get out those platform shoes, turn on those tapes of "American Bandstand," tease up your hair real high, put on that mini skirt and party. This is a must read for everyone of every age. *Beyond Vinyl*: Beyond the record; beyond disco. Beyond Compare!

JOURNAL OF A RUSSIAN BUSINESSMAN: –40˚F

Page Count: 236

Star Rating: ★★★★★

REVIEW BY FRAN LEWIS

Right Out of the Headlines — Lives can be changed when you least expect them to be and great jobs on the surface might be a camouflage for something else. Dmitry Pototskiy is the author of this outstanding memoir, *Journal of a Russian Businessman: -40 degrees F.* This is a true story told in his own words with actual events taking place across many continents: Russia, Europe and the United States. As a government employee working in Russia, how could he resist a job as the president of a financial company? Added in is the fact that his immediate superior is one of the richest developers in Moscow. Gennady Shulman is the man who roped him in. Boredom is his reason for taking the bait.

As the principal owner and president of the Keystone Group, this man was able to gain the contracts for building an office complex on a small island in front of the Kremlin. But, as we listen to the deal being formed and the position described, we later learn that his group's financial standing is anything but solid. He is in dire need of money in order to be able to finish this project. What happens will create a chain of events that take many people down and change their lives in the wrong direction forever.

Learning more within the first two chapters of this intricate memoir we are introduced to the Sberbank, one of the biggest state-owned savings banks in Russia. This bank is difficult to deal with and Shulman decides to look in another direction for help.

The plot really thickens within the first few chapters as we learn that before Pototskiy joins the Keystone Group and becomes president of Universal Investment and Finance Company, he receives a letter earmarked for the mayor of Moscow. This letter is in the hands of Mervin Layton, an American businessman with a lot of power and clout with the Russian Federation. The letter proposes to combine the huge international debt incurred by City Hall into U.S. T-bonds and notes. This would change the problem with this debt into a sustainable source of money within five to seven years. Trade Programs is what Layton called it. He inferred that he was representing a Trade Program where those who invested would come out with quite a return on their investments. He also stated that the U.S. Treasury was selling its bonds and notes to specifically chosen, valued investors at a huge discount. The scam begins when these investors are informed that in order to become part of these Trade Programs it is a necessary to help those nations that are struggling with poverty and also poor nations whose economy needs help and where terrorism ran high. So, why did he fall for this and what would make him say yes?

This is the true story of what happened to this businessman and his company in Moscow. As you hear the voices of those involved, you will begin to wonder just who can be trusted, which assets are real, which documents are authentic and why some things were taken at face value. What happens when one business deal with a bank falls through? Why were there investigations in the U.S., Russia and Europe? Why didn't anyone realize this was one huge scam? Listening to the original players and hearing the voice of Layton, even a novice would suspect that there was something unsavory going on. Conditions were not crystal clear though. These Americans helped to defraud many wealthy people in Russia and the United States, and believe it or not, the Russian Prime Minister. You have heard of hit men who are hired to take out someone for money. What about a hit man who was hired to take out your company, ruin your integrity and steal your money?

Across many oceans and continents Dmitry Pototskiy flies from Moscow, to Munich and other places to participate in what is called "Trade Programs." This was the participation in the buying and the selling of bank debentures. Debenture, is a general debt obligation backed only by the integrity of the borrower, not by collateral. Depository Trust Corporation (DTC): A domestic custodial clearing facility owned by all of the major banks and securities firms which is monitored by various banking regulatory agencies and the Securities and Exchange commission.

In order to fully understand what the author is saying, let me explain it in his own words: [He was] Offered the job to head the Department of City Investment planning and was tasked to create the first government agency that could function as an investment corporation in the residential building industry without public funding. He agreed. But, as I described the offering made by Mervin Leyton, things were about to change. Transactions as Mervin explains have to be approved by a manager. There is a chain transactions involved in order to complete the deal, "Not the bank but a program manager who is responsible for everything and is authorized by the Feds to select investors, prepare all documents and upon receipt of the proceeds, to use some part of them to buy a new portion of U.S. Debt to lock into an approved bank."

To get into a trade Program, you have to be qualities or be able to comply with all of the requirements, which is to "provide a project and we capable of investing a minimum amount of funds. So, Layton, is what you would call a Trade manager. But, there are so many other players you will need a scorecard to follow them but the author is so methodical and meticulous in his descriptions that even someone like myself that has no background in this field can easily follow the events.

Pototskiy listening, heard and then decided to go into this venture where we meet Mark, who seems to be the strongest player along with him. Not fully versed in this field or if he had been would have been aware that these special programs outlined by a man named Mitchell, introduced to him by Mark, and others did not and never did exist. Now, you get it, this was one big fact SCAM that sent a chain of events across the ocean and back and billions not millions of dollars were lost by so many. Hiding behind banks, names that sounded real, government agencies that were made up and told that in order to be approved, as Layton claimed, you needed an approved manager, no one thought to look into the one man that started it all and no won ever saw the huge red flags that kept coming up every time there was a snag.

Lies, betrayals, espionage, fraud, deceit, double talking and definitely some fancy financial footwork, our author was positive that Layton was a certified manager, bought he what he said, hook, line and singer, called in favors to get his visas renewed, spent tons on travel, gave upfront money and never bothered to look back. With Layton saying that he would be able to get the financing need to complete the real estate project that was given to them by the Russian Prime Minister. Told that the assets he needed to procure the deal were happily housed or deposited in a Swiss security house and insured by a reputable insurance company. Never trust the word of anyone and always triple check.

Journal of a Russian Businessman: -40°F takes readers inside the minds of those who aim to defraud. Hard to believe after reading this that the events are real, the maze of transactions quite extensive and the end result you have to read it for yourself. Just how far would you go to get rich? Before all is finally said and done you will not believe how many transactions were posed, those that actually might have done through, the money that changed hands and the events that finally awaked the FBI and other law enforcement agencies to what was going on. From the FBI to Interpol to other police agencies the investigation was worldwide and the traveling to try to get these deals done extensive. As a high- ranking government official why would he decide to go into business in order to find Trade Programs that hide behind the curtain you might say and hopefully will yield his new company millions. So, naïve yet so anxious to succeed he never realizes he is being blindsided by the very company he working for.

When the truth comes out and the final accounting occurs you just won't believe how many links are in this fraudulent chain, how many people are involved and what happens when our author is brought into speak to the police and learns just who was behind the scam. According to the books from Keystone the money was spent on the original project or the Tsar's Garden. But, checking into it they learned some harsh realities. When you read page 219 you will learn just how you gain government approval. Why the author left working for the government and Shulman's difficulties in getting the loan. Sometimes someone right in front of you needs to be watched even closer. One shrewd woman would bring it all down but how: you will never guess. Banks playing by their own rules. Two men caught in the crossfire and So, when the person in charge or his old friend Vasiliev asked him to write down the events I guess I am reading it now. If you want it summed up read page 229.

This is one story that kept this reader glued to the printed page for every transaction, deal and the final result. What happens who thinks he/she can get away with it all? Find out when you read *Journal of a Russian Businessman -40°F* equals -40C. Interesting to say the least.

SEBASTIAN

Author: Christoph Fischer

Page Count: 321

Star Rating: ★★★★★

REVIEW BY FRAN LEWIS

Courage is defined as the "the quality of mind or spirit that enables a person to face difficulty, danger, and pain without fear. But, it can mean even more. Once that initial fear or obstacle is defined and the person overcomes that hindrance, drawback or impediment, something has to take over to keep them going. Handicaps are defined as conditions that restrict a person's ability to function physically, mentally or socially.

Sebastian is a uniquely crafted story that has many layers and characters that often appear to have myriad flaws. Each character strives to find a place in the world that is so filled with hate, prejudice and the threat of war, that they often overlook the simple things in life like family, joy and just love. Sebastian is a teenage boy who does not dwell on an injury when there are more important things to concentrate on. However, not focusing on the pain in his left leg and hiding the fact that the leg was infected cost him more than any young teen should have to endure. The accident that caused his injury and resulting leg amputation causes his family to think he can no longer contribute to their business. They think he is unable to run their family grocery store and is limited to few careers. Vienna, Austria is the setting and the loss of his leg had nothing to do with his brilliant mind.

Franz and Vera Schrieber, Sebastian's parents, seem happy to those who know them, but their reality is surprising. Franz, the owner of a grocery store, has many responsibilities and feels the pressure of having to provide for his immediate family and his elderly parents who reside with him. He thought his son's accident represented a Sebastian's weakness and he doesn't bother visiting him in the hospital, leaving his care to his invalid grandparents.

With his father's family living at home, his friends and the many employees that come through their door, the author graphically depicts pre-war Vienna, including the struggles and day-to-day lives of people during a time of war when the Monarchy was taken down. Just how would this man manage to fend for his family and find time to care for his wife and son? Franz treated his family more like a business and was so concerned with his personal wants and needs that he overlooked what was happening right in front of him.

Vera, his wife, is the definition of a woman who has no idea what is happening in the world around her. Current events elude her, working in the store greeting customers is her only way of interacting with people.

The author's research into the war, the government of Austria, the arrival of technology and the changes some were trying to make is extensive. Many people don't understand change, Vienna, like other countries, embraced a class system and often those employed as household workers had to be of other faiths in order to work in certain homes. From the Five Star author of *The Luck of the Weissensteinters,* comes another five star novel that deals with many of the same layers, themes and ideals. Sebastian focuses on a family that needs to embrace their identities as individuals, prejudice among their own and others, fears, deceit, lies and even betrayals and hope.

When Sebastian is told about his infection from a rusty nail and that it would result in his losing the leg. We wonder how he will deal with the news. His mother worries that he won't be able to handle the news and requests the operation be done that night and not in the morning as the doctor suggested. Convincing the doctor, the young man goes through this operation only to prove that not only he is resilient, smart and courageous but he will not be deterred by this setback and hopes to attend school and take his exams.

The story makes twists and turns along, and the plots and subplots help define a character that goes from being weak to growing an inner strength and beauty. Sebastian's story is the story of his family, the women who enter his life and the war that surrounds and defines them all. The family lives above a grocery store. Picturing all of these people in this small environment how tough things were then. This young man only wanted to bring some joy into the lives of others, and was only embraced by one person, his grandfather, the original owner of the store. Sebastian's injury did not affect his mind, ability to learn or his will to succeed.

His grandfather, Oscar, was there for him every step of the way, tutoring him and making sure that his lessons were done so that he would pass his exams.

Vera needs an ally to bring her out and show her she can do more than just take care of the store and deal with problems. Enter Mathilde and her family who seem to have influence in many important places. She joins a women's group whose goal is to help women understand and fight for the right to vote and voice their opinion. Vera agrees with her, but stands to the side the entire time. With the help of Theresa, Mathilde's mother in law, she begins to thrive in many different ways and learn more about herself.

In walks what is supposed to be relief and help but turns out to be more than Vera can handle. An eighteen year old girl named Ingeborg is sent to work in the home and, when needed, in the store. Hoping to become more than just an employee, she bides her time, endears herself within the family and eventually hopes to replace Vera in Franz's bed. Vera is naïve and does not suspect anything until her friend, Mathilde, enlightens her. What happens is right out of a soap opera. Replaced but not really knowing why, Eva comes to work for the family and Sebastian is taken with her. Her secret as to why she lost her previous job is well kept. The situation heats up until she leaves and is replaced by Margit and her mother. Here is where the story gets really hot and very interesting as Vera's friends will help change the dynamics of her life. She becomes involved in séances, the afterlife and communicating with the dead.

The primary cast is Jewish and the questions raised are many as the family needs to cater to people of many nationalities. Lives are unsettled and the country is about to undergo many changes. WWI is about to begin and many men have enlisted to fight for their country. The war has caused Sebastian to step up before his time as Franz is drafted and sent to the front lines.

Each family member seems to have his/her agenda, and when Oscar passes away leaving them without his wisdom and guidance, Rebecca and Vera are left to deal with the store, Franz's absence and

Sebastian's issues. But, Sebastian decides for himself with the help of a special nurse where he wants his life to to; school is not an option, it is his choice.

Things change, Eva leaves, and a mother and daughter came to live with them. Sebastian soon had feelings for Margit, the daughter. Her mother, although depressed, loud and abusive at times, finds her way into the family on a limited basis. With her mother hiding her own treasure, her distrust for the Schreiber family and people in general, the plot takes on a different tone as the war is in full swing. The draft has lowered its expectations as Sebastian has now left what was a great position in a library to have to teach school. People are cruel, no allowances for his disability are made and the family seems to come unglued as Eva reappears. Sebastian and Margit are still together and have a child.

Joining her two friends and others in a séance, Vera thinks that her job is to care for her granddaughter. When both the mother and grandmother disappear withoua clue, she is left to deal with the fallout. Just where did they go and how did they get there? These questions take the reader on a remarkable train ride from Vienna to Galicia where we learn the probable fate of Margit's father, who is now living in their home. We also learn how they feel about the Jewish people and the history behind what happened in Poland and Russia.

The times are changing, and Piroska, Markit's mother, decides to venture out on her own with the help of some of her husband's contacts. She wants to find out where he is and if he is coming back to her. What she learns is startling; whether she believes what they tell her remains to be seen.

With an ending so dramatic and heart-wrenching you won't see it coming, and characters that are so true to life you will definitely identify with many of them, this book is full of interesting plot twists. There are betrayals, lies, and deceit. Family loyalties are tested as is the human spirit. Sometimes a miscommunication can change your life. Find out how when you read this outstanding novel. Courage: What's your definition?

SHEDDING LIGHT ON THE HOLLYWOOD BLACKLIST: CONVERSATIONS WITH PARTICIPANTS

Page Count: 262

Star Rating: ★★★★★

REVIEW BY FRAN LEWIS

Blacklist: A list of persons or organizations that have incurred disapproval or suspicion or are to be boycotted or otherwise penalized; a list of persons who are under suspicion, disfavor, or censure, or who are not to be hired, served, or otherwise accepted. Just how legal is this and what will be revealed by Stanley Dyrector in his open and honest interviews and conversations with so many that have endured this fate? Is this legal? In some cases yes, in others it's viewed as discrimination. Just where did this begin and how do people wind up on these lists?

Merchants can blacklist someone by denying him or her credit especially if the person has declared bankruptcy. These lists are made public and the person faces more than just simple embarrassment. Imagine having your image permanently tarnished in this way?

These lists are used to determine whether someone is denied the right to belong to social clubs, dine in particular restaurants, act in a play, etc. Some, as you will learn when you read this book, are blacklisted for what others have stated as illegal activities.

Companies can be blacklisted too. A strong comparison can be made when many of us block private calls from our home phones or refuse to answer calls listed as restricted. Some of us even block specific callers or numbers from our phones. There are many reasons why someone is blacklisted. Let's start with the first conversation in this book and learn more.

The author brilliantly introduces the reader to ten writers, movie stars and Hollywood figures, and others who were blacklisted. He begins with three shows that focus on four specific people. As we hear their voices and their stories, we come to understand what they endured. We also hear several audience members voice their opinions and dissension.

The people who were focused on during the McCarthy era were suspected communists, and some of these people readily admit to having ties to the Communist Party. Hollywood was hit hard as many actors, screenwriters, directors and producers were blacklisted. He begins the The Hollywood Blacklist Part 1 with guest Jean Rouverol, Bernard Gordon, Oliver Crawford and Robert Lees. Each presents the reasons why they were blacklisted and shares their back-stories, explaining what led them to join the Communist Party. Each also relates what they went through when they were blacklisted.

The first ten to be black listed were called The Hollywood Ten and refused to cooperate with the investigation that was against them, invoking the First

Amendment. Some were successful, but others were not. The Waldorf Statement issued by Hollywood executives would change the dynamics greatly as these ten were fired. Eight were sent to prison for one year and the other two were in prison for six months.

Compared to the Salem Witch Trials, this time period and what you are about to learn from reading their stories was equally as volatile. The author shares information before we begin our journey into the past with these artists about a pamphlet called Red Channels, which focused on broadcasting. In this pamphlet 151 members of this industry were named and referred to as "Red Fascists and their sympathizers."

The United States government concerned itself with finding links between Hollywood and the Communist party. They created The House Committee on Un-American Activities or HUAC, which released a report in 1938 stating that communism was strong in Hollywood. More than 42 movie professionals were named as communists, including Humphrey Bogart, James Cagney and Fredric March. Much of this information is related to readers in the introduction.

Blacklisting began in 1946. William R. Wilkerson, founder and publisher of *The Hollywood Reporter,* published a column in *Trade View,* "A Vote For Joe Stalin." In it, he named many sympathizers, dubbing this list "Billy's Blacklist." Events that occur because of this will surprise you. Wilkerson's son apologized for the paper's role in the blacklist article. He said that his father wanted revenge when his own ambitions did not pan out to own his own studio.

Robert Lees' story continues, as he shares how and why he was blacklisted and his experiences. Sterling Hayden named him. On the stand for quite some time, he left knowing that he was blacklisted and working in the industry was over for him. The Hollywood Ten were fined by the Committee and sent to jail. He pleaded the Fifth and the First Amendment.

Robert says, "The sad part is that the Committee was not the one to hand out ultimate punishment, the industry did." So, how did he survive? His story is quite compelling. He went into something entirely different. Many writers involved realized they could work if they changed their names. Actors could not do it because they would be recognized. He changed his name four times. His story continues and he relates what happened to Fred Rinaldo, his partner, and then we find out more about Bernard Gordon and his involvement with 55 Days At Peking and then we hear more from Oliver Crawford.

So many amazing actors and writers were fired and the impact on so many lives changed the complexion of the time period. This book lets you hear every voice and details their experiences, and their reasons as each one is interviewed, questioned and allowed to voice his or her side of a very sad story.

To really understand what Jean, Oliver, Robert and Gordon endured, I listened to the shows aired in 2001 and heard their voices, their opinions and their intuitive and insightful comments about the government at time and how they survived.

The author states that his book *Shedding Light on the Hollywood Blacklist: Conversations With Participants* is the result primarily of transcriptions of my guest interviews with blacklisted screenwriters and actors from my cable television show over a decade ago, (with the exception of the audio interview I did with actress Marsha Hunt a few months back in 2012). Several of the shows won WAVE AWARDS for Excellence in local programming." He wrote this book in order for readers to hear what happened to his friends that had been blacklisted.

We then hear the voice of Abe Polonsky and learn what films he wrote, such as "Body and Soul." Listening to the interview, hearing why his father named him Abraham Lincoln Polonsky and finding out why he was blacklisted and how he managed to become one of the highest paid writers in the industry is truly great. His interview was compelling.

He was an American Film director, screenwriter, and essayist and blacklisted by the Hollywood movie studios during the McCarthy era. During these interviews he relates information about the novels that showcased his career, becoming a Marxist and joining the Communist Party. He even tells readers about how he participated in union politics. He created a paper called *The Home Front* and he signed with Paramount Pictures. He served in WWII, returning to Paramount after his tour of duty. The first film he directed was "Force of Evil." He was blacklisted and called "a dangerous citizen." To learn more you need to read his interviews for yourself. His sense of humor will bring smiles to your face and the courage he shows is compelling.

Next, the author includes Norma Barzman and Joan Scott and we hear their stories. We learn about Joan and Norma's careers, their husbands and Adrian Scott's time on the blacklist and how they survived.

Richard Powell is next. He created some of my mom's favorite shows like "Topper," "Life of Riley" and one for the other Dick Powell. The interviews are extensive and the cast quite varied as he interviews Robert White, screenwriter and author, along with author Norma Barzman. Talking to Robert about a book he co-authored titled *Hollywood and the Best of Lost Angeles Alive*, he talks about why he wrote it and many of the stories within the book.

The author then talks to Norma about her novel *Rich Dreams* and why she was blacklisted. This story shared along with one about Marilyn Monroe.

The remainder of the book is quite revealing as the author devotes on complete chapter to Oliver Crawford, Robert Lees why he became a writer, his work, movies and much more followed by his time on the blacklist and how he lived and survived.

Next, Jean Rouverol is heard and we learn more about her writing and work. The author once again talks about her life with her blacklisted husband, Hugo Butler, and their friendship with Waldo Salt, who was the primary reason they joined the Communist Party. We learn more about the Freedom of Information Act and how she and many others obtained their FBI files and the information that they were allowed to see. Some pages were blacked out. She talked about the trial, the Fifth Amendment and the end result. The reader is even enlightened about Hugo's condition and the drugs he needed to stay alive.

The final chapters are devoted to Bernard Gordon, Jeff Corey and the interviews conducted in 1999 and 2001. The final two interviews are John Randolph and Marsha Hunt. John was a great actor and he talks about his time in the service, being blacklisted and why he could not work in Hollywood. He did work on Broadway, though, and wrote a book titled *Naming Names* and you can guess what the theme of that book was when you read his interview and learn more about this great actor for yourself.

Marsha Hunt is last and we hear her as the final voice and the final interview. Asking her about the blacklist, she said she did not want to discuss it. She talks about Stanley's book and realizes he discusses where it all began and how it spread. She even talks about HUAC and then about McCarthy. Marsha Hunt devoted her time to fighting for civil rights and working with The March of Dimes and The Red Cross. She wrote a book in 1993 titled *The Way We Wore*.

Stanley Dyrector and Ed Asner.

Flashing back remember that she went to Washington to support 19 people in order to testify at the U.S. Capital in 1947. She believed that what was happening was unfair. Supporting her friend, Anne Shirley, and her husband as well as producer Adrian Scott. She was one of the 151 listed in Red Channels and wrongly accused of being a communist sympathizer.

The rest is really quite compelling as author Stanley Dyrector takes readers back to a time when freedom of speech was halted, or non-existent some might say, and when defending those that you felt were not guilty would cast guilt upon you. A great book with outstanding interviews and mentions of books that I would love to read and interviewees I would love to have on my own radio show. This is a must-read for everyone. As you read each interview you can literally hear the voice of Stanley and the person being interviewed. Listen closely: this book gets FIVE GOLD LISTS and so does the forward by Edward Asner.

INTERVIEW WITH LAURA HAMILTON-FITZ

I fear that one day all my amateur sleuthing is going to catch up with me. Gerry or I could get really hurt or Gerry could get sick of me playing Nancy Drew and leave. What would you give up everything to have? Children What is the biggest mistake you've ever made and are you going to be able to rectify it? Hmm … that's a hard one but getting to involved in the Leena situation in OVER HER DEAD BODY. I could have been Killed and it nearly ended me and Gerry. I tried to lay off but again death found is in DAYTONA DEAD. What food would you never eat? Entrails — I don't do liver, tripe, tongue or kidney – makes me want to yack

Me a fashion maven? I am most comfortable in a pair of sweats and a t-shirt.

Motherhood and a winning lottery ticket.

I am not sure but Gerry and I are trying for that all-important baby. The clock is ticking.

We live in the north end of Toronto in Canada. We just moved from Scarborough.

Building superintendent for a high-rise building and amateur sleuth as it turns out. Some even call me a corpse magnet.

Someone who is trying to find herself and who is insecure.

Not really hate but I do have a few people I would be happy not to see again. Tiny Todd Crawford (*Dead on Arrival*), Leena Dubois Brown (*Over Her Dead Body*) and Killer T. Ford (*Daytona Dead*)

Karen H. Vaugan is a first-time author who enjoys reading and writing. She is a part of Class 1983 at Applewood Heights Secondary School in Mississauga, ON. She is married with one daughter, and four stepchildren. She has two cats at home. She has a warped sense of humor and sees the lighter side of things.

She is the co-author of Dead on Arrival (Julie Faulkner), Daytona Dead, Over Her Dead Body and Dead Comic Standing. Books may be purchased from her website at www.KarenVaughan.info

BOOK OF THE MONTH

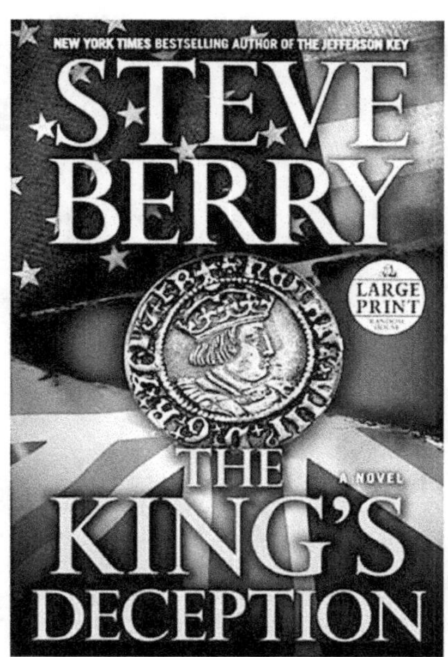

THE KING'S DECEPTION
Steve Berry
Page Count: 432 pages
Price: $27.00 U.S.
$29.00 CAN.
ISBN: 978-0-345-52654-0

Praise for "The King's Deception"

"A Dan Brown-ian secular conspiracy about The Virgin Queen driving nonstop international intrigue." — Kirkus Reviews

"Berry never fails to hit the high notes but he achieves a new crescendo in 'The King's Deception.' This is a textbook lesson in everything a great thriller should be." — Author Magazine

"So pick up this new fast-paced book and have an excellent thrill ride while you also get a wonderfully enjoyable history lesson. Education has never been this much fun." — The Huffington Post

"As smart as it is chilling, as bold as it is brash, Berry's latest is literary entertainment of the highest order further cementing his status as heir to the throne of Ludlum." — Providence Journal

"Interspersed between the modern incidents of betrayals and counter-betrayals are numerous episodes of Tudor/Elizabethan history sure to ruffle the skirts of the most avid Tudor fan. With its great plot and interesting characters, this book is a real page turner and an enjoyable read. Highly recommended." — Historical Novel Society

"Readers old and new will enjoy 'The King's Deception.'" – — The Associated Press

"...undeniably fascinating historical material..." — Publisher's Weekly

"As always it's a perfect blend of history and action and let me tell you, by the time I got to the end of the book I was worn out! So go pick up this great book, and if for some reason you haven't read Steve Berry before, go grab some earlier ones. It's perfect summer reading." — Crimespree Magazine

New York Times and #1 internationally bestselling author Steve Berry returns with *The King's Deception* (Ballantine Books; June 11, 2013) another Cotton Malone thrill ride, which takes readers to the heart of England, uncovering a secret that threatens to rock Great Britain to its royal foundations.

When Cotton Malone's 15-year-old son, Gary, is kidnapped in London, Malone stumbles into a high-stakes diplomatic showdown—an international incident fueled by geopolitical gamesmanship and shocking Tudor secrets. At its heart is the Libyan terrorist convicted of bombing Pan Am Flight 103, who is set to be released by Scottish authorities for "humanitarian reasons." An outraged American government objects, but nothing can persuade the British to intervene. Nothing except, perhaps, Operation King's Deception—a CIA operation that aims to solve a centuries-old mystery that calls into question the legitimacy of the entire 45-year reign of Elizabeth I. With assassins, traitors, spies, and dangerous disciples of a secret society closing in, Malone is caught in a lethal bind. To save Gary he must play one treacherous player against another—and only by uncovering the incredible truth can he hope to prevent the shattering consequences of the King's Deception.

Steve Berry is the *New York Times* and #1 internationally bestselling author of eight Cotton Malone adventures, four stand-alone thrillers, and four short-story originals. His books have been translated into 40 languages with more than 15 million printed copies in 51 countries.

History lies at the heart of every Steve Berry novel. It's his passion, one he shares with his wife, Elizabeth, which led them to create History Matters, a foundation dedicated to historic preservation. Since 2009 Steve and Elizabeth have crossed the country to save endangered historic treasures raising more than $400,000 via lectures, receptions, galas, luncheons, dinners and their popular writers' workshops. In 2012, Steve's devotion to historic preservation was recognized by the American Library Association, which named Steve the first spokesman for National Preservation Week (a role he'll reprise in 2013). Among other honors coming his way in 2013 are the Poets & Writers' Barnes & Noble Writers for Writers Award, the International Thriller Writers Silver Bullet Award and the Spirit of Anne Frank Human Writes Award. The first two awards honor Steve's philanthropic work with fellow writers and historic preservation. The latter is given to the writer who best exemplifies the spirit of Anne Frank in their work; the other recipients have been playwright Arthur Miller and New York Times journalist Nicholas Kristof.

Steve was born and raised in Georgia and graduated from the Walter F. George School of Law at Mercer University. He was a trial lawyer for 30 years and held elective office for 14 of those years. He is a member of the Smithsonian Institution Libraries Advisory Board and a founding member of International Thriller Writers—a group of more than 2,000 thriller writers from around the world—and served three years as its co-president.

For more information, visit www.steveberry.org.

Review of King's of Deception

What secret did King Henry VIII take to his grave? What does he make his wife promise to relate to his son before closing his eyes for the last time? Why does Katherine loathe him and yet takes care of him until the very end? What secret related to the Tudors will come into the present? His former boss Stephanie Nelle of the Magellan Billet has asked Cotton Malone a favor. Hoping to escort a recalcitrant teen back to England should have been an easy feat. But, when arriving at the airport and hoping to present him to the police Cotton fails to notice some discrepancies in the officials that greet him. Entering the limo, falling asleep for fifteen minutes would cost him more than must the missing time. As he prepares to turn over Ian the young man in question he is greeted by two police men and when questioning one and asking for identification what he receives is definitely not a ID you or I would want. Leading him at gunpoint, finding himself in danger he tells Gary to run and take cover with the Ian. But Ian and Gary are on the run and disappear. Just how will Malone find out where and who is behind it.

But what happens next alerts him to the fact that his son has been kidnapped and this young man might have orchestrated the events. As Gary and Ian are running for safety thoughts go through the reader's mind as to where this will lead the boys.

Just who is behind what's going on and why would the CIA orchestrate this event so perfectly? The operation hopes to solve a centuries-old mystery. But, the information might change the course of history and make them question the veracity of the reign of one of their own monarchs.

Blake Antrim is the man who orchestrated the events at the airport. But, one call to Langley sets the events in motion, and lead Stephanie Nelle, the head of the Billet, to enlist Malone's help in delivering Ian, since Malone, was once a powerful man at the Justice Department and agent at the Magellan Billet.

Kathleen Richards is about to be fired when summoned to The Serious Organized Crime Agency where she learns of her new assignment and fate. Katherine new assignment takes her to a vault, and its hidden occupants are none other than King Henry VIII and Jane Seymour, his wife. Learning the reason she was taken there and the fact the coffins were opened and the vault rummaged through, Kathleen would soon learn the reason got her job back, plus who requested her on the case. When Kathleen learns why she was summoned, the author takes us back to find out about Henry VII's secret. The kind relates the secret to his son before he dies and no one hears of it until more than 130 years later. The secret told, and the wealth of a king lays hidden somewhere.

Just what happened to it and what is the King's Deception? Why did a group called the Daedal approach Blake and why did they want him to fail in his quest? As Kathleen learns the history of both kings, Blake faces those who want the secret to stay hidden. Would he find the legal reason for the English to leave Northern Ireland? How does this link to the release of a Libyan Terrorist convicted of the bombing of Pan Am Flight 103 who is about to be released? Why are they killing American Intelligence agents in order to make their point that nothing will stop them from his release by Scottish authorities. Why won't Britain help and what will the American government do? What part does a five hundred year old secret play and what impact will it have?

Kathleen is a member of M16 and the CIA and she is also involved in trying to uncover the clues to this royal mystery. What happens when Gary disappears? Malone needs to find the answers. How does it link back to the Tudors? Piecing it all together will take him from the Middle Temple to the Chapel at Windsor Castle where Henry VIII is entombed and on to Oxford College.

Things take a rough turn as one college professor gives the background of Elizabeth I, including who she named to succeed her, her reign, those she trusted and her final moments. The professor might have the answers to decipher the coded journal, but something happens to change it all. No not only is the professor in danger but someone warns Kathleen what will happen if she does not stop her investigation.

With Cotton and Ian trying to find Gary and learn more about what happened, the author brings to light the fact that one prisoner is about to be released who was responsible for Pan Am Flight 103 and the British are not doing anything to stop his release. Why still remains to be seen as we learn more about the King's Deception.

Operation King's Deception relates to the wealth of the late King Henry VIII, where it is located and how it relates to the Daedalus Society, the group behind the warnings to Blake and Kathleen. But, why did Blake initiate the kidnapping of Gary and what link does it have to Malone and Ian? From Windsor Castle to Oxford college and Hampton Court there is deceit and murder, as well as assassins, spies and much more.

In the end, the author reveals the true deception and the hidden information about Elizabeth I and her reign. With all the players revealed, we learn more about Kathleen Howard, Blake and the woman he was having an affair with who was not what she appeared to be. Just who was behind the attempt to stop the King's Deception? Who killed the agent that was working to uncover the code? Who can be trusted?

The end of this tale will definitely defy all odds and make you wonder what is truth and what is fiction. Once again, author Steve Berry brings the reader inside the tomb, Windsor Castle, Oxford and throughout England to learn the true secret of the *King's Deception*. A completely intriguing book.

INTERVIEW WITH THE AUTHOR

Mark Rubenstein Talks with Author Steve Berry

Steve Berry is the highly acclaimed, bestselling author of historical thrillers, including the *Cotton Malone* adventure series. His novels have been translated into forty languages and have sold in fifty-one countries. His newest novel, *The King's Deception*, as do his other works, combines history with current day events and intrigue.

It started when I was a teenager. When I began writing, I naturally gravitated to what I loved. When I'm teaching writing, I always say to my students, 'Writing what you know is really bad advice. Instead, write what you love.' I love action, history, secrets, conspiracies, and international intrigue.

The *King's Deception* notion came about when my wife, Elizabeth, and I were at a cathedral north of London. I heard a local legend about the village of Bisley. On a certain day, for centuries, the locals would dress a young boy in an Elizabethan costume and parade him through the streets. That's really odd behavior. I looked into it and began to see there was some historical fact behind this ritual. Bram Stoker, in the early 20th Century, came across it, too. He wrote about it in a book called *Famous Imposters*. I read that book and realized there was a novel there. So, I started putting it together. History is integral to all my books, and particularly this one. It deals with Elizabeth I. She was fascinating. All her life she wore wigs; heavy makeup; clothes that didn't flatter her body; refused to marry; refused to have a child; wouldn't let doctors examine her; and forbade an autopsy when she died. She even proclaimed herself "The Virgin Queen." She was then buried with her sister Mary in the same grave, which had never happened before or since with an English royal. All this adds up to she may have been harboring a great secret, and that's what *The King's Deception* deals with — a legend that could well be true. And that oddity becomes central to what's going on hundreds of years later with Cotton Malone.

That's what I strive for. I've got to have something from the past — something lost; or something forgotten. But it must be relevant today. After all, what does it matter if there was a problem with Elizabeth I's reign? That was 400 years ago. Actually, it matters a great deal when it comes to Northern Ireland. It could actually change Northern Ireland completely and reignite a war there. When I came across the connection between Queen Elizabeth and Northern Ireland, I knew I had the thing that makes this secret relevant today. I love the connection between then and now.

History Matters is a foundation my wife, Elizabeth, and I created. We raise money for historic preservation. So far we've raised about $600,000 for various projects that include buildings, documents, rare books, and libraries. History matters because history is who we are; it's where we came from. How can you know who you are, or what you are, or where you're going if you don't know where you came from? That's what I hope people take away from my novels.

Even more so than for a nation. Where people came from; their backgrounds; ancestries; families; how they got where they are today. What could be more important to any individual? Look at it from the standpoint of an adopted child. The child longs to know, 'Where did I come from?' It's a natural human instinct. It's an insatiable quest for one's own personal identity. That's even more important than the greater historical picture of nations.

I actually think we're getting closer to our history. There's a greater fascination today with where we came from and who we are than perhaps at any other time. With technology we possess the ability to actually discover these things. You can sit in your living room and learn where you came from simply by surfing the internet.

I would include James Michener. He's my favorite author and I never got to meet him. I learned so much from him. I would have to put him in there. I would always love to chat with David Morrell. He's my favorite thriller writer of all. I've enjoyed so much having dinner with him over the years. He's forgotten more about writing than any of us will ever know.

Dan Brown has to be on the list. I owe him a lot. He and Doubleday took a great risk with *The Da Vinci Code.* In the end, their success brought a genre back to life and gave me a chance to be published. I need to thank him. I went through twelve years and 85 rejections before I was published. *The Amber Room*, my first novel, was bought because *The Da Vinci Code* was coming out and Random House was looking for something to go with it.

I never was able to speak with Robert Ludlum. I learned so much from his books. I've talked to people who did have dinner with him, and he would definitely be a guy I'd like to ask some questions.

As for people from history, number one would be Walt Disney. He was absolutely a genius, a visionary. I enjoy everything about Disney and I've read many biographies about him.

Elizabeth I is another. I have many questions for the queen. Even if perhaps the secret I've written about in *The King's Deception* is not true, I'd like to know, 'Why did you do all that stuff? What was going on in your brain?' At her death she left the country in turmoil. The Stuarts were incapable of ruling and, two monarchs later, they lost the crown in the English Civil War. Her father broke with Rome and changed everything, yet she apparently had no desire to keep the Tudor family in power. Why? Maybe because Henry VIII wasn't her father?

I would also love to meet Charlemagne. This guy changed everything. The concept of modern Europe goes all the way back to him. He was a remarkable individual. When I wrote *The Charlemagne Pursuit* I studied him in detail. He was fascinating.

It's already written. It's Cotton Malone's ninth adventure. He's going to come home for another American adventure. It's called *The Lincoln Myth.* It deals with something about Abraham Lincoln that will probably surprise most readers. I'm now starting Cotton Malone's tenth adventure for 2015. You try to stay a year ahead in the book business.

Not really. I handled thousands of divorces and also did criminal defense, so there's little that would shock me. That experience did spur me to write because I watched people at their worst. For me, writing was an escape — a way to get away from that. That's what a thriller is — an escape. It's not going to change the world or re-invent literature. But it will entertain you for a while.

Yes, many times. It's just a complete thrill. You would think that after thirteen years, you get used to it. But you absolutely don't. You write alone; you create these stories alone; you don't know if anyone's going to read them or care about them. And then, when you actually see someone reading your book, it's such a rush. One time, I was on an airplane and right across the aisle — not two feet away — was a guy reading my book. My picture was on the back in full color, yet no one made the connection. That's the great thing about being a writer. No one recognizes you. There's anonymity. It was great watching this guy being enthralled. He forgot his flight and read for two hours. I never, ever say anything to anyone. But seeing people reading my books is gratifying.

RECOMMENDED READING

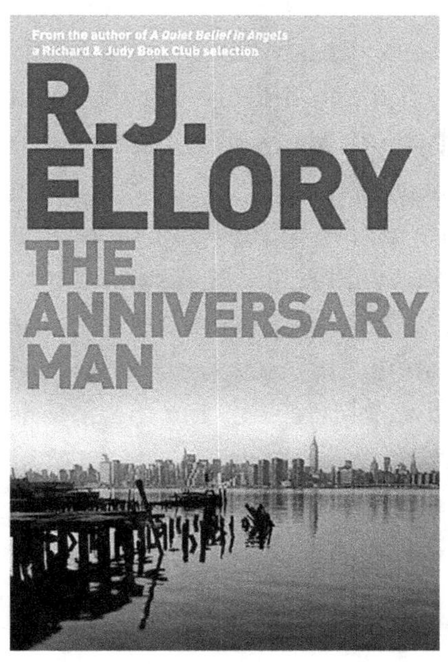

THE ANNIVERSARY MAN
Page Count: 400
Formats: Hardcover, softcover, audio and ebook

You are 16 years old and you have your whole life ahead of you. Working hard in school and helping out in your father's store you just want to be a typical teenager and enjoy life. In walks Nadia, a beautiful redheaded teenager, and your whole world changes. Getting to know her and developing strong feelings is normal when you are 16 years old, but what happens as a result of this relationship is anything but normal. It is tragic. After getting to know each other, John and Nadia decide to meet at the beach to discuss that she is leaving to study art in New York City. The events of that afternoon will embed themselves in John's mind and forever scar him not only physically but mentally. "I am the Hammer of God," he states as he comes upon the young couple and lifts his hammer to kill Nadia and critically injure John. This brings me to my review of a riveting thriller, *The Anniversary Man* by R.J. Ellory.

Twenty-two years after this horrific event, the unthinkable happens. A string of what appears to be random murders of teenagers plagues the police department in NYC. The murders appear unrelated, but are they. John Costello, a crime researcher for the *New York Herald*, works for Senior Crime Correspondent Karen Langley. Detective Ray Irving is determined to solve these murders before the cases become cold and the killer gets away. Karen Langley will do anything to put roadblocks in his way and barrels into his life demanding answers and threatening to run the story marking the murders as the work of a serial killer. Along with John Costello they begin to uncover the pieces that might tie all of the murders together.

Most people celebrate wedding anniversaries, the day they first met or the first time they went to a dance with that certain someone, but few celebrate the anniversaries of murder. Our murder, dubbed the "Anniversary Man" does just that. New York City is playing host to a serial killer who kills on the exact date of previous murders using the same methods. He is copycatting the murders executed death row inmates. He is killing and targeting teenagers and what brings this home to John

Costello is the memory of the murder of his girlfriend 22 years before by the "Hammer Of God" killer who this present day killer is mimicking with the murder of Mia Grant.

Detective Ray Irving is determined to find out how John Costello was able to link the murders. Finding out about Costello's past and learning a little about his present makes the detective suspicious of him. John Costello a relative recluse who belongs to the Winterbourne Club, a group who meets weekly to discuss serial murder cases. Irving is on a quest to find the killer and Costello might be the only source to help him succeed. Through John's researching expertise and his connections, Detective Ray Irving begins the daunting job of trying to connect the murders before the body count rises. Ray Irving and John Costello along with Karen Langley form an unwritten bond to bring this man to justice and it forever changes all their lives.

With limited resources, the body counts rising and the suspect list remaining sparse, Detective Ray Irving and the NYPD are at a dead end until something changes to blow the case wide open. Suspicions rise and one phone call puts the entire city on alert and sends the police force on a deadly chase for a sadistic killer. Sometimes we have to go back to the beginning in order to come to the end. Starting with Mia Grant and intertwining many others involved in trying to find her killer, author R.J. Ellory creates an ending with twists, turns, deceit, lies and more that will send the reader on a wild ride. The resulting conclusion is more deadly than a Category 4 Hurricane and equally as devastating. *The Anniversary Man* isn't someone you'd want to celebrate with, but the book is a definite must-read.

REVIEW BY SUSAN ROSS

OUTSTANDING CHILDREN'S BOOK

SNACK ATTACK
Marsha Cook
Page Count: 32

OTHER CHILDREN'S TITLES YOU MIGHT CONSIDER:

The Keeping Quilt, Patricia Polacco

Where the Wild Things Are, Maurice Sendak

Something Good, Robert Munch

The Very Hungry Caterpillar, Eric Carle

Goodnight Moon, Margaret Wise Brown

Susan's first recommendation for outstanding children's book is *Snack Attack* by Marsha Cook.

The main character in the book is a boy named Addison. One morning Addison goes into the kitchen to see a bowl of oatmeal on the table for breakfast. He's not too happy with this choice but he takes a spoonful and keeps it in his mouth for a little while. When he manages to swallow it, he has to decide what to do with the remainder of the oatmeal in the bowl. This brings back memories of when I was a kid and would go to my cousin's house and watch my aunt make them eat soft-boiled eggs for breakfast. One of my cousins looked like she was about to get sick just from the sight of the eggs and the other one refused to eat them until they were hard boiled. Could you blame them?

Addison is smart and gives his oatmeal to his dog Sammy. Sammy eats the oatmeal leaving Addison wondering what he was going to eat. Addison is so hungry, he grabs as many cookies as he can from the cookie jar and puts them in his mouth. The cookie jar breaks and Addison has to leave for school. He leaves the broken jar and cookies on the floor since his mom is waiting for him in the car and he does not want to be late.

When Addison comes home from school his mom is already there and she sees the broken cookie jar. As a result Mom decides to give him a choice of anything he wants to eat for breakfast, lunch or dinner the for as long as he likes. Addison was so happy he thought his mom was the best. He chooses ice cream, marshmallows and all kinds of junk food.

Soon, Addison learns these choices aren't the right ones. The next morning his mom makes oatmeal and Addison eats the whole bowl.

This shows we learn from the choices we make. Sometimes the choices we make are good and sometimes not so good. His mother let him make the choice, which was a good learning experience. Would you like junk food for breakfast? Decide after reading this FIVE SNACK BOOK!

Murder in Duplicate, Fran Orenstein
Bertha and Tillie — Sisters Forever, Fran Lewis
Bad Choices, Fran Lewis
Rebels Divided, Lance Erlick
Dizabeled Princess, Jewel Kats
Koko's Gift, Sarah Granahan

Strong Rain Falling, John Land
Taking Eve, Iris Johansen
Road Kill, Stuart Yates
Indian Summer, Dellani Oakes
Where Have All the Pop Stars Gone: Volume 2, Jeff March, Marti Smiley Childs
Deadly Pleasures, Mary Firmin
Maxwell The Raindrop Who Wouldn't Fall, Joe Moore
A Quiet Vendetta, R.J. Ellory
Seeking Salvador, Max Mitchell
It Started With The Count, My Mother and Me, Jane Congdon
The King's Deception, Steve Berry
Mad Dog House, Mark Rubinstein
The Preservasionist, Justin Kramon
Devil in the Hole, Charles Salzberg
One Gay American, Deniis Milam Bensie
The Secrets They Kept, Suzanne Handler
Pieces of You, J.F. Elferdink
Hunting Eve, Iris Johansen
Stolen, Daniel Palmer
Deadline, Sandra Brown
Ophelia Cut, John Lescroart
Memoirs from the Asylum, Kenneth Weene
Codecrafter, Erica Sandbothe

FOR THE HUFFINGTON POST

Power, Bad Behavior and Who We Are

Author, *Mad Dog House* and *Love Gone Mad*

Eliot Spitzer is running for comptroller of New York City. He's currently ahead in the polls. In 2008, he was forced to resign as governor of New York State after it was learned he'd repeatedly frequented prostitutes, even *violating federal law* by transporting one over state lines. *He sent money to off-shore shell companies* to surreptitiously pay for these illegal activities.

Mark Sanford resigned as governor of South Carolina in 2009 after it was revealed he'd disappeared for six days to join his paramour in Argentina. He not only *abandoned his post* as governor (no one knew where he was), but *misappropriated state monies* for his own personal use. In May, 2013, despite the initial public outrage at his prior scandalous behavior, Sanford won a seat in the U.S. House of Representatives to represent South Carolina.

Anthony Weiner resigned from the U.S. House of Representatives in June 2011, after repeatedly *lying* in public about his involvement in telephone sexting activities. We've just learned such activities continued until the summer of 2012 (he admits that; who knows if it's still going on?). According to polls, Weiner is ahead in the New York City Democratic primary battle for mayor. Despite calls to withdraw from the race, Weiner says he'll push on. People wonder why he would expose his family to public humiliation and shame.

But do these politicians *possess* a sense of shame?

Shame is a painful feeling arising from one's awareness of dishonorable, disgraceful or ridiculous behavior in the presence of *others*. It denotes awareness that others ridicule or disapprove of one's behavior. It differs from *guilt* which is a feeling of not having measured up to an *internal* standard. You don't need the disapproval of others to feel guilt.

So, certain questions arise: are some men running for political office today able to experience shame? Are they *capable* of feeling embarrassed, humiliated or disgraced? Or, are they insulated by some impenetrable emotional armor against cringe-worthy feelings that would cause most people to forever avoid the public eye?

Are today's politicians so narcissistically self-absorbed and so power-hungry, they've lost any sense of vulnerability to feeling judged as unworthy by others? Do they lack an internal barometer for self-evaluation? Do they even possess an inner core serving as an arbiter of propriety? Can they even *imagine* themselves as others see them—pathetic, lying, deluded narcissists who feel entitled to wantonly betray the public trust?

Do they even care?

Does the fact that these men either have been, or may be elected to office, say something about *us*? Have we become so coarsened that ignominious behavior no longer disappoints voters? Have vitriolic radio talk shows and "reality" TV inured us to outrageous behavior? Do we care if the officials we elect lie, cheat, steal or mislead us?

Does anything truly shock us anymore?

Despite congress having the lowest approval rating in its history, we re-elect ineffectual incumbents. Is it worrisome that our federal government is paralyzed in partisan deadlock? Have we so little expectation of office-holders that we view politics as simply a side-show; and if we vote at all, do we pull the lever based on nothing more than name recognition?

Do these societal questions have ready answers?

I think not; but we had better look at ourselves more closely. Great nations have declined due to a malignant confluence of these factors.

It's not just the politicians' bad behavior that has us where we are; but our own indifference could take us where we would never want to be.

Mark Rubinstein was born in Brooklyn, New York. Before turning to fiction, Rubinstein coauthored five medical self-help books: *The First Encounter: The Beginnings in Psychotherapy* (Jason Aronson); *The Complete Book of Cosmetic Facial Surgery* (Simon and Schuster); *New Choices: the Latest Options in Treating Breast Cancer* (Dodd Mead); *Heartplan: A Complete Program for Total Fitness of Heart & Mind* (McGraw-Hill), and *The Growing Years: A Guide to Your Child's Emotional Development from Birth to Adolescence* (Atheneum).

Rubinstein lives in Connecticut with his wife and as many dogs as she will allow in the house. He still practices psychiatry and is busily writing more novels. *Mad Dog House*, his first novel, was named a Finalist for the 2012 *ForeWord Reviews* Book of the Year Award (Thriller & Suspense).

My World

By Fran Lewis

If my Mom could tell you about her world:

In my world everything stays the same
I see your face but cannot recall your name
You have been in my life for many years
But, when you look at me why so many tears?

I am still here and I am glad you came to see me
Don't worry about what I say or do I can't help it you see
My world stays the same and the days run into each other you know
I get up and they feed me and then I watch television with the aides but their favorite show

I eat when they feed me and then I sleep on my chair
I will not sleep in a bed my habits won't change this I share
My world revolves around decisions made by others I know
There is nothing I can do about it but hope for the best before I go

My world is so dull but I am glad that I am here
I may not understand you but I still make a difference and I have a fear
That someday I will get worse before I can tell you how I feel
So, understand that I am grateful for everything and to you I appeal

Work hard as you have done to help find a cure to me
For others who have this illness and whose voices cannot be heard you see
We are the ones who have been dealt a hand that nobody wants or needs
It is a hand that you get whether you have done good or bad deeds

My world is my own and no one can take that from me
No one can see into my heart and learn how sad I can be
But if you look into my eyes you will know what I feel
That if there is a miracle from God to him I do appeal

Find the source of my weakness and the reason my mind has gone
Find a medicine or cure that will let me be restored before I am too far-gone
My world begins and ends with the same thing each day
Someone comes into my home and cleans me and feeds me in her own way

My world changed without notice and I had no control of it I know
It is a world filled with no hope and no future where I sustained a hard blow
Although I have a hard time expressing my feeling to you
Remember my heart is yours and I love you through and through.

Dedicated to my mom, Ruth Swerdloff
If she could tell you about her world these are the words she would express.

I spoke at an organization that she belonged to on Novemeber1. I spoke about her and her journey with Alzheimer's and what it has done to her life, her mind and her soul. I spoke about the disease and all that I have done to make sure that she gets the care at home that she needs and deserves. I spoke to her friends. It was sad. I told them how sorry I was that no one wanted to come and see her and how she would love to see a familiar face. They understood but the fear of seeing my mom now frightens these people who feel that this disease can and might strike them too. To everyone out there with a loved one who has this awful illness: Visit him or her or just call him or her on the phone and let him or her hear your voice. They may not answer you but they will know you love them and hear your voice. My sister and my brother call my mom everyday. She might not answer but she smiles when she hears a familiar voice.

Today a dear friend of my mother called and told me she read my Alzheimer's book. I gave her an author's copy to read. She told me she was going to share this book with everyone in her complex and added to the library in her community. I am so proud.

Help me fight for a cure.

To make my point even more, imagine this:

Today is the first day of the nightmare, which is my life. I woke up and the sun was shining so I thought I would go food shopping. I went into the kitchen and found my car keys on top of the microwave. I don't remember putting there. Going to the supermarket is really routine expect today I wound up getting lost. When I got to street that I thought the market was on it wasn't there. So, I turned around and headed for home. Thinking that the market might have gone out of business I decided I would call the corner grocery store and ask them to deliver what I needed. But, things went from bad to worse. Riding along in my car I began looking at the houses in the area and the cars in the driveways and did not recognize any of them. What color is the front of my house? What's my address? I started to panic because in all honesty I could not remember the answers to either question. Even worse I was in someone else's car. How, I don't know. But, what I do remember is going to the doctor the previous week and having him tell me that I might have a slight memory loss but not to worry. It could just be an aging problem. But, now I am beginning to wonder if he was right or if he was just sugarcoating what was about to become my new life. Panic began to set in. I could not even find my cell phone and hoped to find a pay phone on the street in order to call someone for help. Riding around in circles, not begin able to find any familiar landmarks I finally pulled over and started to cry. The feeling of helplessness, despair and loneliness set in and what was worse I could not remember why I was in my car or even where I was going.

Alzheimer's is deadly. There is no cure and at this point no one really knows what causes it. As time went on my mind drifted off and I started to live within myself and could not express my inner most thoughts to anyone. At times I would stare at people that I knew and tried really hard to place them or remember their names. This is a cause that many are passionate about. Help find the cure and remember: if you have a family member with this illness be patient, kind and understanding. There are times they will smile when you walk into the room and might even say your name. There are times they will look at you and wonder why you are there. This is their World.

You can promote www.GiveToMonteFiore.org/franlewis in order to direct donations to Dr. Mehler and his Alzheimer's and dementia research.

A Plea From a Tree

Anne Stanmore

What memories I have, what treasures I hold
Maybe it's time that some should be told
I watched as the young men fought to the death
Saw so many fight then draw their last breath

The couples who came with secrets to share
They kissed and they cuddled to show that they care
Tired folk also came who just needed to rest
They had worked very hard and given their best

Little boys they would come just now and then
To build in my heart their very own den
I hoped I would remain so strong for us all
That no little boy from my branches would fall

I have many friends and it would be wrong
Not to mention all those who give me a song
There are also some who are very small
In fact they are difficult to see at all

They live here and share my home with me
I wish all you humans could really see
How we all help each other and live side by side
And I can look over them all with such pride

There's been many changes in the land all around
But one thing I know that I have found
There will always be bad folk among you out there
I know that most people really do care

I hope you'll allow me to be standing here
So people can come from afar or so near
To take shelter when they are tired and lost
I'd like to be here when you need me the most

To cut me down would be such a shame
I really don't want you to play that game
I provide many things that help you each day
So please, please allow me to stay.

To Life

Marsha Casper Cook

The question is to be curious
To be curious is to care
To care is to love
To love is to forget
But if we forget
Who will answer the questions
Who will be there
To make sure
The deaths of our loved ones
Will have not have been in vain,
So please don't ask us to forget
The pain and the sadness
The outburst and
The tears
They belong to us
They are dreams,

They are the sparks of light
That survive in us
To remind us
Of love and honor
And of being who we are
We have been spared by G-d
To hold in our hearts
All that is dear to us,
For we as a people have
Survived
We are not just Jews
We represent honor
And courage

We are the inspiration
We represent love,
We are not only survivors
We are teachers
We are friends
We are the assurance that
The Holocaust did happen
We are here to repeat
The facts
So it can't happen again,
Yes, we are the reminders
But you my children
You are the future
You have the power
To say no
We didn't …

DELLANI'S STORIES

NEW AT LOVE

CHAPTER ONE

Amanda Bitterson shrugged off her heavy winter coat, sighing as the heavy, damp garment fell from her shoulders. Kicking off her shoes, she closed the door to her apartment, looking around for Muse.

"Here, kitty kitty," she called, knowing the stubborn gray Persian was probably not going to come when she called him. "Here, kitty. Mommy brought some num-nums."

Mentally chastising herself for talking to a cat like he was a two year old human, she took her hair down out of the severe French twist and padded into the kitchen in her stocking feet. She set the tea kettle on to boil and headed toward the bedroom, shedding her clothing as she went. The kettle was just coming to a boil when she came out in her favorite sweats and fuzzy slippers. She fixed her tea and thought about what she wanted for dinner.

The contents of the fridge were pretty disheartening. Shutting the door with a thud, she carried her tea to the cozy living room, clicking on the DVR. Moments later, Muse arrived, tail erect, long fur standing out with static electricity. He curled up in her lap, nuzzling her hand.

Amanda set down her tea, stroking the cat with both hands. He rolled on his back, exposing his stomach to her ministrations. Batting at her playfully, he purred softly as she warmed her hands in his fur.

"Hey, buddy. Decided to come out and be friendly for once, huh?"

They watched TV in silence, watching yet again, reruns of "Lost." Jack was just running into the jungle, followed by Kate, when her phone rang. Hitting the pause button, she answered.

"Mandy, hi!" It was a colleague of hers, Evan Wilson.

"Hi, Ev. What can I do ya for?"

"I've got a problem, Mandy. I was supposed to sub tomorrow for an English teacher at the high school." He coughed and sneezed. "Only you hear me? I've been like this since last night. You were the only person I could think of who could take this for me."

"Evan!" She was understandably annoyed. He did this to her fairly often.

"Is there a big race at the track? Is that why you're faking a cold?"

"Seriously, Mandy." He sneezed again. "This is for real. I picked up something when I was in the kindergarten last week. I can't shake it." He blew his nose, sounding very authentic. "I've been sleeping all day, guzzling chicken soup and popping vitamin C trying to kick this, and I can't. Please? I'm begging."

"You owe me dinner," she said grudgingly. "Steak, all the fixings."

"When I'm not dying of the rot, I'll take you out. Scout's honor."

"You were never a Boy Scout," she teased.

"Shows what you know," he coughed loudly. "Eagle Scout, so there!"

"Go back to bed, Ev. I'll take it for you. Which teacher?"

"Tyler. She's out with this same crap."

"She's got seniors, right?"

"Yeah. I was looking forward to it. Some of those chicks are smokin' hot!"

"And way too young for you. Ev, you're forty."

"Doesn't mean I can't dream! Oh, the kind of naughty dreams I'd have if I were well."

"Go to bed, old man."

"Young whipper snapper. I swear, if I were ten years younger..."

"You'd still be too old for me."

Evan laughingly hung up.

Amanda ordered a pizza and got her things together for the next day. She always dressed in a business suit to sub at the high school. In her early twenties and barely out of college, she tried hard to look more mature. High school students had a tendency to push the limits of substitute teachers, especially the pretty ones.

Her pizza arrived as she was feeding the cat. He was a nice looking young man, tall and broad shouldered with dark blue eyes and shoulder length blond hair. He looked like a surfer, dressed in baggy jeans and a sweater. His smile warmed her on the uncharacteristically cold night. She gave him a nice tip, thanking him for such prompt delivery.

"Stay warm!" He said, tipping his hat. His voice held a slight accent she couldn't place.

"I'm sure gonna try." She started to close the door.

"Tell your boyfriend to buy you an electric blanket."

"Don't have one," she admitted rather shyly.

"Bummer." He looked less disappointed than she did to find that out. "Take care!" Reluctantly, he hopped in his car and took off with a screech of tires.

Muse wrapped himself around her ankles, purring loudly.

"Oh, you liked him, huh? Probably because he smells like anchovies. He was pretty cute, though. You're right about that."

She ate her pizza, watched a little more TV and went to bed. High school started at seven thirty-five. She wasn't looking forward to the early morning.

Her alarm went off at five thirty, startling her out of a deep sleep. Her dreams were somewhat chaotic, full of blond surfers with washboard abs and snowshoes. She got ready on autopilot, doing her hair and makeup carefully. Satisfied that she looked older than her students, she headed out the door. Finding a place to park wasn't easy, but her car was small enough to squeeze in between a couple of mud covered pickups. She reported to the office and was directed to her classroom.

Walking across the courtyard, she received the anticipated whistles and cat calls. It was inevitable. Young, tall, athletically built with long blonde hair and gray eyes, she attracted a lot of attention. She felt awkward and self-conscious as she went up the stairs to her room. She reviewed the substitute plans and waited for the first class to arrive.

They thundered in about ten minutes later. Some were loud and boisterous, others more subdued. The morning people vs. those who weren't, she suspected. The boys were all huge, the girls more poised and sophisticated than she'd ever been in high school.

"Where's Mrs. Tyler?" One loud young man with a buzz cut and earrings asked her.

"She's sick."

"You gonna be here all week?"

"I've only been asked for today and tomorrow."

"I was planning to skip otherwise."

Amanda raised a skeptical eyebrow. "What's stopping you?"

"Shit, baby. Eye candy." He winked at her, making kissing noises and rude gestures.

"Want a referral to go with that attitude?" She asked, whipping one out of a stack on the desk. "I'll give it to you, no problem." She let the subtle double entendre hang in the air, waiting for his response.

The cockiness forgotten, he settled back in his seat looking deflated and embarrassed. She didn't think he'd challenge her again. Smiling politely, she took attendance and gave instructions for the lesson. Once they were all busy, she walked around the room, checking their progress or answering questions about their essays. Overall, the first three classes went well. When the students for her fourth period walked in, she knew she was in trouble. Ninety percent of the class was male. The few girls there were fell into the "I'm to shy to assert myself" category.

Taking a deep breath, Amanda began to explain the lesson. "Today you'll be writing an essay on the symbolism in 'Hamlet'. It's due at the end of the period."

"Is it true that Hamlet's mom was boffing his uncle before his dad died?" One of the football player types in the back of the room asked loudly. He and his buddies tapped knuckles, grinning at her challengingly.

"Have you read the play, Jason?" She asked pointedly. "If so, that's pretty self-explanatory."

He stared at her blankly. "So, was she?"

"Read it and see. I'm not telling you."

"Oh, come on! Are you a virgin or something? Why won't you answer?"

Amanda's gray eyes flashed as she exhaled slowly. "That plot element isn't important to your essay. If you really want to know the answer to that question, read the play. Otherwise, shut your mouth and do your work."

Tossing his pencil on his desk, he crossed his arms, refusing to work. "Blow me, bitch," he mumbled, thinking she couldn't hear him.

Rather than giving him the satisfaction of losing her temper, Amanda walked to the desk, filled out a referral form, handing him a copy before he knew what she was doing. Pointing to the door, she invited him to leave without a word. Jason picked up his books, walking slowly to the door. To speed him along, she opened the door, standing next to it as he passed her. He purposely tripped, falling into her, grabbing her breast in the process.

"Dudes, hey, they're real!" He grinned over his shoulder, flashing his friends a thumb's up as he winked luridly at them.

The entire classroom burst into laughter, including the girls. Amanda was mortified. She wanted to break his fingers, but as a teacher, she couldn't touch him. She could add it to his referral, but that meant he was in the classroom longer. Slipping away from his groping fingers, she tried to go back in the room.

"What?" Jason said, leaning close to her. "You got a problem? Don't like a man's hands on you? You some sort of religious freak? Virgin!" He yelled it like an insult.

Amanda blinked hard against the angry tears she felt welling up. Just as she was about to say something to him that could have gotten her fired, a strong, male hand separated them. Afraid at first that it was an administrator, Amanda took a step back toward her classroom. Catching her hip painfully on the doorknob, she risked looking up.

The man's face was familiar, but she couldn't place him. He inserted himself between Amanda and Jason, taking a step toward the huge teenager fearlessly. Jason took his referral, walking toward the stairway. With a silent smile of thanks, Amanda nodded to her savior, ducking back in the classroom.

The rest of the hour went fairly smoothly. Jason never came back, but the vice-principal called her to let her know he'd arrived and would be staying in the office. No one else challenged her.

Fifth was her free period. Straightening up after the students filed out, she took her lunch down to the courtyard for some fresh air and much needed warm sunshine. As cold as it had been yesterday, today made up for it by being warm, breezy and cloudless. She sat on a planter in the courtyard, enjoying the sunshine on her shoulders. Someone approached from her left, but the sun was in her eyes, so she couldn't see details until he sat down. It was her rescuer from earlier.

"Hi." He smiled, extending his hand. "Large pizza, extra cheese, pepperoni, bacon and pineapple. I'm Derrick Butler."

"I thought you looked familiar! I'm Amanda Bitterson. Do you work here?"

He laughed, tossing his blond hair out of his eyes. "Not exactly. I'm visiting from Australia. Might have noticed?" He put on an exaggerated Aussie accent.

"No, not really. We didn't talk much last night."

"True, that. So, shit for brains giving you trouble, eh?"

"He would have, except for you. Thank you. He had me pretty scared."

"Never show fear of the enemy," he said with a chuckle.

"I was more afraid I was going to break something," she laughed. "It's reflex to knee a guy in the balls for grabbing a boob unless I want him to. I don't want to lose my job."

"Can't say I blame you. Besides, little shit's not worth it."

"So, you never said if you worked here or not."

"I'm mostly an observer." He shrugged, eating one of her potato chips. "It's an exchange program for instructors. Kind of like foreign exchange students. I've come for a semester to teach a class while a teacher from here works in mine. I hope he's having more fun than me."

"What do you teach?"

"History, mostly. Though, mind you, I'm only here for the surfing and the hot chicks."

"I see."

"I'm team teaching with a guy who's near retirement. He doesn't even notice if I'm there or not, so I wander around having lunch with beautiful women after rescuing them from horny football players."

Amanda laughed, covering her mouth with her fingers so she wouldn't spew her food.

"Though there's no one to save them from horny Australian history teachers. Pity that."

"Who says they want to be saved?"

He raised an eyebrow. "You drink coffee?"

"What?" She was puzzled by his abrupt subject change.

"Do you," he pointed at her. "Drink coffee?" He mimed drinking from a cup.

"Yes."

"Want to have coffee with me later? My treat. I even have American money."

"I'd like that. Thanks."

"Cool! Can we make it right after school? I have to deliver pizzas again this evening."

"Sure. That'd be great."

"I'll meet you by your classroom then." He was gone as suddenly as he'd arrived.

Amanda had never met anyone quite like Derrick Butler before. He completely took her breath away, bouncing in and out of her life like a beach ball. He was unlike any other men she knew. Somehow that was comforting.

The last two hours of school passed Amanda in a blur. As soon as the last student handed in the essay, she set out what she would need for the next day, waiting for Derrick. He tapped on her door a few minutes later.

"Got hung up in the classroom. Mr. Snooze wants me to teach tomorrow."

"He's not really named Snooze, is he?"

Derrick laughed, placing his hand at the small of her back as he opened the outer door, letting her precede him.

"No. His name is Murray, but he's a real snooze. I'm actually looking forward to class tomorrow. I get to talk about my favorite subject."

"What's that?"

"Besides myself and beautiful blondes? I wax virtually poetic on the subject of my homeland. He's asked me to talk about the settling of Australia by the Brits."

"I see. Fascinating! I'd like to hear that."

"Sweet! Come by during your free period and listen in."

"I'd like that. I know very little about Australian history. Ned Kelly and prisoners, that's about it."

"Oh, love, what I could teach you!"

Amanda laughed, thinking there was a lot more than Australian history couched in that remark, but she didn't draw attention to it. She liked Derrick a lot, finding his boyish enthusiasm refreshing. She wasn't all that experienced in love, but her last boyfriend had burned her badly before dumping her for someone new.

Their conversation over coffee was as diverse and entertaining as the one over lunch. Derrick was familiar with a wide variety of subjects. His easy going, lighthearted style kept Amanda laughing. He asked a lot of questions about her, giving equal information about himself.

"You know, I've told you more in the last thirty minutes than I've told my best friend in the last year?"

"Really? Not talk to her much?"

"Not that. It just seems like when she and I talk, it's all about her."

"Well, I know I talk a lot, Mandy, but I listen damn well, too." He flashed a smile.

"Thanks, Derrick. Same applies."

"Oi! I need to get my arse in gear and get to work. Can I see you later? I'm off at nine."

"Sure. I'd like that. I can't stay up too late. These early mornings don't agree with me."

"I'm lucky, Murray's off for planning first period, so I come in at eight thirty."

"Lucky!"

"How many more days do you have for Mrs. Tyler?"

"Tomorrow. Past that, I don't know."

"I really do need to leave." He sighed, a wistful look filled his eyes. "I'll see you after nine, yeah?"

"Oh, let me give you my number." She jotted it down for him.

"Thanks." He kissed her hand, folding the paper carefully before putting it in his wallet.

"Later."

Amanda watched him drive away, already missing him. The coffee shop lights seemed dimmer, the air cooler than when he'd been with her. She headed home, greeting Muse at the door. He wrapped himself around her legs like he had the night before.

"This is unusual for you, young man," she chided him gently, carrying him to the kitchen to start her tea kettle. "You usually can't be bothered with me."

She set Muse down to change her clothing and he purred as he rubbed against her phone. A moment later it rang.

"Hi, it's me, Derrick."

"Hi, Derrick. It's me, Amanda."

"Fancy that. Thought maybe some stranger would answer your phone."

"Nobody here but me and the Muse. I thought you were working."

"Seems I mixed myself up, or the bastard changed the schedule. I'm off today. Would you like to exchange my dropping by with a pizza to a proper meal?"

"I'd like that." She couldn't believe her adventurousness. She usually didn't accept invitations from men she'd just met.

"Super! What's a good time? I know you've got to get your beauty rest."

"What works for you?"

"Love, I'm free as a bird, it's not even four and I'm talking to a gorgeous woman. I'd come get you now if I wasn't afraid you'd think I was some sort of horny, stalking pervert."

There was a stunned silence for a moment, then Amanda started laughing. "No danger of that. You seem harmless enough."

He chuckled, his voice dropping to a more seductive range. "Oh, you've got a pretty laugh. So, dinner. What time?"

"Depends on how fancy we're going?"

"Something comfy and casual. That describes most of the restaurants around here."

"True. How about six? We should miss the early birds and late diners then."

"Excellent. Six it is."

"You need my address?"

"Memorized it. I'm brilliant, me. I'll see you at six."

"See you then." Puzzled by his call, she hung up the phone, moving to her window.

Derrick's beaten up, surfboard sticker covered car pulled away from the curb with another squeal of the tires. Amanda wasn't sure if she should be alarmed or flattered by that. Choosing to be pleased instead of appalled, she went about choosing her wardrobe for her date. She laid out three outfits on the bed, standing back to get a more objective view.

"What do you think, Muse? The black jeans and avocado top? Or do you prefer the red top? Maybe white slacks with the rose sweater?"

Muse hopped onto the bed, eying each outfit with disdain. He flicked his whiskers at the avocado top, laid his ears back at the red one, but nosed the pink sweater with curiosity. The black jeans earned a cursory tap of his paw, but the white slacks got the same treatment as the pink sweater.

"Glad you approve. I was leaning that way myself."

Muse's behavior was certainly erratic. He'd never done anything like that before. She wondered what had brought it on. She spent the time before her date checking her e-mail, Facebook and Word Press pages. Soon, none of that held any real interest, so she made herself another cup of tea and sat down with her DVR. Even "Two and a Half Men" couldn't keep her attention for long. Picking up the phone on an impulse, she called Derrick.

"I had an idea," she said right after he answered. "Have you seen much of the sights?"

"Besides the beach? Not much, and very little of that. Too bloody cold to surf. Why?"

"If you aren't busy at the moment, would you like to sight see a bit before dinner?"

"You volunteering to be a tour guide, then?"

"Absolutely."

"I'll be there in fifteen minutes. Does that give you a chance to freshen up?"

"I'll be ready. Time me." She hung up the phone, trotting to her room.

Dressed and ready in thirteen and a half minutes, she waited for Derrick on the porch of her apartment building. He pulled up a moment later, glancing at his watch as he got out of the car.

"You're good. I'd have thought you'd still be at it. You look lovely, by the way." His lips brushed her cheek in a more than friendly manner, his hands lingering close to her.

"Thanks. You look good yourself. I like the Oxford tweed look."

"These are my intellectual duds," he explained as he opened her car door. "I wear these when I want to look studious and professorial."

"All you need is a pipe."

He pulled one out of the pocket, clamping it between his teeth. Amanda could hardly stop laughing.

"I think it would make a better impression if it wasn't a bubble pipe," she giggled.

"Best I could do on short notice. I don't smoke. Where to?"

"Silly of me. I could take my car."

"I take directions well. I'll follow you anywhere."

Amanda gave him directions to her favorite part of the beach, a national park at the end of the barrier island. It was windy, the beach nearly deserted except for them and a few late afternoon joggers. They took a walk along the beach until the chilly wind forced them to abandon the sand for the sanctity of the car.

"Brr! It's not supposed to be this cold here," Amanda shivered.

"I'm starving," Derrick countered. "Let's find something to eat."

"We'll hit early bird traffic."

"I don't care. I want warmth and food immediately."

She directed him to her favorite steakhouse on beach side. Pulling into a parking place, Derrick turned the car off, facing her across the car.

"In case I forget later, I had a great time at the beach."

"You won't forget later." She smiled shyly, ducking her eyes, not meeting his intense gaze.

"Why is it you do that? When someone looks directly at you, you duck your head?"

"Do I?" She glanced up at him, puzzled. "No one ever pointed that out before."

"Maybe it's just me, then?"

"No," she smiled, forcing herself to meet his gaze. "Not just you. I guess I do it because it embarrasses me."

"Why? You've got so much to be proud of. You're bright and witty, you're beautiful."

"I wasn't always that pretty," she mumbled. "And everyone thought I was dumb."

He touched her cheek tenderly, brushing wind blown hair from her lips. "Then they were stupid wankers. You're amazing, Amanda."

She giggled, tossing her hair casually over her shoulder. "You make me sound like a super hero, The Amazing Amanda!"

"Sweet! You're smiling again. And you're my super hero." He grinned. "Let's get some dinner. I don't know about you, but the cold is making me hungry as hell. I hate being hungry."

"I do too."

He opened her door, helping her out of the car. His fingers lingered on hers, his other hand brushing the small of her back as he shut the door behind her. Guiding her to the restaurant, he let his arm slide around her waist, holding her close in a fond embrace. Amanda enjoyed the touch of his hands, finding herself at ease with him as if she'd known him for years.

They got a table in a relatively quiet corner away from the elderly early birds. Amanda told Derrick about various menu items, making recommendations based on what she liked the most. Their waitress came to the table, pen poised over notepad.

"Oh, I know you!" She pointed at Derrick. "You're in with Mr. Murray, right?"

"Yeah. Let me ask you something." He leaned toward her conspiratorially. "Which of us do you think's better looking? Me or Murray?"

The waitress, whose name was Brandi, eyed him curiously. "You're kidding, right? He's like a hundred years old. Who in her right mind would find him attractive?"

"So I win based on the fact he's ancient. Is that it?"

She giggled, tossing her short, brown curls. "If Mr. Murray was your age and the two of you stood side by side, you'd still so totally win. It's not even a contest. Blond, Australian and charming or old and fat? You do the math."

"Sweet! Are you always such a scintillating elocutionist?"

"A what? Mr. Butler, you're confusing me."

"Never mind, love. What will you have, Mandy?"

They placed their orders and sipped mixed drinks while they waited for their food to be prepared. So wrapped up in one another, they didn't notice the clutch of young men who walked in as their food was being served. Brandi set down their plates and a large, male body blocked the light. Looking up, Amanda saw Jason, the boy she'd sent from the room earlier that day.

"You got me suspended, bitch."

Arms crossed, massive muscles bulging, he gave a very convincing impersonation of a thunderstorm. Derrick looked at him calmly, smiling slightly.

"What a unique greeting," he said conversationally. "Though I think calling her a bitch is a bit over the top. As I hear it, you weren't very gentlemanly in the classroom."

"I asked a simple question and she went off on me."

"Really? Did you do that, love? Did you, in fact, go off on young Jason?"

"Hm, I remember telling him to read the play and shut his mouth," Amanda said. "If he chooses to interpret that as *going off*, I suppose I did."

"You go yelling at people, mate, you're going to get yourself in trouble. Telling the teacher to blow you isn't going to find you much favor either."

"You banging her?"

"I beg your pardon?"

"Her." Jason pointed at Amanda. "Are you riding her?"

"I don't see that's any of your business."

"My buddies and me think it is. In fact, my buddies and me want to talk to you outside."

"As you can see, gents, I've just received my meal. Though the idea of settling this is quite appealing, I believe I'd prefer to eat with a pretty lady and save your ass whipping until later. If you'll excuse me."

Jason upended Derrick's drink into his dinner, dropping the glass on the floor. He dusted his hands together, flicking his fingers in Derrick's face. Derrick considered the implications of Jason's behavior a moment, then stood, excusing himself politely. Pointing at Jason, he jerked his head toward the door.

"Order me another platter, love." He told Brandi as he passed.

Stunned, she watched him as he moved slowly toward the door, unbuttoning his jacket. Amanda grabbed her purse and was going to follow Derrick outside, but Brandi stopped her.

"I've called the cops," she said quietly. "Jason's got a mean temper. Mr. B better watch himself, or Jason's gonna hand him his balls on a plate."

Derrick walked the boys to the parking lot. Standing on the blacktop, he spoke quietly to Jason and his buddies for a moment. The football players exchanged an amused look as the Australian surfer explained something to them. None of them looked convinced. Taking off his jacket, Derrick laid it on one of the outside tables. Rolling up his sleeves, he stood there silently.

Jason laughed, pretending to walk away. He took a step or two, turned and threw a punch, putting his superior weight behind it. Derrick grabbed his wrist, tugging toward him. He clamped the football player's head to his chest, turning slightly to his right as he threw him to the ground. Taking his jacket, he was putting it back on when one of the buddies jumped him. Followed by the other three, they swung at Derrick, who gracefully eluded them.

Suddenly, all of them were on the ground, moaning loudly, holding various parts of their anatomy as they cried out in pain. Moments later, a police car pulled up, blue lights flashing. Derrick waited patiently for the officer to approach, hands in plain view. Brandi and Amanda hurried out of the restaurant to explain what had happened. The manager followed them, yelling loudly at Derrick.

"What the hell are you doing? You just beat up five people! Officer, I want this man arrested."

"Harry," Brandi hastened to assert herself. "Wait. No, officer, Mr. Butler didn't attack them, they all jumped him. He tried to talk to them, but Jason swung at him and then the others came at him."

"Is that how it happened?" The female officer asked Derrick.

"Yes, ma'am. I brought the boys out here to calm them down. I explained that their behavior was inappropriate. Apparently they didn't care. Jason turned to go, then took a swing at me. I took him down."

"So he threw the first punch?" The African-American woman took hurried notes.

"He threw the only punch. I never hit him. I did grab his arm and tossed him down." He said a something in Japanese that the officer seemed to understand.

"I see. And the others?"

"I told them I was going back in to join my date, but they took it rather personally that their leader was lying on the ground. They came at me all at once, so I took them down too."

"Did anyone else see this?"

"I'd say at least half the restaurant," Derrick replied, pointing to the windows. "They didn't exactly keep their hostility a secret. I thought I'd do the right thing and take them outside."

"You're on my property," the manager said angrily. "I want to press charges."

"The boys are all on city property, sir," the officer replied tersely. "Mr. Butler was standing within the easement when I pulled up. You can't press charges. From what I'm hearing, Mr. Butler has every right to press assault charges on these boys."

"What? That's my son!" He pointed to Jason.

"Oh, really? Is your son in the habit of attacking innocent people in restaurants?" the officer asked.

"I can explain that," Amanda interjected, taking Derrick's arm. "Mr. Butler works at the high school. I was substituting in Jason's English class. He said some inappropriate things, so I sent him to the office with a referral. Jason grabbed me aggressively on the breast and Mr. Butler interceded on my behalf."

"Oh, so you punched him in the hallway?" Jason's father was red in the face.

"I never touched him," Derrick explained. "I put my arm between him and Miss Bitterson. That was all. I also talked to the assistant principal about what I had witnessed. You could ask anyone in that classroom, they would all tell you the same thing. I never laid a hand on your son until he tried to hit me."

"Mr. Butler, do you want to press charges?" The officer asked him.

"No, ma'am. I just want to eat my meal and spend time with Miss Bitterson." He leaned toward the woman, speaking quietly. "It's our second date, ma'am. I thought I was doing rather well until young Jason poured my tea in my dinner and threatened my date. I couldn't let a big fella like that intimidate a lady, could I?"

"Well, if you won't press charges, I will." The officer said with the authority of her position.

"I don't want trouble," Derrick said. "I was hoping to settle this quietly. But if you must, you must."

"I think an hour or two in the tank will make these boys think twice about acting like barbarians." She called for additional cars to come and cart the boys to jail.

"I want you two to leave now," the manager said loudly, pointing at Derrick and Amanda. "I want you both out of my place right now. Don't ever come back."

"You couldn't pay me to come back," Derrick said with a smile. "Though I do hope you treat your other customers more politely. Hey, love, fancy Mexican?" He pointed to another restaurant in the complex.

"I could go for some fajitas and black beans," Amanda took Derrick's arm.

CHAPTER TWO

After giving the officer all their information, they walked up to the Mexican cantina arm in arm. They arrived just as the live entertainment was beginning. A middle aged man with long graying hair sat on a stool with a guitar and a laptop.

"Hi, I'm Rick." He smiled and waved as Amanda and Derrick sat down. "I'm your entertainment for the evening. I hope you enjoy listening to me as much as I enjoy performing for you."

His fingers were already plucking the strings, playing *Maria, Maria* by Santana.

Amanda wanted to get up and sing with him. Dancing in her chair, she snapped her fingers, singing with Rick as he played one of her favorite Carlos Santana songs. When the song finished, she clapped and cheered loudly, making the rest of the patrons clap louder as well.

"I've got a fan, I see. What's your name, young lady?"

Amanda didn't want to say anything, because suddenly everyone was looking at her. Derrick nudged her, but she wouldn't speak.

"Her name's Amanda," Derrick said, laying on the accent.

"Pretty name for a pretty lady. You like Santana, Amanda?"

"Yes!" She bit her lip, blushing deeply.

"A woman of taste as well as beauty. See if you know this one." His fingers flew over the strings once more. Closing his eyes, he sang *Nothing At All* in a sweet, clear tenor.

Amanda ordered her meal, totally distracted by the song. Derrick watched her as she was transformed by the music. She dipped and swayed as she listened to the guitar music. He beckoned one of the waitresses over, asking her a question.

"Sure. Right up by the stage is fine."

"Thanks. Mandy. Oi, love." He held out his hand to her, leading her to the dance floor.

Interplanetary Party started to play with Rick really wailing on the guitar as he sang. More couples joined Amanda and Derrick as they danced and clapped in front of the stage. After the song finished, their food had arrived, so they sat down to eat. As soon as they were done, they got up to dance again, with Rick watching them.

"I'd like to dedicate this next song to my number one fan here." He held out his hand to Amanda, smiling. "Amanda, this one is for you and your date. What's your name, buddy?"

"Derrick."

"You're an Aussie boy, right, mate?" He did a fair imitation of Derrick's accent.

Derrick laughed, nodding as he spun Amanda under his arm.

"This is for you two. Because Amanda, the way you've made me feel tonight, you are truly a *Black Magic Woman*."

After that song ended, he took a break, putting in a CD of himself playing more songs with a Spanish flavor. He asked Amanda and Derrick if he could join them at their table. A waitress brought him a Corona with a slice of lime. Rick sat across from them, grinning happily, his pale blue eyes sparkling.

"I never had such an enthusiastic audience." He laughed, toasting them. "You're a big Santana fan?"

Amanda nodded, taking a sip of her drink. "My dad used to play his albums all the time. He taught me to play *Oye Como Va* practically before I could read."

"You play guitar?" Derrick was stunned. "You never told me that."

"It never came up," Amanda laughed. "Why are you so surprised?"

"Dunno, I thought it might be something you'd tell me. Hello, I'm Amanda and I play Carlos Santana on the guitar. Perfect introduction."

"I don't play that much anymore." She looked down at the table.

"How come? I bet you were marvelous."

"I stopped playing when my dad left." She wouldn't meet his gaze.

"Shit. Now I've done it, Rick. I hurt her feelings."

"I'll cheer her up. What's your favorite Santana song, Amanda?"

"You already played *Maria Maria*," she said. "But my next favorite is *Europa*."

"Then *Europa* it will be." He kissed her hand. "And your meal is on me."

"Oh, I can't let you do that," Amanda stammered.

"I own the place, I can do anything I want. Sit, enjoy." He got up, heading back to the stage. "I've got one more song to play, then I'm going to grab a bite to eat. Once again, for Amanda, her second favorite Santana song, *Europa*."

His fingers brushed the strings, playing the haunting melody. Amanda felt like he was playing it just for her. She could feel the tears in her eyes, struggling to get out. Instead of giving in to them, she closed her eyes, listening to the guitar sing. When the song was over, she stood up, clapping and cheering loudly once more. Rick took a bow and hopped off the stage.

"You come back anytime," he said, taking her hand. "You've made this old string plucker

feel nineteen again. Derrick, this is a fine lady. Treat her right."

"I have every intention of doing just that, Rick. Thanks for the meal, mate."

"No problem, kid. Thanks for the enthusiasm."

They headed back to Amanda's apartment, talking happily about their evening of music and dancing. Derrick was amazed at the change that came over Amanda when she talked about playing the guitar. Gone was the shy young woman. In her place was a sparkling, bubbly teenager.

Her phone was ringing as they walked into her apartment. Picking up, she wondered why Evan was calling her.

"Hey there. I've been trying to reach you for hours. Where you been?"

"Out. What's up, Ev?"

"I'm feeling better. I wondered if you'd mind my taking the day tomorrow. I could use the cash."

"No, that's fine. I'd honestly rather not sub in high school. I only did that as a favor to you. I wouldn't do that for anyone else."

"Thanks, baby girl. They didn't give you any trouble, did they?"

"I'll tell you about it later, Ev. I've got company."

"Really? *Male* company?" He sounded excited and mildly disappointed.

"Yes. Is that such a shock?"

"Honey, in the last two years, I can count the male company you've had on one hand and miss a couple fingers."

"That's only the ones you know about. I've had more dates than that!"

"Not trying to start an argument, baby. Enjoy your date. I'm history." He hung up.

"My friend, Evan." She explained. "He's the one who gave me the job today. He was sick and couldn't take it."

"Remind me to thank him tomorrow." He brought her fingers to her lips. "I'm not stepping on his toes, am I?"

Amanda laughed loudly, almost incredulous. "Ev's old enough to be my father," she giggled. "He used to date my mom and kind of took me under his wing. Super nice guy."

"I'll drop in and say hello. Are you still going to come hear me speak?"

"I wouldn't miss that for anything."

"Super!"

"Would you like a cup of coffee?"

"I'd far rather have a kiss," he said, leaning toward her.

Taken somewhat by surprise, Amanda closed her eyes, leaning toward him. His lips met hers with a small spark. Kissing her harder to rid himself of the sting, Derrick took her in his arms, drawing her close. They stood a long time by the desk, oblivious to everything else as they kissed. The phone dangled from Amanda's fingers.

Muse darted between them, wrapping himself around Derrick's ankles, then twining around Amanda's. Extending his claws, he tried to climb Derrick's leg. Giving that up, he leaped from the floor to the couch, then from couch to the man's shoulder. He lay comfortably behind Derrick's head like a large, furry boa. Laughing, Derrick let go of Amanda to study the large gray cat.

"Is he always like this?"

"You know, he's never done that before? He's been acting strangely since I met you." She told him about the cat picking her outfit.

"Good taste, mate. She looks stunning."

Muse leaped down to the floor, twining around his ankles again, purring loudly.

"He usually hates everyone," Amanda explained, picking up the noisy feline.

"I feel very honored then," Derrick scratched the big tomcat under the chin. "Not often a fella gets the blessing and endorsement of the ranking male of the family. Thanks, Muse." He chuckled, rubbing behind the cat's ears. In a fit of feline pique, Muse dove suddenly for the floor, flicking his tail arrogantly.

"Cats!" Amanda exclaimed. "That's more like it. *That* is the real Muse."

Derrick led her to the couch as she launched into a story about her cat. He waited patiently for her to finish, then put one finger on her lips as she started to say something else.

"Mandy, love, much as I like cats, I don't really want to talk about them. Point of fact, I don't especially want to talk at all."

His lips brushed hers once more. She had enjoyed his first kisses, soft and sultry as they were. This one took her breath away. He'd been holding something back before, that he suddenly released. Had she been standing, she'd have gone weak in the knees. Amanda clung to his shoulders as if she were drowning. She felt like she was falling, but it was a good fall. She knew that Derrick was there to pick her up.

Derrick's heart pounded hard in his chest. Careful where he put his hands, he kissed her with barely contained passion. He didn't want to frighten her with the power of his emotions, but he was finding it hard. He'd been attracted to her since seeing her the night before. She'd been on his mind for hours during the night. Seeing her at the school was like having a dream come true.

Now that she was in his arms, kissing him, her full lips caressing his, he wanted to carry that attraction to its logical, noisy, sweaty conclusion. He sensed that Amanda wasn't the kind of girl to succumb to his charms quite that rapidly. He'd overheard a bit of her conversation with Evan. He had very good hearing and Evan didn't exactly speak softly. He figured that she didn't date much, which would explain the older man's caution. Naturally protective himself, he could understand the concern.

Pushing that from his mind, he concentrated on seducing her with his lips. He felt the shivers run up and down her spine as his mouth explored hers, moving to her neck and ears. Nibbling her ear, he allowed his hands to travel the length of her back, feeling her shiver with anticipation. His lips traveled to her neck, brushing the skin below her ear, making her jump against him.

Of their own will, his fingers found her waist, encircling gently, moving upward. She shivered once more, pressing hard against him. She didn't yell or pull away, so he tried once more, testing his boundaries.

Amanda pulled away, confusion in her eyes. Did he really think she was going to go to bed with him that fast? She was horrified.

Derrick could see he'd stepped over the line. Backing off, he apologized, holding his hands away from her body. "Sorry." He whispered. "Perhaps I should go."

Amanda took his hand, holding it with both of hers. "Derrick, perhaps I need to explain."

"This isn't the part where you tell me you're studying to become a nun, is it?"

Amanda's eyes twinkled. "No. Nothing like that. I really like you and I find you devilishly attractive—"

"There's a *but* hanging about in there. I can almost hear it."

"But—not yet. I'm not in the habit of making that kind of commitment this early on."

"Entirely my fault. You're beautiful, seductive, luscious. . . . I apologize. I couldn't help myself. If I promise to behave, may I kiss you some more?"

She laughed as he pretended to pout, holding his hands away from his body. Taking one hand, then the other, she put them at her waist.

"How about the hands stay in this area. Your lips stay up this way." She put her hand at the base of her throat, motioning up. "If you stay within that range, you're fine."

"So many rules!" He chuckled, rolling his eyes. "None of this, eh?"

He let his hands gently cup her breasts, brushing the nipples with his thumbs as he licked her neck from her ear to collar bone. Amanda shivered, moaning as she pressed against him. The reaction was instinctive, unpremeditated. Unlike his own actions, which had been premeditated in the extreme.

"No." She gasped. "No. Derrick!"

His lips effectively stopped her objections. He didn't touch her like that again, but was satisfied that when he did finally make love to her, it was going to be an incredible experience for them both. Smiling to himself, he planned his next move with care. He had found his limitations, not nearly as restrictive as he'd anticipated, and was happy to comply. Even if it wasn't quite as much as he wanted, it was at least progress.

Amanda was breathless, her heart fluttering in her chest. Derrick's lips left sparkling, hot, erotic trails in their wake. She imagined that making love with him would be an amazing experience that would long define her list of *Life at its Best*. There was something that Derrick didn't know and she was loathe to tell him. While Jason had thought he was merely insulting her by calling her a virgin earlier that day, he'd actually been right. Amanda had never been with a man. But how did she tell Derrick that? She couldn't find the words.

Somehow, it had never been particularly important to her to date a lot. Nor had she found a man she considered worthy enough to give him the ultimate gift of her virtue. Now she had found one, she was worried about what he might say when he discovered the truth.

"Mandy, are you alright?" Derrick's eyes held concern.

"I'm fine. I'm sorry, I should never let myself get distracted when I'm with you."

"Still upset by what happened with Jason?"

Was she? "A little, I suppose. I don't want you to get in trouble for helping me."

"I won't. Don't worry. Mr. Granger, the assistant principal, and I are good friends. He knows what Jason is like. It was his call to suspend the little wanker."

Amanda giggled, loving his accent and mannerisms. He could be so funny with so little effort. Relaxing somewhat, she leaned against him, lips parted in anticipation. Derrick took his time, playing with her mouth as he explored her body within the specified parameters. Testing his boundaries a tad, he let his fingers stray. When he did, she took his hand, moving it far away from his intended goal.

"You're very good at that," he mumbled, his mouth next to hers.

His breath tickled her nose and mouth and she laughed.

"Yes, I am. Years of practice as a substitute teacher. Kids test their boundaries all the time."

"Yes, but I'm not a kid."

"Which makes you that much more dangerous."

"I'm not dangerous, love. You're the one who's a danger to me. I could lose myself in you — so easily." He nibbled her lip, kissing her passionately.

Amanda was frightened for a moment, then realized she had nothing to fear from him. He was crazy about her, but he wasn't going to hurt her. This was what real passion felt like, not that cheesy version most guys carried in their back pocket with their packet of condoms. He wanted her specifically, not just some woman to satisfy his lust.

It made her feel empowered to realize she had such control and influence over him. If she were the kind of woman to exploit it, she could have driven him wild and sent him away. But Amanda wasn't like that. When she whipped him into a frenzy, it would be because she had decided to go to bed with him.

That wasn't going to happen tonight, nor anytime soon. If Derrick wanted her, he'd have to woo and win her. Old fashioned standards maybe, but she was an old fashioned girl. She was just thinking about the best way to break off gently, but she couldn't think clearly when he was kissing her. Her phone ringing startled them both.

"Damn," he whispered as she reached for the offending appliance. "Bother phones."

Giggling, Amanda answered. "Hello?"

There was silence, though she was sure someone was there.

"Hello?" She hung up. "That was odd."

"What? Wrong number?"

"No one at all. I guess they dialed wrong and hung up."

"Rudeness, it's reached epidemic proportions." He chuckled, leaning on his elbow, gazing into her eyes. "I've had a wonderful time this evening, Amanda. You're still coming tomorrow?"

"Of course. I wouldn't miss it. What time should I arrive?"

"Come for seventh, then we can grab another coffee after school. That's if you want to?"

"I'd love to. Are you delivering pizzas tomorrow?"

"You know, I have no idea. I'm thinking of quitting anyway, he keeps jerking around my schedule. I think he wants me to quit."

"Why? I'd think you'd be an asset."

"Owner wants to give me the manager's job. I don't want it, but he's used it as a threat so often, the other guy believes him."

"He must know good manager material when he sees it."

"It's just my accent. Folks go wild for it. Buy lots of pizza."

"I'd think it would be your dashing good looks and charming smile."

"Gawd, he's a dude! Perish the thought!"

The phone rang again. Frowning, Amanda looked at the clock. It was late for anyone to call. Evan didn't even call this late, and he was the only one likely to call her after nine.

"Hello?"

There was a sound of heavy breathing. "You having fun with the wimp from down under?" The deep male voice was gruff, distorted. "Bitch." He hung up.

Amanda dropped the phone like it was alive. Staring at it, she froze.

"What's wrong? Mandy?" Derrick held her shoulders, giving her a little shake.

Amanda forced herself to focus on his eyes. "Someone said, 'You having fun with the wimp from down under' and hung up. Derrick, what's going on?"

"Got Caller ID?"

"Yes, of course, but it showed up unknown name."

"If it rings again, answer and I'll call 911. Someone's got a sick sense of humor."

"Derrick, I'm scared. What if it's Jason?"

"I doubt it. That officer arrested him."

"But he could get out on bail."

"Will it make you feel better if I call the station and ask?"

"I don't know. Not if he's gone."

"We'll fall off that bridge if we come to it. Find me the number, eh, love?"

She dutifully complied, looking it up quickly on her cellphone. After a short conversation with the desk sergeant, Derrick hung up.

"He's gone, isn't he. He's out on bail?"

He nodded sadly. "I told them what happened. They can't do anything yet," he said. "No threat has been made. They will send a police officer by here to check on the neighborhood and one will drive by Jason's house. That's really the best they can do."

"It's better than nothing, I suppose."

"No, love. It's bloody nothing."

The phone rang again. Reluctantly, Amanda answered, putting it on speaker.

Derrick hit redial on his phone, waiting anxiously for the phone to be answered. Stepping into the bathroom, he explained, then hurried back out to the living room.

"Is he still there?" The voice sounded husky, dry, wicked. "Put him on if he's man enough to talk to me."

"He doesn't want to talk to you, Jason. I know it's you. Stop calling or I'll call the police!"

"Cops won't do shit, angel face. You can't prove anything. All they have is your word and that ain't worth much, bitch." He hung up again.

"Please tell me you heard that," Derrick said into his cellphone. "Great. Thank you."

"Was that the police?"

"Yes. Smart of you to put the speaker on, they heard everything. They're going to increase patrols on your street."

"Can't they send someone here? I'm terrified! Derrick, I don't want to be alone! What if he breaks in when you leave?"

"I won't leave, then. I'll sleep on the couch. Got a spare toothbrush?"

"I can't ask you to stay. I'll call someone."

"Mandy, it's nearly one in the morning. Who are you going to call at this hour?"

She burst into frightened tears. Derrick held her close as she cried, wetting his shirt. He made comforting noises, not really saying much, as she clung to him. Sniffling and snuffling, she buried her face in his chest. His arms provided much needed comfort for her, driving the demons away for awhile. Still, the chilling knowledge of the mysterious phone calls made her shiver with fear.

"Who would want to do this to me?" She mumbled into his shirt. "I just sent a kid to the office because he was being disruptive."

"It's okay, Mandy. We'll figure this out, love. Meanwhile, it's late and one of us has to work tomorrow." He squeezed her arms gently, pulling away from her. "Don't suppose you've got something I can sleep in?"

She laughed, beckoning him to follow her. "My older brother always gives me weird gifts for Christmas. For some reason, he gave me men's pajama pants last year. I kept hoping he was going to find me a man to fill them, but he hasn't yet. You can use them."

She tossed him a pair of Sponge Bob pants. They landed on his head, one leg slid down so his face was framed by a horizontal 'V'.

"Cute," he smirked. "Sponge Bob, my favorite cartoon character. Swell."

"Oh, sarcasm. Original. I like it."

The next thing she handed him was a toothbrush still in the package.

"It's pink." He wrinkled his nose.

"Do you want clean teeth? Beggars can't be choosers, love." She imitated his accent perfectly.

"I'll remember you said that." He winked.

"You go ahead and use the bathroom first. I'll make up the couch. It folds out into a very comfortable bed."

"I bet," he sounded dubious.

"I got that particular couch on purpose. The futon is actually a queen sized mattress. It's got a wooden frame, so there's no bar or springs to poke in the wrong spots." She let her eyes drift to his belt buckle and back up before turning away.

Derrick could feel his body react to her stare, glad she'd turned around. How embarrassing to be holding a pair of Sponge Bob pj's with a hard on. The ignominy of the situation made him laugh as he went to the bathroom.

"If you want a shower, there's clean towels in the closet," Amanda called from the living room.

"I'll get one in the morning, if that's all right. Makes me feel shower fresh all day long."

"I thought that was feminine hygiene spray." She laughed, opening the couch.

"Well, for you birds, yes. For me, it's a manly shower."

"What's the difference between a manly shower and a womanly shower?"

She was standing in the bedroom doorway, the light of the living room giving her a golden aura. Derrick's breath caught in his throat. Swallowing with difficulty, he managed to smile. She was obviously waiting for an answer, so he tried to formulate one while his brain did mental jumping jacks.

"A m-manly shower, eh? Well, that would be the one that — uh. . . . Strewth, I don't know, love. You got me there."

"Probably the one that has a man in it instead of a woman."

"Yeah, that's the one. Be out in a tick."

He closed the door rapidly. Taking deep breaths, he hoped he hadn't made a terrible mistake being here. He wanted her desperately, more than any other woman he'd ever known. She was sweet and naive, intelligent and able to keep up with his smart mouth and quick wit. She was beautiful and vulnerable, a deadly combination for a man like him.

Derrick thrived on danger. He loved extreme sports, constantly taunting and tempting death. More than once, he'd nearly gotten himself killed, but he always went back for more. The more dangerous, the bigger the thrill. Conversely, he was very protective of those around him. His mother and sisters always told him he was smothering them with his concern.

Now here he was in the apartment of a beautiful, vulnerable woman who needed him. It was an aphrodisiac of gargantuan proportions and he couldn't do a damn thing about it. Leaning against the sink, he gazed at himself in the mirror.

"You're insane, mate. You've finally dropped off the edge of the sanity cliff and are hopelessly lost, falling to your death." Death by love sickness. Was it a death he could handle? "Hell yes," he confided to his reflection.

Amanda tapped on the door. "You about done?"

"Just got to brush my teeth," he replied. "But I can do that in the kitchen."

He folded his clothing carefully, laying it over his arm. Grabbing his toothbrush, he squeezed toothpaste on it and opened the door. Holding it up, he grinned.

"It's all yours." He gestured broadly with his arm, ushering her in the bathroom.

She slipped by him, casting her vivid blue eyes up at him as she smiled her thanks. The scent of her perfume tantalized him, making his head spin. Castigating himself again, he walked to the kitchen to brush his teeth. He didn't bother to turn on the light, using the illumination from the living room behind him to find his way. Glancing out the window, he saw something that made his blood run cold. A man stood on the curb, leaning against a light colored four door sedan, staring intently at Amanda's building. Digging his phone out of his pocket, he called the police. Anxiously waiting for an answer, he didn't hear Amanda come in the kitchen.

When she flipped on the light, he startled, nearly dropping his phone. With a yip, he fumbled it just as the dispatcher picked up.

"911 emergency. What is the nature of your emergency?"

"Hi. There's someone outside my girlfriend's apartment. He's staring up here, leaning against a car by the curb."

"Sir, there's no law against leaning against your car. How is this an emergency?"

"My girlfriend got several strange phone calls this evening, one of a threatening nature."

"Are you calling from Amanda Bitterson's?"

"Yes, ma'am. I'm looking at the bloke now."

"Can he see you?"

"I don't know. We're in the kitchen and he's staring at the building, but not up here."

He pressed Amanda behind him, moving slowly to the light switch. She got to it first, turning it off quickly as she ducked into the living room. Her hands were shaking, her face pale.

"Oh, my God," she said quietly, in a panic. Her eyes grew large as she thought about the implications of the man standing on the curb. "What does he want? Why is he here? God, Derrick. Who is he?"

"I don't know, love."

"Is Miss Bitterson there? I'd like to speak to her."

"Yes." He turned to Amanda, handing her the phone. "She wants to speak to you."

"Miss Bitterson?"

"Yes?"

"I'm sending a squad car by. The officer will talk to the man by the curb and see if he can explain himself. Stay inside, make sure all your doors and windows are securely locked."

"Yes, ma'am. I already did."

"There's no reason to panic, Miss Bitterson. May I speak to your boyfriend again?"

"Sure. Thanks."

She handed the phone to Derrick, clutching his arm with both hands.

"Sir, may I get your name and address?"

Derrick told her all his pertinent details, watching the window as he spoke. "Oi, the officer just pulled up. He's talking to the fellow now."

"I'm going to hang up now. The officer will speak to you when he's done. His name is Waters." She gave him the badge number. Derrick wrote it down on a pad by the phone. "He's about six foot two, brown hair and eyes. If anyone else comes to the door, do not let them in. If you aren't sure who he is, call me back. My name is Tina."

"Thanks, Tina. You're my hero."

"Thanks, Derrick. I never was anyone's hero before." Laughing, she hung up.

Derrick watched the police officer get out of his cruiser, approaching the man by the curb carefully. He stood out of reach, one hand on his gun, the other on his nightstick. The man stood up, pushing away from the car. Dropping his cigarette, he seemed to get belligerent, gesturing wildly. They couldn't hear what he was saying, but his voice, raised in anger, was audible.

The police officer spoke calmly, taking another step toward the man. Making rude finger gestures, the man spun away from the police officer. Instead of getting back in his car, he lunged abruptly at the officer, taking a swing at him. Waters grabbed the man's fist, bringing his arm behind his back. Holding it with one hand, he shoved the man face first over the hood of his car as he grabbed his cuffs. Once the man was restrained, Waters spoke into his radio as he led him to the back of the squad car. He put the man in the back seat, shutting the door with a snap of his wrist. He came toward the building, looking at the apartment windows as if he were looking for someone.

Derrick handed the phone to Amanda as he headed briskly for the door. He was waiting when Waters showed up. Peering through the peephole, he read off the badge number and name on the man's chest. He opened the door, welcoming the police officer inside.

"Mr. Butler?"

"Yes, that's me." He shut the door, holding out his hand.

Officer Waters shook his hand. His grip was like a vice. Derrick was glad the man wasn't mad at him. What the dispatcher hadn't mentioned was that Waters was about six two and two hundred pounds of solid muscle. His shoulders were so broad, they almost brushed the door frame on either side. His brown hair was closed cropped, his blue eyes appraising, taking in details as he examined the interior of the apartment.

Amanda stood in the doorway between the kitchen and living room, clutching the phone like a life preserver. Waters approached carefully, smiling warmly, as if he were dealing with a frightened animal. He stopped about three feet away, thumbs hooked in his belt.

Derrick walked to Amanda's side, taking the phone from her white knuckled hands. "Mandy, this is Officer Waters."

"Hi." She managed a smile, holding out her hand.

Waters shook it carefully, gauging his actions well. "Shall we sit down a moment, Miss Bitterson?"

"Sure. Okay."

"How about a cup of coffee? I think I can find my way around," Derrick offered.

"I thought you were the boyfriend?" Waters led Amanda to the couch.

"We just started dating. This is my first time up here."

"Oh. I kind of assumed you lived here." He eyed the Sponge Bob pants.

"I'm sleeping on the couch tonight. Mandy didn't fancy being alone. And I didn't fancy taking advantage." He shrugged, smiling casually.

Officer Waters smiled. "Coffee would be good if you can find everything."

"Sweet. It may take a moment, but I'll get it." He walked back into the kitchen and started opening cupboards.

"Miss Bitterson, I have some questions for you."

"Okay."

Her voice was steady. That was a good sign.

"Did you recognize the man outside?"

"No. I couldn't see his face. He had that cap on." She made gestures like she was putting on a baseball cap.

"Is there anyone who would wish you harm?"

"I– I don't know." Her voice now held an edge of panic. "I had a problem with this kid at the high school. He got mad and jumped Derrick at the restaurant tonight."

"Yes, the dispatcher told me about that. Tell me exactly what happened at school and the restaurant."

"Derrick can tell you about that better than I can. I was inside when Jason jumped him."

"The boy from the school is Jason?"

"Yes."

She explained in careful detail what had happened. Waters took notes as she spoke, asking questions from time to time to clarify something.

"And you'd never had an altercation with him before?"

"No. I've never been in that class before. I don't go to the high school often."

"Why's that?"

Amanda gestured at herself, a sweeping motion that went from her shoulders down her body. It was a graceful, dance-like movement that flowed along the lines of her figure. Both men were struck momentarily dumb.

"Look at me," she said softly. "I'm barely older than they are. Even some of the girls are bigger than I am. They don't always take me seriously in the classroom. But I've never had any problems like Jason. He just wouldn't let up. Then he copped a feel as I escorted him to the door."

"He had the balls to grab a boob in front of everyone?" Waters' professional demeanor fell away, shattered. "And you didn't knee him?"

Amanda giggled. "Believe me, it was tempting. But I need my job. Not exactly going to endear myself to the administration if I accost a student."

"Oh, but he can grope you? Dude!" He said to Derrick. "Please tell me you broke his damn arm."

Derrick chuckled. "Not quite, but I think it dislocated. I heard a pop when he went down. I got between him and Amanda at the school. He wasn't ready to let it drop. I encouraged him to."

"Sweet! Sorry. Totally unprofessional." He rubbed the back of his head nervously. "When guys abuse beautiful women, I go into monster protector mode. Guys like that need to be locked up with Bubba."

Derrick guffawed, spewing his coffee. Amanda blushed deeply, hiding a smile. Officer Waters grinned, putting away his pen and bid farewell. Amanda filled a cardboard travel mug with coffee and he left to take his prisoner to the jail.

"If you have anymore trouble, you call and ask for me personally. Anytime, okay?"

"Thanks, Jasper. I appreciate that." Amanda closed the door and he waited until he heard it locked and chained before he left.

CHAPTER THREE

Once Officer Jasper Waters had pulled away from the curb, Amanda and Derrick looked at one another uncomfortably. Derrick was especially nervous around her, feeling vulnerable in her Sponge Bob pants and no shirt. Amanda made it worse because she couldn't stop staring at his chest.

"I could go," he said quietly. "Seems no need for me to be here now."

"We don't know that he was the one making the calls. I'd feel so much better if you would stay, Derrick. I hate to put you out, I know it's — awkward."

"Yeah, that's one word for it." A random chill passed over his skin, giving him goose bumps.

"I like you a lot, Derrick. You've been so kind and protective. I can't tell you what that's meant to me. You're an incredible guy."

"There's not a *but* lurking, is there?"

She grinned, placing a hand on his firm chest. "No. Only a request to let me get to know you better. I really want to."

"Me too." The touch of her hand set him on fire. "I want to get to know you very well." Realizing how that could be interpreted, he blushed slightly, eyes downcast.

"Me too," she admitted shyly. "Just not tonight."

"Right." He pointed with his thumb to the couch. "This is me going to bed now. Night, Mandy."

"Night, Derrick." She leaned forward to kiss him, then thought better of it. Her lips brushed his cheek.

That small gesture disrupted his exterior calm, making his chaotic interior explode. She couldn't have ignited him more if she'd stripped naked and given him a lap dance. He wanted to grab her and make passionate love to her. Instead, he waved good night and scurried to the bed before she noticed that Sponge Bob's nose was growing.

Amanda closed her bedroom door, leaning against it with a deep sigh. Something about Derrick set her insides on fire. She'd never been so attracted to a man in her entire life. All through school, she'd been too busy with her advanced classes to pay that much attention to boys. In college, working on a double major in English education and Theater and Dance, she hadn't had time to date much. After college, her life took a turn for the worse.

Her parents had financial difficulties, leaving her on her own to fend for herself. Once her dad left, her mother couldn't afford to help her. She did her substitute teaching as well as tutoring students in English and typing term papers. Amanda could turn her hand to all kinds of tasks, making a little money here and there to pay her bills and save a bit for a rainy day. Overall, things hadn't been going to badly, until Jason walked into her classroom.

Flopping on the bed, she wondered how her life had suddenly gone from pretty good, to pretty bad in the blink of an eye. Crawling under the covers, she huddled in the middle of her bed, clutching her body pillow. Wrapping her arms around it, she buried her face in it and started to cry. Loud sobs shook her as she gulped for breath. She couldn't control it. No matter how hard she tried to be quiet, she made a lot of noise. Moments later, Derrick was by her side, sitting on the edge of the bed.

"Here now, what's all this, then? It's all right, Amanda. We'll get through this together, love. You're not alone." Murmuring quietly, he ran his fingers through her hair. Crooning comfortingly, he lay down next to her.

Amanda curled up in his arms like a little girl. Laying her head on his chest, she fell asleep. Derrick slept very little. Holding Amanda was the third greatest thing in his world. Second was kissing her, and only one activity topped that. Stroking her hair, he dozed a couple of hours until her alarm went off at five thirty. Startling awake with the buzzer right near his head, he nearly threw Amanda on the floor.

She reached calmly across him, turning off the alarm. "Sorry. I forgot to reset it. I had to get up early yesterday."

"God, was it only yesterday? It feels like a week!"

"Didn't you sleep?" She looked concerned, frowning.

"Not much. I'm not used to being a pillow."

"I'm sorry!" She jumped away as if he'd stung her.

He pulled her back down, cradling her head on his chest. "Don't be. I stayed awake because I liked it, not because I was uncomfortable. It felt good to hold you all night, Mandy. How I'd like to wake up with you beside me every morning." He mumbled as his eyes drifted shut.

"I'd like that too." She murmured, kissing him. "I hate to be the bad guy, but don't you need to get up for work?"

He groaned. "Not this early. Off first period, remember?"

"I'll reset it for — what time?"

His brain refused to function on so little sleep. Forcing himself to concentrate, he thought about how much time it would take to get ready. "How 'bout seven thirty? Yeah." He drifted back to sleep.

Amanda reset the alarm, snuggling next to him. Derrick held her close, his hands drifting over her body in his sleep. Unwittingly, he caressed her breast and buttocks, his hands roaming over the curves of her body. Amanda realized happily that she didn't mind this level of intimacy nearly as much as she thought she would. Somehow, it felt right to have him touch her like a lover, even if they hadn't actually been lovers yet. Her cheek on his chest, she too fell asleep.

The alarm going off at seven thirty was not quite as bad as the earlier one had been, but was still far too early for Derrick. This time, when Amanda leaned across him, he watched the movement of her breasts under her nightshirt. He reached out a tentative hand, allowing his fingers to trace the lines of her cheek, neck and shoulder.

Amanda couldn't find it in herself to resist him. His touch electrified her senses, making her feel the most alive she had in years. *Not like this*, she thought. *Not yet*. Pulling gently away from him, she rose from the bed, allowing his fingers to fall away from her ever so slowly.

Derrick's blue eyes held so many emotions, she could hardly look into them. Passion, affection and desire were mixed with longing and regret. Amanda looked away, scooting off the opposite side of the bed.

"I seem to keep finding reasons to apologize," Derrick murmured. "Sorry, once again."

"No, don't be. It's natural to be attracted to one another. I mean, you're gorgeous. Any woman would be a fool to tell you no. I can't imagine anyone but me being that dumb. God, how stupid can any one girl be? You're handsome and charming, intelligent and gallant—"

Standing with her back to him, she tossed her nightshirt aside angrily as she spoke. She pulled her sports bra on, flinging a T-shirt hastily over her head, completely forgetting that he could see everything. She continued to babble, dropping her pajama bottoms to the floor. She pulled on her jeans, zipping them with a note of finality.

"And I bet you always get the girl." She faced him again.

Derrick lay on the bed, watching her intently. His blue eyes glittered with suppressed humor and passion. Which took precedence would completely depend on her. Amanda blanched, then blushed a dark, lingering red. Derrick's mouth quirked up at one corner as he started to laugh. Amanda threw her pillow at him, pommeling him angrily as she roared at him.

"You let me do that! You lay there and let me! Oh, I could kill you!"

"Hold up!" He laughed, grabbing the pillow from her.

Amanda collapsed against him, aware once more of how strong his arms were, how broad his chest, how tight his abs. And what else was there about him? Something was different. Realization dawned and she blushed even more. He had a whopper of an erection, a fact that not even Sponge Bob could conceal.

"Oh, God." She ran from the room, into the kitchen.

Derrick lay on the bed, willing his body to cooperate. Standing awkwardly, he followed her, wishing he had more control over involuntary vascular responses. Now he owed her yet another apology. How could he be expected not to react when she was hitting him like that? After the show she inadvertently put on, he was so hot, he couldn't stand it. He was already attracted to her, he just woke up, she dressed in front of him and beat him across the hips with a pillow. Was it his fault he'd gotten excited? He could hardly be held responsible for that.

Stopping to dress, he felt less vulnerable in his khakis and T-shirt than he did in the Sponge Bob pants. He followed her to the kitchen where she had just started a pot of coffee. He slipped onto a bar stool, clearing his throat.

"It seems I owe you *yet* another apology," he said softly.

"Entirely my fault," she countered, getting the coffee things out and setting them on the table.

"Perhaps I should explain a bit about the male anatomy..."

"Look, Derrick, I get it. You're horny. Sorry I can't accommodate you."

"Dammit, Amanda! It's not just that! I don't want just anyone, I'm hot for you."

"What's the difference?"

"A huge, unimaginably enormous difference. If I just wanted to get laid, I could pick up some bird in a bar and boff the hell out of her. If all I wanted was sex from you, Mandy, we'd have done it already."

"Pretty sure of your charms, huh?"

"As a matter of fact, most women find me irresistibly charming, yeah!"

"Who says I'm one of them?" Her eyes flashed dangerously.

That could have hurt his feelings, but he didn't let it. Instead, he moved toward her, as non-threateningly as possible. Holding out his hands, he took her elbows in his, pulling her close. She came without resistance. Leaning over her, he kissed her deeply, pressing his firm body against hers, his hands running up and down her back.

"If you weren't, you wouldn't let me do that." He kissed her again, his tongue probing her mouth. "Tell me you don't want me, and I'll go and never come back."

"Derrick, I..." Her voice caught in her throat. Dropping her head, she stared at the floor.

Determined to get an answer one way or another, he lifted her chin, gazing deeply into her eyes. She saw so much in his face, reading everything he was thinking with one glance.

"Amanda, I'm not in the habit of apologizing so much for my actions as I've done with you the last twelve or so hours. I'm not apologizing anymore for being attracted to you. If I do, I'm never going to say anything else. I refuse to be sorry for thinking you're the most beautiful, charming, deliciously seductive woman I've ever met. If you don't share that opinion of me, I'm not going to force my affections on you. But know this." He kissed her longingly, deeply, pouring every ounce of desire he could into that one act. "Once you've tasted me, you'll never want anyone else."

Grabbing the rest of his things, he headed out the door, closing it with a bang. The noise made Amanda jump. Dropping the spoon she'd been holding, she ran after him, but he was already in his car and pulling out of the parking lot. She wanted to go after him, but she was barefoot and it was cold. Weeping and gasping, she collapsed on the living room floor. Leaning against the closed door, she sat with her knees drawn up to her chest. Miserable, she didn't move for quite awhile, until her stomach growling made it apparent that she'd better eat soon.

She tried to fix herself some food, but she couldn't stop crying. Her eyes were puffy and red, her nose sore from rubbing away the tears that accumulated on the tip. The phone rang, making her jump. She looked at the caller ID, hoping it was Derrick, but the number wasn't familiar. Picking up hesitantly, she spoke.

"Yes?"

"Hi, Miss Bitterson. It's Officer Waters."

"Oh, hi."

"I'm about to go off shift. I was calling to see how you are."

"Fine, thanks. It's kind of you to be concerned."

"Well, our mystery man still hasn't spoken. I did get an ID off his plates. Do you know a Trevor Johnson?"

"No. Should I?"

"No reason you should. I was just checking. This Jason kid, he's not got the last name Johnson?"

"Not that I know of. Why?"

"Curious, that's all. He got out on bail last night."

Amanda nodded, even though he couldn't see her. "Derrick told me."

"Don't worry. He went right home and stayed there all night. They put a house arrest anklet on him. Apparently this wasn't his only brush with the law, nor was it his first assault case. We're keeping a close eye on him."

"But he might have friends or family who aren't restricted. That's what you're saying, right?"

"Sorry to say, but yes. Listen, one reason I'm calling is the captain here suggested that if you have any relatives or friends you could stay with for a couple days, you might feel better. You know, until this blows over some. Or have your boyfriend stay the next few nights."

Amanda hiccupped, trying not to start crying again. Jasper Waters didn't miss it.

"Amanda, what's wrong?"

It all came bubbling out. She couldn't stop it. Feeling like a fool, she told a total stranger her life's story. He listened quietly, sighing heavily before speaking.

"Look, Amanda, you sound like you could use a friend right now. How about I come pick you up and take you to breakfast. We can talk about this, maybe I can give you a little objective perspective. Will you come?"

"Sure, I'd like that. A girl's gotta eat, right?"

"She sure does. I'll be over in about thirty minutes, okay? I want to get home and get out of this monkey suit."

"Okay. I'll see you then. Thanks, Jasper."

Amanda got a quick shower, but didn't wash her hair. It was chilly and would take far longer than thirty minutes to dry it. She grabbed a pair of warm jeans, a white turtleneck and a heavy cable knit sweater in bright red. Digging her lumberjack boots out of the bottom of the closet, she put them on with a pair of heavy socks and waited for Jasper to arrive.

He pulled up a few minutes later in a black sports car. Amanda wasn't up to speed on car models, but this one had the lines of a muscle car. Somehow she couldn't see Jasper driving anything else. It had a solid, reassuring feeling like he did. He hopped out, walking to the front of her apartment. He was dressed in jeans and a brown leather jacket. His breath left white plumes behind him as he jogged up to the porch.

Amanda trotted down the steps to meet him. He was just opening the outside door when she came down, her jacket flung over her shoulder.

"Hi, there!"

He looked startled, but smiled. "I was expecting to have to wait for you. Most women can't get ready in thirty minutes."

"I'm not like most women. I was ready in ten." She grinned as he helped her put her jacket on.

Jasper lifted her hair out of her collar, his chilly hands brushing her neck. She jumped, giggling.

"Sorry. I couldn't find my gloves. The car was pretty cold when I got in. You look nice. Did you sleep okay?"

They made small talk as they walked to his car. He'd left it running by the curb, the motor rumbling with a deep, comforting thrum that sent a shiver down her spine when she sat on the seat. It was warm and toasty in the car. Jasper helped her find the seat belt, then trotted around to his door.

"Where to? Lady's pick."

"Oh! My favorite restaurant is on the beach side. Smokey Jo's."

"Really? Well, you'll be pleased to know my Great-Aunt Jo owns that place."

"You're kidding! I've gone to church with her forever. Why haven't I ever seen you there?"

He looked embarrassed. "I'm the black sheep of the family," he admitted dourly. "I converted to Episcopalian a few years ago. I thought I was going to get tossed out of the family on my ear, but they took it well. If I'd gone any further from the fold, I think they would have."

"Oh, my!" She started to laugh, covering her mouth with both hands to muffle it. "Your middle name isn't Michael, is it?"

"Yeah. Why?" He looked puzzled.

"Once a month, someone dedicates a mass to you. Jasper Michael Waters, for whom this mass is said," she quoted. "I've been praying for you for years and didn't even know it."

He rolled his eyes, putting the car in gear. "That would be my grandmother's doing. She's sure I'm going to hell."

"Why did you convert, if you don't mind my asking?"

"I've always had a problem with the whole *sex* issue."

"Oh? Which sex issue?"

"First, the whole idea that you're going to hell for having sex outside of marriage. That's bad enough, but then to force men and women to become celibate to take religious orders? I really have to draw the line there."

"I can see how it would be hard for some people to accept that. You didn't have to leave the church over it."

"I was going to school with the idea of becoming a priest."

"Really? I can't picture that, somehow." She smiled, her eyes twinkling.

"I hope that's a compliment."

"Trust me, it is."

His smile broadened. "I tried. I really thought I'd heard the call for vocation, but then something happened my freshman year in college that changed my mind."

"What?" She was leaning toward him, hanging on every word.

He glanced at her as he slowed for a red light. "I had sex."

Laughing, Amanda bounced on the seat, clasping her hands. "A big, gorgeous, buff guy like you didn't get laid before that? I find that so incredibly hard to believe."

"Believe. I wasn't always this big and buff. The new me." He spread his hands, pointing to himself. "I dropped the idea of being a priest, changed majors to criminal justice and the rest is history. If you'd seen me ten years ago, you wouldn't recognize me. I was scrawny, weak and nerdy. Amazing what the right exercise routine can do for a man."

"Oh, I completely agree."

She realized she was staring at him like he was the main course at a banquet for starving virgins. Laughing at herself, she sat back in the seat with a happy grin as they pulled into the restaurant. Jasper parked the car and came around to open her door. Helping her out, he held her hand a little over long, gazing into her eyes.

Amanda was overcome with the desire to kiss him, but fought the impulse. Jasper was just being friendly, helping her because he was a police officer. This was a casual breakfast, that's all.

They were the first customers in the restaurant. Jo herself was sitting at the bar reading a newspaper. Looking up at the door, she smiled when she saw who it was.

"Amanda! You brought my wayward nephew to visit."

"Actually, he brought me, Jo. How are you?" She embraced the frail older woman gently.

"I'm better. This cold weather is awful. It's not supposed to get this cold in Florida."

"Do I get a hug?" Jasper asked, holding his arms wide.

"Of course!" Jo embraced him, kissing both his cheeks. "You look so good. Your father to a tee, I've always said that. Such a handsome boy!" She squeezed his cheek. "Sit. What are you eating? Paul!" She called over her shoulder.

"Yeah, Ma!" A tall, broad shouldered man in his forties came out of the kitchen wiping his hands on a towel. He wore a white butcher's apron and red shirt with blue jeans.

"Mikey?" He bellowed, coming over to Jasper. "No, it's Jasper. Damn, you look so much like your dad, I got you confused."

"Your eyesight must be going, Paul. Dad's twice my age."

"Yeah, well, I don't need glasses to cook. Who's this?" He hugged Amanda, kissing both her cheeks. "New girlfriend?"

"No, a friend. We just met, so don't start making wedding plans yet, okay?"

"I know you! You always sit up front near the Mary statue every Sunday. Ma, it's that pretty blonde from church."

"Paul, you need to work on your people skills," his mother said with a grin. "This is Amanda. She assists me with religious education as well as always sitting near the Mary statue. You've met her half a dozen times already."

He shrugged expansively. "I remember faces, I don't do well with names. What are you eating? Your usual, Amanda?"

"You remember what she eats but not her name? You're an idiot, Uncle Paul."

"So sue me. What are you eating, moron?" He punched Jasper in the chest.

"Whatever Amanda's having. And coffee, Auntie. Lots of it."

They sat down at a table and waited for his aunt to finish filling mugs of coffee. New customers arrived and she went off to greet them.

"Finally! I was beginning to think she'd never leave," Jasper chuckled.

Amanda could tell he didn't mean it. He obviously loved his great-aunt and his uncle a lot.

"So, what happened between you and Derrick?" He asked casually, but there was more to the question than he was letting on.

"A silly argument. It's my fault for not understanding."

"Don't blame yourself. There's always two sides to every conflict."

"On my side, there were a lot of misconceptions and assumptions. My interpretation of his actions was based on a variety of bad relationships. I thought he was acting like all those other guys and he wasn't."

"Bummer," Jasper didn't sound nearly as upset as he was trying to. "And what were these misconceptions and assumptions? If you don't mind me asking."

"That he just wanted to get in my pants and then leave me."

"That's happened to you?" He sounded shocked. "How could any guy do that to someone like you?"

"Not so much the getting in the pants part," she admitted with an embarrassed blush. "The leaving part. I'm a pro at that."

"So they don't love you and leave you? They just leave?"

"When I try to make it clear that they aren't getting into my pants, that's when they leave."

"Ooh. . . ." He looked at her with a totally different expression. "So, Derrick tried to get more friendly than you wanted?"

"Not really, no. That's the assumption part. I read him totally wrong."

"So he didn't try to take advantage?"

"No. I'm not making any sense, am I?"

Jasper laughed, taking a sip of his coffee. "Not a lot."

"Okay, let me go over events and see if that clarifies it for you."

She told him what had happened that morning between her and Derrick. Jasper nodded, listening politely as she talked.

"So I drove him away. I've totally ruined a great relationship with a wonderful guy because I'm an idiot."

"Did you try apologizing? Just a suggestion." He held up his hands like she was holding a gun on him.

"I didn't have the chance. He drove away before I could get outside."

"Phone?" He held his thumb and finger up by his ear like a play phone. "I bet those two little words, *I'm sorry*, would go a long way right now."

"What if he's still angry? What if he won't forgive me?"

"My grandmother would say, *what if doesn't pay the bills*. Amanda, speaking from the perspective of a man who's been on the hard side of an argument, I think you should call him. I think you'll find him receptive to an apology."

"Why would he be?"

"Because if he's not, he's an idiot of the first order. He probably forgave you before he'd even driven away."

"How do you know that?"

"Because I would have." He attacked his food like it had threatened him with bodily harm. He didn't look at her for several minutes as he concentrated on his food. "Look." He set his fork down. "I'm not going to pretend that I'm not attracted to you. I see this from his perspective and I know why he left. He doesn't see any way to convince you that he's not what you think. He seems like a good guy, Amanda. Not every man would have stayed the night in the first place. Any guy who's only interested in bedding you would have used your fear to his advantage. Derrick didn't do that."

"Why are you taking his side?"

"I have *no* idea. Really, I kind of hoped you two would break up so I could ask you out."

Amanda was so shocked, her mouth fell open. "What? So this whole friendly breakfast thing was your attempt to get in my pants?"

He set his glass of orange juice down with a click. "Can I explain a few things about men so you know where both of us stand? You've obviously been burned a few times by real jerks. Okay, I accept that. Please, don't judge all men by the dweeb squad standards, okay? Some of us are actually gentlemen who take more than five minutes to get to know a girl.

"Like for instance, if this was dinner instead of breakfast, I wouldn't take you home and try to screw your brains out on the first date. Give me a few dates, yeah, I'm gonna try. By that time you'd have made up your mind how far you were going to let me go, and I'd have a pretty good idea of my limitations."

"So, what are you telling me?" She looked completely confused.

Jasper sighed a little, scratching his ear. "I'm telling you that Derrick and I are just a couple of red blooded, heterosexual males who see a gorgeous woman we'd like to get to know better. Believe me, if you weren't already involved with him, I'd try to kiss you myself."

Amanda tossed her napkin on the table, blinking hard against tears. She wasn't sure why she was crying, but she couldn't stop it. Lips trembling, she blinked again, but the tears fell anyway.

"I've messed it all up, haven't I?"

"No. I think you can still salvage this, more's the pity."

"What's that supposed to mean?" She picked up her napkin, dabbing her eyes.

"Nothing would make me happier than to have you two split up. I'm a guy, I'm not above being a little mercenary. If you aren't with him, I have a chance."

"Why would you want a psycho like me?"

"Because you're the prettiest, most amazing psycho I've ever met," he admitted. "And if you don't patch things up with that crazy, Aussie bastard, I'm gonna throw you in jail."

"You confuse the hell out of me, Jasper."

"That's okay, Amanda, I confuse the hell out of myself. I can't believe I'm sitting here giving you the advice to get back with another man, but he's a good guy and deserves his chance. If it doesn't work out, it's not because you didn't try. Then you call me and I'll console you until I win you over." He shrugged, grinning.

They finished eating and he took her home. She didn't invite him up, knowing that he needed to get home to get some sleep. Amanda glanced at the clock and thought about going to the school. Better than calling, she could go listen to his lecture and try to talk to him afterwards.

It was early yet, so she cleaned house, fed the cat and made her bed. About one o'clock, she got dressed in a suit, putting her hair up. Redoing her makeup, she gazed at herself in the mirror.

"You can do this, Amanda. You can make it work."

At the school, she signed in at the front desk. The clerk at the desk gave her directions to the classroom and handed her a name tag. Ignoring the stares and occasional cat call, she walked to Derrick's classroom. She had timed her arrival for the interval between classes so she could slip in with the students.

He wasn't in the room when she arrived. She introduced herself to Mr. Snooze, and he showed her to a seat at the back of the class. Derrick walked in a few minutes later, chatting with another couple of history teachers who had come in to observe. Taking his place at the front of the room, he set up his Power Point and waited for the students to settle down. Mr. Snooze took role and dimmed the lights.

Derrick seemed distracted, but once he started speaking, his enthusiasm for his subject was evident. The pictures he used for the Power Point were pictures he'd taken himself. He had traveled extensively, visiting parts of Australia that many white people never went to. He'd even been adopted by a native tribe and had pictures of their dances and ceremonies.

After the Power Point was over, he took questions from the class. Most of them were silly questions, like had he ever met the Crocodile Hunter or any of the other countless famous people from Australia. Some of the questions were insightful, getting Derrick's full attention as he answered. His excitement was contagious. By the time class was over, all the students were making plans to visit Australia as soon as possible.

"You'll take us around, right, Mr. Butler?" One pretty little brunette asked him, going up on her toes, nearly shoving her tits in his face.

"Um, not until you're at least eighteen and no longer my student."

She giggled, tossing her hair with an expert flick of her head. "Oh, well. It was worth asking, right? Thanks, Mr. B." She waved, walking out of the classroom on her toes.

The girls left in gaggles of giggles while the guys talked about hunting crocodiles and dancing with the Aborigines.

CHAPTER FOUR

Amanda waited until the classroom was clear before walking toward to the front of the room. Derrick was putting his laptop away, his back to her.

"Excellent lecture, Mr. Butler," she said softly.

"Thanks," he replied, turning to greet her. "Mandy." The smile faltered, his eyes took on a haunted look. "You came!"

"I couldn't miss something this important. You were great."

"My favorite subject. . . ."

"I'm sorry about this morning."

"Me too."

"I don't want to talk about this here. Have you time to go for coffee?"

"Yeah, I do. I quit that other job." He cast about for something. Spotting his laptop case, he picked it up.

"Great, then I don't have to feel guilty about monopolizing your time."

They talked quietly about inconsequential things as they walked to the office. She checked out, turning in her name tag, and Derrick walked her to her car. She stood with her back to the driver's door, facing him. He put his arms on either side of her head, smiling.

"See you in a few minutes," he said, leaning close.

"You sure you want to kiss me in front of the entire school population?" She grinned at him as he leaned over her.

"To hell with them." He chuckled seductively. "Not like they've never seen two people kiss."

His lips descended on hers, slowly, seductively, leaving a trail of sparks in their wake. One by one, the students saw them. Hoots and cat calls attracted attention, so Derrick gave them a show. Taking her in his arms, he pulled her close. Amanda held his belt loops, enjoying the kiss as well as the attention. She found that for once she didn't care that a man was kissing her in public. Usually, she felt like she was hiding her attraction to a man. With Derrick, she didn't have to. In fact, he challenged her not to. He finally let go of her, amid the cheering, clapping students.

"She your wife or something, Mr. B.?" One tall young man asked.

"Her? Just met her five minutes ago." He shrugged, putting his arm around Amanda's shoulders, grinning like crazy.

"Yeah, right."

"Honestly. Didn't we? What's your name again?"

"Amanda."

"Right. I'm Derrick. Nice to meet you."

"You too." She gave him a firm handshake.

"Meet you back at your place, then?"

"I thought we'd have coffee first, so it's more like a date," she said, trying to look serious.

"Oh, right! Of course! Okay, I'll meet you there then. Bye, all!" He waved at the students, saluting happily as he walked to his car.

After getting their coffee, they went for a walk along the river, enjoying the chilly sunshine. They made no mention of the morning's events. As if by mutual consent, they set the misunderstandings aside. Derrick turned thoughtful, not speaking for a few moments.

"I was wondering. What gave you this sudden insight into the male psyche? Surely Muse didn't reveal our secrets?"

"No," she smiled, her eyes tender. "I had a long conversation with Jasper Waters."

"The cop?"

"Yes. He took me to breakfast."

"Oh, did he?" He sounded mildly put out by that announcement.

"He called shortly after you left, to check on me. I was upset, so he took me to breakfast."

"Did he make a pass at you?" He tried to sound casual, but didn't quite pull it off.

"He told me if I wasn't so hung up on you, he'd pursue me himself, if that's what you mean by a pass."

"Up front, isn't he?"

"Calm down, Derrick. I don't want him."

"Apparently, you don't want me either," he mumbled, stirring his coffee angrily.

"I never said that." She paused, pursing her lips. "Look, we aren't going to have this argument again, are we? I like you, Derrick. I'm incredibly attracted to you. Women have an advantage over men."

"Oh? What would that be?"

"When we're interested in a man, it doesn't show." She smirked, winking at him.

"Good one, love. Think that up all by yourself?"

"Be nice. You know it's true. I could be having all kinds of fantasies about you, but unless I do something overt, you haven't got a clue how I feel."

"And how do you feel, love?"

She kissed him, running her tongue over his lips. "How do you think?"

"I think that if you're teasing me, it's a cruel joke."

"What happened this morning scared me, Derrick."

"I scared you? How?"

"I'm not used to a man's attentions. When I saw — that — I panicked."

"My big, scary boner made you panic?"

"Yes. Well, sort of. What scared me was what your expectations might be, waking up in my bed."

"I didn't have any, except a good morning kiss."

"I haven't dated all that much, Derrick. In fact, hardly at all. I could probably count the number of times I've kissed a man on my fingers and toes with at least a foot left over."

"What are you telling me, Mandy?" He took her hand, halting her progress along the sidewalk.

There was a small gazebo nearby, overlooking the water. He led her to that, sitting with her on the bench.

"Do I really have to say it?"

"It seems so, because I haven't any idea what you're trying to tell me."

She shivered, pulling her collar up. It was warm in the sunshine, but not in the gazebo.

"I'm inexperienced, Derrick — because I haven't ever been with a man." She mumbled the last part, so embarrassed she couldn't stand it.

Derrick wanted to laugh because it was such a minor issue. He had it fluffed out as being some major, complicated problem that couldn't be worked out. He allowed himself to smile as he took her hand.

"Is that it? You're a virgin, that's the big secret I can't extract from you?"

"I'm glad it isn't that big a deal to you. It's rather important to me, however."

"Please, don't get in a huff over this. I thought it was something horrible I'd done, or some baggage left by another guy. I was fleshing it out like you'd been molested or raped and I was going to have a huge battle of epic proportions on my hands before I could make love to you. This isn't insurmountable, Mandy."

She said nothing, looking stunned. "What?"

"I mean, we can work with this. Now that I know what the problem is, I can deal with it. I can't promise Mr. Sparky won't hop up to say hello, but at least you know I'm not going to leave you. If I only wanted sex—"

"I know, we'd have done it already."

"There wouldn't have been any *no* for an answer. I would have circumvented your objections and gone right for the g-spot."

"Have you done that?"

His coffee became very interesting. He stirred it rapidly, watching the foam on his latte swirl and disintegrate. "Yeah." He met her stare with one of his own. He neither smiled nor frowned. "I think every guy does at one point or another, especially when he's young. I didn't rape anyone, if that's what you're worried about. But yeah, I got what I wanted despite her objections. She wasn't fussing much by the time she had her first orgasm, though. But I was a bastard and I knew it. She

didn't want to do it and I made her. That was our first time. I felt so bad about it, I never did it again."

"I'm sorry, it really wasn't my business."

"Kind of is, right? You want assurance that I'm not just trying to boff you. I'm perfectly capable of being a selfish prick. I hope you can appreciate now that I haven't been."

He was so formal, she was worried. He didn't sound like himself at all. His expression was stone cold, bland, immovable.

"You're right. I do appreciate that. I apologize for my assumptions. I'll try not to do that anymore."

"Thanks," he mumbled. "I appreciate that. So," he paused. "These other guys. Why did they leave?"

"I wouldn't let them in. I kept them all at arm's length. You're the only man who's come close to me."

"Are we talking literally or figuratively in?"

"Both. Not in my pants, not in my heart. I thought if I cared for someone, I'd do something foolish. I didn't want to be another teenage statistic. My older sister — she had a baby when she was sixteen, I was twelve. I watched what she went through, and decided that wasn't going to happen to me. She gave him up, and she's regretted it every day since."

He took her hand in his, kissing her fingers. Looking deeply into her eyes, he spoke quietly. "Can I tell you something to set your mind at ease?"

She nodded, placing her other hand over his.

"I've never been happier than where I am right now. This is what I want, *you're* what I want. I could fall so hard and deep in love, I'd lose myself in you. You're everything I want, Amanda. I'm not going anywhere. So the next time Mr. Sparky pops up, don't panic. He's not going visiting unless you want him to."

His clever euphemisms amused and reassured her. Leaning forward, she kissed him, feeling his warm breath on her cool cheeks. They stayed in the gazebo a long time, kissing one another, their coffee forgotten on the bench. They were interrupted when two elderly ladies walked up with their dogs.

"Oh, don't let us stop you," one of them said in a broad New England accent. "We've stepped into young love in bloom, Effie."

"It's all right, Millie. They'll go back to it once we leave. Carry on, children!"

The women waved at them, walking rapidly past without another word. Their presence threw a bit of a blight on their enthusiasm.

"Why don't we head to your place?" Derrick suggested.

"We could go to yours," she countered. "I haven't seen where you live yet."

"Yes, but I'm less likely to have extremely naughty thoughts outside my own environment. At your place, they will simply be somewhat naughty."

Amanda giggled. "If you stopped having naughty thoughts, I'd think you didn't care anymore."

"Rest assured, Amanda," his voice dropped almost an octave, his eyes filled with a seductive passion she'd never seen before. "I will always have naughty thoughts and I will always, forever be interested in you."

"I guess we'll have to give Mr. Sparky his own room then, huh? Cause he's here to stay."

"Oh, love, what I could make of that remark!"

Realizing what she'd said, Amanda blushed deeply, dropping her gaze to the ground. "Oh, God. Someone just shoot me now."

He laughed, putting his arm around her. "Let's go get some dinner. Where would you like to eat?"

"Hmm, good question. I've got an idea. It's a surprise. Follow me to my apartment, let me change into something more comfortable and I'll drive us there."

They headed to her place and he parked in her guest spot. She trotted up to her apartment and he followed her, admiring the view as she climbed the stairs. Muse greeted them at the door, leaving Amanda's ankles in order to tangle with Derrick's. He purred, rubbing his head against the tall man's legs.

"Why does he like me so? I thought cats were aloof."

"I'm still trying to figure that one out. I don't know. He's never even greeted me like that when I brought him food! I'll be out in a minute. Have a seat. If you want a soda, there's some in the fridge."

"Got a beer? I'm not driving, after all."

"Yeah, I've got that or Woodchuck's Cider. Help yourself."

Derrick half hoped she'd forget again and leave the door open so he could watch her change, but she closed the door carefully behind her. At least she didn't lock it. Whistling, he went to the fridge and helped himself to a Woodchuck's Cider. It tingled and sparkled in his throat. He sipped at it as he looked at her DVD collection.

"You've got some good flicks here," he said loudly so she could hear him in the bedroom.

"Lots of action movies. Don't tell me you don't like chick flicks."

"Not a lot," she came out, breathless, in her jeans and sweater. "I'd rather watch Mel Gibson or Bruce Willis smack around the bad guys than some smarmy sniffler. I want tight asses and beefcake, baby!" She took a sip of his cider, raising it as if she were toasting him. "Then again, I've got enough eye candy right here. Who needs Bruce and Mel?" She winked, handing his bottle back to him.

He took a step back, clutching his heart. "Oh, be still my heart! She thinks I'm eye candy! Love, that's quite a compliment. I'm hoping you are comparing me to Mel and Bruce in their prime. They're looking a wee bit long in the tooth these days."

"Of course! I love '80s action movies. I like just about any action flicks, but my favorites older than I am."

Derrick laughed, finishing off his cider. "I'm ready, you?"

"I'm set. Let me feed Muse and we can be on our way."

He rinsed and filled the water bowl while she sprinkled food into the cat's bowl. Derrick got the ankle treatment again as Muse expressed his delight in being fed.

"See what I mean? I gave him the food, you just did water, and he's all over you. I tell you, there's no justice."

"Well, if it's any consolation, I'd love to be all over you." He winked, knowing what a whopping double entendre that remark was.

"Stinker." She nudged him with her elbow as she closed her front door and locked it.

They drove to the beach side to a comfortable family style restaurant with a view of the beach. It was too chilly to sit on the deck, but the hostess seated them near the huge glass windows so they could see the ocean in the warmth and comfort of the inside.

"Oh, seafood!" Derrick's eyes widened. "Is it good here?"

"It's excellent. I recommend the grouper or the red snapper. It's all good, but those are my favorites."

"I'm easy to please as long as it doesn't have tentacles. No squid or octopus for me."

Amanda shuddered, wrinkling her nose. "Eww, don't even mention it! I went on this horror date once when I was in college. He wanted to show me how cosmopolitan he was and ordered in Italian at this restaurant."

"Did he order the wrong thing?"

"No, that's what's so awful! He knew perfectly well he'd ordered calamari." She gagged as she remembered, fanning herself with the menu. "It was so disgusting, I can't even begin to describe it."

"I thought it was like eating rubber bands, myself."

"But rubber bands don't taste like that! Ewg."

Derrick laughed, flipping through the menu. "I don't see any on the menu, you're safe."

"I think I'm going to have a steak. Our steak meal got interrupted."

"Sounds delicious. I'll do the same."

Their waitress, who was probably about seventeen, came to the table. She carried her pad and pen, wearing her uniform of black pants and a white shirt. Her hair was dyed black and streaked with pink and blue.

"Hi, I'm Elicia, your server for this evening. Hey, aren't you Mr. Butler?"

"The one and only."

"You were kissing in the parking lot after school, weren't you? I knew it was you!"

"You're in one of my classes, right? Sit in the back and you're always drawing in a notebook."

"Yeah, that's me. What can I get you this evening?

They placed their orders, taking hands when she picked up the menus. Derrick leaned across the table, kissing Amanda.

"So, are you two married or something?"

"Dating, is all, love. I can't convince her to make it more permanent."

Her eyes grew wide again. "Oh, you should totally commit. He's too yummy to let go, you know? My boyfriend isn't nearly as jacked at hot as Mr. B." She grinned sheepishly. "But he's pretty cute!" Biting her lip, she walked to the kitchen to place their order.

"You do attract an odd element." Derrick shook his head, taking a sip of his drink.

"Me? You're the one who kissed me!" She laughed, happily incredulous.

"Yes, well, if you didn't have such full, red lips and luscious — mm. . . ." He bit his lip, closing his eyes. "Everything. . . ." He took a deep breath, exhaling slowly before continuing.

"Then you wouldn't have given me such an incredible kiss. I see how it is. You're just interested in my tits."

"No, I'm also interested in what's south of your belly button, but I'm mostly interested in what makes you tick, Amanda Bitterson."

"I'll never understand a man like you." She shook her head, mind boggling.

"There are no chaps like me. I'm unique, me."

"Yes, you are, which is why I find myself so attracted to you."

"Do you, now? That's good to know. I thought maybe I was the only one totally besotted."

"I wouldn't call myself besotted, more intrigued. Yes, decidedly intrigued."

"May I still be besotted? I really want to be."

"You may be anything you want, love," she imitated his accent beautifully.

"Sweet!"

Their meal arrived, served by Elicia and three other girls. Two had an entree, the other two refilled their drinks.

"That's what I call service," Derrick grinned, winking at them. "I wonder if they each expect a tip," he whispered when the girls had gone.

"I think they just wanted to see the gorgeous Mr. B."

Derrick looked shocked. "You think so? How odd."

"I think you're going to be the fantasy of more than one underage girl tonight, my sweet."

"Oh, God. So long as they can't arrest me for it, that's fine."

"I promise, I'm of age. My fantasies can't get you in trouble. Well, maybe if we put them in practice. In which case, I hope you have good health insurance."

His eyes grew wide, his mouth hanging open. "You're not one of those kinky, S&M types are you?"

She giggled, shaking her head. "No, I don't get off on pain, Mr. B. My fantasies are much less painful, but no less taxing." She raised her eyebrows, taking a bite of food.

"God, do you have any idea what you're doing to me?"

"Mm hm. Mr. Sparky wants to play." She winked at him, licking the food off her fork very seductively.

"You can't blame him when you act like this. What's gotten into you?"

"Nothing, yet."

"Amanda, seriously, love. Enough!" He lowered his voice, speaking in a very earnest whisper. "Please. Unless you're going to allow this to progress to a sweaty, sensual encounter, don't."

The expression in his eyes made her stop and think that she'd gone too far.

"My turn to apologize. I admit, I enjoy talking dirty. I think I'd be very good at it."

"You can be the strict teacher and I'll be the naughty school boy."

"Only if you wear those cute short pants like Angus Young." She countered with a grin.

"Are you a closet AC/ DC fan?" He frowned at her, smiling.

"I am a huge closet AC/ DC fan!" Her voice dropped to a conspiratorial whisper.

"Wicked. Me too. Pink Floyd." He matched her tone.

"Ooh, love them. Gary Moore."

"Grand! Led Zeppelin."

"Love Robert's hair! Prince."

"You mean the Prince of Wales?" He sounded startled.

"No, funky Prince with the cut away chaps." She clapped her hands on her hips.

"Oh, you kinky darling. Next you'll tell me you like Michael Jackson."

"Only the Thriller album. Maybe a few other songs. Sugar Ray."

"You don't like that pussy, pop crap do you, really?"

"A few songs, and Mark McGrath is. . . ."

"Eye candy. I get it. I'm sensing a pattern develop here. Bare asses and buff biceps."

"So I like to look. You're better built than any of them."

"Well, thank you. Glad you noticed."

"I noticed a lot when you were sporting Sponge Bob," she whispered.

"Ah, yes." He blushed, dropping his head slightly. "Good old Bob. Let's do Derrick a small favor and not go there, eh?"

"How about this? I'll make you a deal. We'll talk about it from time to time so you know just how attracted I am to you. When the time is right, Sponge Bob's nose can grow all it wants and Mr. Sparky can play."

He set his fork down, staring at her with his mouth open. "You mean that?"

"I do. Just don't rush me, Derrick. Give me a little time. It's only been a couple days. I promise, it will be worth waiting for."

"I — um. . . ." He cleared his throat, trying to speak. "I promise."

"You up for dessert?"

"Baby, I'm up for anything." He winked, casually brushing her leg with his foot.

"You *are* the naughty school boy, aren't you?"

His blue eyes twinkled as he gazed at her. "You've no idea how good I am when I'm naughty." He lifted her hand to his lips, kissing her fingers. He motioned to Elicia, who came immediately to the table.

"You two want dessert?"

"We need two house specials, please, Elicia," Amanda said.

"Sure! I'll set them up myself. Whipped cream?"

"The works," Amanda said with a grin.

"Two house specials with the works. You got it!" She grabbed their dirty plates and carried them to the kitchen.

Five minutes later, she came back with two plates on a tray. Setting them carefully in front of Derrick and Amanda, she stood back to watch them take the first bite.

"What is it?" Derrick eyed the plate with skepticism.

The item on the plate looked like a tortilla that had been folded in half, stuffed with something and dipped in bread crumbs, then deep fried. It was topped with strawberries, chocolate syrup and whipped cream.

"Don't be such a wimp. Taste it." Amanda cut into hers, taking a big bite. Rolling her eyes, she licked the fork to show him how good it was. "It's positively sinful. Yum!"

Derrick bravely took a bite, waiting for the flavors to blend on his tongue. "Oh! Oh, my God, that's good!" He took a bigger bite. "That's like deep fried, chocolate covered sex!" He gobbled up his dessert, savoring every bite. "I swear my mouth is having an orgasm." He licked his lips to get every drop of syrup off them.

"It's just fried cheesecake, Mr. B. No one ever described it like that."

"I can't help if they didn't think of it," he laughed. "This is delicious. If I were at home, I'd lick the plate," he confided to Amanda when Elicia was gone.

"I love it. That's my one indulgence. It's so decadent, it's almost a mortal sin."

"Yeah, but what a way to go. I could eat this forever and never get tired of it."

"But think how fat you'd get."

"Not me, I've got a crazy metabolism and an extreme workout routine."

"Let me guess, body by P90X?"

He looked stunned. "How did you guess?"

She motioned to her figure. "I'm a P90X'er myself."

"Strewth, we're a match made in heaven, Amanda. I always wanted to know what it would be like to make love to a P90X lady. One of my tawdry little fantasies."

She grinned, giving him a look that set his loins on fire. He knew at that moment she was his. She'd never give that kind of look to a man she had no intention of going to bed with — at least he hoped not.

After dinner, they took a very short stroll on the beach. The cold, damp spray drove them back to the car, where they stood for a few minutes, kissing. There again, the chill forced them inside and they headed back to her apartment for a hot chocolate and, Derrick hoped, more kissing.

Driving up to her place, they saw police cars in the parking lot. They were three of them, clustered around the far end, near where she would normally park. Amanda pulled up on the street in front of the building. Getting out, they were greeted by a police officer, Jasper Waters.

"Amanda, there you are! No one knew where you'd gone. Your cell must be off, I've called at least ten times. Hey, Derrick." He looked worried.

"I shut it off when I was at the school for Derrick's lecture. I guess I forgot to turn it back on. What's wrong? Why all the cars?"

"Let's go inside," he suggested, motioning to the front door.

"Jasper, you're scaring the lady. What's up?" Derrick put a protective arm around Amanda.

"Did you lock up when you left?" Jasper asked quietly.

"Of course I did. I never go out without locking the door. I always double check, I'm a little paranoid about locks."

"Someone broke into your place, Amanda."

"My — what?"

Pale and shaking, she leaned against Derrick for support. He and Jasper helped her sit on the bench just inside the entry way.

"Why? What did they do in there?"

"They took your cat," Jasper said quietly.

"What? Muse? Where is he? Is he okay?" She tried to stand. The men restrained her, gently.

"Yeah. He's okay. We sent him to the vet. Someone shaved him and taped him to the hood of Derrick's car." Jasper's voice held disgust and a fine edge of anger.

"*My* car? Why the hell would they do that?"

"I was hoping you could tell me."

"Was it Jason?"

"First person I thought of. No. Our records confirm he was home all night. He can't get that anklet off and he can't go more than a hundred yards from his house or it will set off an alarm. They're pretty tamper proof."

"So someone else has targeted us? His family or friends, maybe?"

"Immediate family is being interviewed, as are his close friends. If anyone knows anything, we'll find out. I've got forensics going over the car for evidence right now."

"And her apartment?" Derrick asked.

"Untouched except for a note they left. Computer printout, of course. It was taped to the door, telling us where to find the cat. Nothing more."

He handed her a plastic evidence bag. Inside was a note printed in huge block letters. "If you want to see your cat, look out the window."

"How did you find out about this?"

"Neighbor called. Your cat was yowling his head off. I guess the guy didn't count on that. He was probably hoping you'd come home and find him missing."

"Poor Muse! Can I see him?"

"He's being examined right now. They'll call me when they're done. You can see him then."

"Thanks, Jasper." She hugged him, kissing his cheek.

Closing his eyes, he patted her on the back. "Doing my job, Amanda. They called me in on this since I came over last night. I asked if anything else happened for them to contact me."

"Can she go inside now? It's pretty cold down here," Derrick asked quietly.

"The lock on the door is damaged. I'd suggest you stay somewhere else tonight. You can go get your things, though."

Amanda's next door neighbor, Miss Hook, came out about that time and took Amanda into her apartment so she could warm up. She was a delicate, elderly lady with the looks and mannerisms of a fine boned bird.

"She can come home with me," Derrick decided.

Jasper's face clouded as he hung his head.

"Look, mate, nothing's going on, okay? She'll be in the guest room."

"Hey, not my business," Jasper said, rubbing his face with both hands. "You saw her first, I'm just the beat cop with a heavy crush." He tried to smile.

"Thanks for what you did this morning, man. It meant a lot to us both."

"I guess that means you're trying to work through your issues, huh?"

"Yeah, we aired a few little demons we've been hiding. Cleared the air. I'm just sorry you had to get in the middle of it. It's not exactly a position I'd like to be in."

Jasper's sardonic laugh filled the small entry hall. "Believe me, I don't like it either, but I couldn't let her suffer. If she's meant to be with you, then that's where she needs to be. But I'll be honest, Derrick, it wouldn't upset me if you broke her heart and I was here to pick up the pieces."

"Having been on both ends of that kind of relationship, I understand. I don't envy your position, mate."

"No, but I sure as hell envy yours." He sighed heavily. "Well, that was refreshing, huh?"

Derrick punched him lightly on the shoulder. "Yeah. A catharsis has that effect. Want to help me pack her bag?"

"Shouldn't you let her do that?"

"Oh, I'm gonna ask her before I rifle through her pantie drawer," Derrick chuckled, his eyes twinkling. "Maybe."

Jasper laughed, a happier sound this time. "Mr. Butler, I think it's only right to warn you that going through a lady's pantie drawer can be construed as misconduct on the part of a police officer."

"Okay, I'll go through it and you stand lookout."

"Then it's aiding and abetting."

"I won't tell if you won't."

Laughing and joking, the went into Amanda's apartment. She and Miss Hook were already there packing up some things for an overnight bag.

"She can stay with me," Miss Hook said with a happy smile. "That way she's close to home. Poor little pussy," she said sorrowfully. "I don't know how they got out of here with him and me not hearing." Shaking her head, she wandered into the other room.

"Deaf as a post," Amanda said, pointing to her ears. "The neighbors on the other side were the ones who called and reported it. They were out when he was taken, but heard him as they were coming home."

"You'll be alright next door?" Derrick looked concerned and rather disappointed.

"Yeah." Amanda stood close, holding the lapels of his jacket. "It's better, really. There's no temptation."

"I like a little temptation," Derrick pouted, kissing her.

Jasper cleared his throat. "Okay! If you're all right, I'll head back down. We'll put a security lock on this for the night and you can call a repairman in the morning. My cousin does repairs." He handed her a business card. "Tell him Aunt Jo sent you and he'll give you a discount."

"Why not just tell him Jasper sent me?"

"Cause he likes her better." He winked. "Take care, Mandy. Call if you need me." Saluting, he went out.

"I've hurt that poor man's feelings," Amanda said softly, resting her forehead on Derrick's muscular chest.

"Been there myself more than once," Derrick replied. "If it's any consolation, he knows he did it to himself. It's not your fault."

"Doesn't make it any easier on my conscience. What did I do to make him like me?"

"You smiled." He kissed her gently, holding her close.

"Oh, sorry!" Miss Hook came through with a pile of clothing. "Mandy, is this all you'll need, dear?"

"Probably. I don't know how long I'll be staying. The officer interviewing the neighbors said to pack for at least three days."

Miss Hook leaned close, whispering. Well, what she thought was whispering, it was really rather loud. "Did you remember feminine supplies, dear? I don't have those anymore."

"I'm set, thanks," Amanda blushed.

Miss Hook left, muttering to herself. Derrick was laughing at Amanda's embarrassment.

"I've got four sisters. I've bought more boxes of feminine supplies than any man I know. It's easy to boss baby brother around and make him run to the store."

"I'll keep that in mind if I need something." She grinned, kissing him.

"There's only one thing I need," Derrick's lips lingered next to hers. "Another of those kisses before I go."

Amanda was happy to comply. They kissed a long time, standing in her apartment. They were interrupted again when a police officer, not Jasper, tapped on the open door.

"We're all done here, Miss Bitterson. I need to put the security lock on the door."

"Oh, thanks. I think I've got everything."

"If not, we'll give you the code. You can come back in."

CHAPTER FIVE

She and Derrick went out hand in hand. The officer secured the door, giving her a card with the code on it.

"Night, Miss Bitterson."

"Night. Thanks."

Miss Hook met her at the door. "I'm going to bed, honey. Your young man is welcome to stay for awhile if he'd like."

"Thanks, Miss Hook. I think I'll head home. Call if you need me, yeah?"

"I will. Thanks, Derrick."

"My pleasure," he smiled, kissing her once more.

Miss Hook, who was still standing in the doorway, sighed happily, clasping her hands in front of her chest.

"That's so romantic! Good night, young man."

"Good night, Miss Hook."

He kissed her hand, bowing over it. With a flourish, he bowed again, bidding them farewell, and left. Amanda's cellphone rang as she was putting her things in Miss Hook's guest room. It was Jasper.

"Hi!"

"Hi. I called to tell you the vet wants to keep Muse for the night. He got pretty cold out there without his fur."

"At least he didn't rape him or something perverted."

"Yeah, that would be pretty bad. I've been desperate for pussy before, but that's twisted."

She giggled despite herself. "I shouldn't laugh at that. It's my pussy!" She knew she'd made a double entendre, which was exactly what she meant to do.

Jasper laughed so loudly, it echoed in the tiny guest room. "God, that's too funny. Anyway, have a good night. I'll keep you posted on what we find out. Oh, the vet's name is Albert Simpson. I don't have his number, but it's in the book."

"Thanks again, Jasper. You're such a good friend."

He was silent a moment and she knew she'd just hurt his feelings. "Yeah. Well, we all need one of those, right?"

"I can't promise anything more, I'm sorry."

"Nothing to be sorry about. Sleep well, Mandy." He hung up rather abruptly.

Amanda felt horrible. She'd never been in a position where two men interested in her at the same time. She liked Jasper, he was friendly and funny, handsome and charming. Derrick was all of that and he set her insides on fire. Jasper didn't have the same effect on her, taking her breath away just by being near her. Had she met him first, he would have been a good match. Yet there was just something about Derrick that simply defied words.

Her phone rang again as she was getting in bed.

"Hello, Derrick." She grinned. "I was just thinking about you."

"Yeah? What were you thinking?"

"Are you sure you really want to know?"

"I'm a sucker for punishment. Of course I do."

"I was thinking about how special you are."

"That's a good thought." He inhaled deeply, exhaling slowly before replying. "I was thinking the same thing. I'm not keeping you up, am I?"

"It's nine thirty. I'm not the least bit sleepy, but Miss Hook doesn't have a TV or computer. I'm glad I brought my laptop and my Kindle, at least I can read and listen to music."

"I couldn't survive without my music. I've got my place at home wired for sound in every room. Here, I just crank it up and hope the neighbors don't complain."

"Where do you live?"

"You'd have seen it if you'd come home with me," he admonished playfully.

"I couldn't tell Maisey, no, it would have broken her heart. She felt so bad about Muse being catnapped and not hearing it."

"Guilt is an amazing motivator, isn't it? Makes fools of us all."

"I thought that was love."

"That too, but guilt works faster."

"Derrick, why did he hurt my cat? There's no reason for it. That's just mean!" Amanda sniffled, wiping her eyes with the sheet.

Derrick's sharp ears picked up on the soft sound. "Hey, he'll be okay. Don't worry about him."

"Why is someone doing this to me? What did I do to deserve this?"

"You don't deserve it, love. Some sick bastard is just trying to upset you. It'll be okay."

"But when? I'm so confused! I can't even think straight. I just want to curl up in a fetal position and gibber incoherently."

"Oh, if you do that, can I take advantage of you? I've always wanted to do that to a gibbering, fetal person."

She laughed despite herself. "You're a nut," she giggled.

"No, but I've got a couple," he mumbled, letting her interpret it as she liked.

"I'm sure you're more than willing to share."

"Sure am! I'm very generous, me." His voice dropped to a soft murmur. "And I'll share anytime, anyplace, anywhere. Just say the word, and I'm all yours."

"You're going to get yourself all worked up."

"Too late, Mr. Sparky already wants to come out and play."

"Mr. Sparky needs better manners."

"Yeah, well, you want to tell him? Maybe he'll listen to you."

"I think I'll pass." She chuckled as he sighed at her.

"You could beat him into submission again."

"Don't you have to work in the morning?"

"Yeah, but it's not all that late. I figure a nice, cold shower and I can call it a night."

"Derrick?"

"Yeah?"

"You won't have to take too many more of those."

"Promise?"

"I promise." She paused, gathering her courage. "I need to figure a few things out, get out from under this mess. I have to resolve my issues before I can start anything more with you. But you've given me the motivation and the courage to do it."

"Yeah? That's great. Any way I can help, I will. You know that."

"I know. You're a very special man, Derrick Butler."

"You're a special lady, Amanda Bitterson. Is it okay if I fall in love with you now? I can't wait until you get your issues cleared up."

"Sure. You have my permission to fall deeply in love."

"You'll be there with me, yeah?"

"Yeah." His phone made a funny clicking sound. "Oh, sweet cheeks, I've got another call coming in. It's overseas. I'll call you tomorrow, okay?"

"Okay. Bye now."

"Bye." He hung up, glaring at the caller ID. "Yes, Persephone. What do you want?"

"Nothing much, Derrick." A hostile sounding woman with a chilly voice answered. "Just calling to see how my long, lost hubby is."

* * *

Amanda plugged in her laptop and put on her headphones. She got her Kindle out and found the page she'd of the excellent romantic suspense novel she'd been reading before meeting Derrick. Somehow, the problems of the main character paled next to her own. Instead, of reading, she dug out her phone and called her mother.

"Manda? Why are you calling?" She sounded mad. She always sounded mad when Amanda called. "What's wrong? Do you need money?"

"Mom, I'm fine. I don't need money. I just wanted to tell you what's been happening the last few days."

"Make it fast, I'm watching TV."

"This is important, Mom!"

Amanda raised her voice, nearly shouting. She never did that with her mother, but it felt good to take command of a conversation for once.

"It's on a commercial. What?"

"I met someone," she said softly. "This really great guy named Derrick. He's from Australia."

"Austria? Is he German?"

"Mom, I said Australia. Can you turn down your TV? Maybe you'd have a chance of hearing me."

The sound in the background was immediately muted.

"Okay, you happy now?"

"Someone broke into my apartment today."

"Did they take anything?"

"Don't you want to know how I am?"

"You're obviously fine. You're talking to me, aren't you?"

"For all you care, I could be in the hospital! Don't you even care that your youngest child had her apartment broken into? They shaved my cat!"

An explosive sound like someone spewing liquid on the phone filled her ear. "You're kidding, right?" There was muffled laughter.

"Why would I kid about something like that?"

"Who is it, Stella?"

She heard a familiar voice in the background. What was her father doing there?

"Mom! Dammit! Is Dad there?"

"Sure, talk to your father." She heard sounds of the phone being moved. "It's Amanda. Here's Daddy. My show's back on." She handed the phone over. The loud TV noise returned.

"Hey, baby. What's wrong?"

"Hi, Daddy. What are you doing there?"

"Stella and me decided to try and work stuff out. What's up?"

Amanda told him everything that had happened over the last couple of days. Somehow it was easier telling her father, whom she hadn't see or spoken to for three years, than it was to tell her mother.

"Oh, honey! That's terrible. Is Muse okay?"

"Yes, I guess so. I haven't seen him yet. He's at the vet."

"Do they know who did it?"

"Not yet. I hope they're working on it. I have this feeling it's weird enough to get swept under the rug."

"Got any friends on the force?"

"Actually, yes."

"Ask him to keep a fire lit. Is he a good friend?"

"He could be. But there's Derrick—"

"Ah, my baby girl in a love triangle."

"Not like that. I mean, we're not involved like that."

"Honey, I don't want to know about your sex life."

"Well, if I actually had one, I wouldn't tell you anyway, Daddy. Ew."

He laughed. She could picture him cradling the phone as he talked, his blue eyes dancing happily. As uninterested and uninvolved as her mother was, her father had tried hard to make up for it. After awhile, it became impossible for him to sustain the farcical marriage any longer and he left. Amanda asked him once why her mother was so distant. What he'd had to say was even less satisfactory than not knowing.

"Your Mom's an alcoholic, Manda. You were a late life baby that she wasn't expecting and I don't think she ever accepted you." Harsh words for a girl of sixteen to hear, but she had found the truth often hurt.

"You there, Manda?"

"Yeah, Daddy. It's been a long day and I didn't get a lot of sleep last night."

"Keep me posted on the break in. And call if you need me. You know you can always come home if it gets really bad."

"Dad, it would have to mean the end of the world before I'd come home."

Her father sighed heavily and she knew she had hurt his feelings. "I know, honey. It's there if you need it."

"Thank you, Dad. Let's hope it doesn't get that bad."

"Good night, sweetie."

"Night, Daddy."

Hanging up, she wiped her tears on the sheet. She turned out the lights and eventually cried herself to sleep.

* * *

Derrick eyed the phone as if it had somehow violated him. "I signed those bloody papers before I left, Persephone. God, can't you do anything right?"

"Your lawyer lost it or failed to file," she commented with an ugly snarl. "Is it my fault he's incompetent?"

"So we're still married, is that what you're saying?"

"That's what I'm saying, lover. So whatever fun you're having in the States, it's at an end. You have to get those papers signed."

"Fax them to me. I'll sign whatever it takes to get you out of my life."

"Well, there's just one tiny problem, sweetie."

"What's that, you blood sucking fiend?"

It was then he heard a small, snuffling sound near the phone, then a wailing cry.

"Meet Derrick Butler, Junior," she said and hung up.

Furious, Derrick threw his phone across the apartment. It hit the glass window leading to the balcony with a resounding crash. He thought at first he'd cracked the expensive glass, but it was just his phone falling apart. He was rather impressed it didn't break completely, but the cover just fell off it. Cursing loudly, he picked up the pieces and dropped them in the kitchen drawer.

"Unbelievable!" He yelled. "Un—believable!"

He knew Persephone had done something with the papers. She had to have screwed it up somehow. Glancing at his clock, he saw that it was still mid-morning back home. He put his phone back together and called his lawyer's office.

"Sam, it's Derrick."

Sam Hudson was a little older than he was, a college friend. They'd roomed together when Derrick was a freshman.

"Derrick, how's it hanging?"

"Could be better. It could be free of the bonds of matrimony."

"What?"

"I just got a call from Persephone. She informed me that not only are we not divorced, but she'd bouncing little Derrick Junior on her knee. As we speak, my life is falling apart. What can we do about this?"

"Dude, totally not cool." Sam was several decades behind in his verbal skills.

"Tell me something I can do, Sam. I can't have this right now. I've just struck up a new acquaintance, someone I really care about. I can't have the beast from the abyss lurking in the netherworld trying to suck me dry. And what's this about a baby? No one told me!"

"Dude, I swear I didn't know. I filed your papers, I promise. I did it the day you handed them to me."

"She said you didn't."

"I'm looking at the file now. I did do it just like I said. Must be on her end. I have no clue why. I'll check it and get back to you."

"I want a paternity test on the kid. If he's mine, so be it. I don't want to shirk my responsibilities. If he's not mine..."

"You don't want her to work you. Got it, dude. Word."

"Talk like a normal human, Sam. This is serious."

"I'm aware of that, Derrick. I'm working on it. Trust me, if she's done something skunky, I'll find out."

"Thanks, man. I appreciate it."

"I'll get back to you today, may not be until afternoon."

Derrick sighed. "Fifteen hour difference, remember? If you can't call me back in the next couple hours, call me tomorrow around this time, yeah?"

"Will do, buddy. Sorry, Derrick. I don't know how she slipped that by me."

"Because she's Medusa's Roommate," Derrick growled. "Later, Sam."

Hanging up, he almost threw the phone again, but he didn't want to risk losing his lifeline to Amanda. Shit! Amanda. What would she think of all this? Would she think he'd lied to her just to take her to bed? Wondering how to handle it, he risked a call to his sister in Atlanta. As a flight attendant for a major airline, she'd married a pilot and settled in the states. The phone rang twice

before her husband picked up.

"Yeah?" His broad Texas drawl elongated the word almost comically.

"Holmes, it's Derrick. Is Tammy there?"

"Sure is! Lemme get her for ya! Honey, it's your brother! She's coming. How's life treating you, buddy?"

"Like shit, Holmes. You?"

"Hell, kid, it's pretty damn good here. What's up?"

"Put Tammy on the extension, I'll tell you both. I need your help, Holmes. I'm desperate."

His sister got on a moment later, concerned layering her voice. "What's wrong, Derrick?"

The funny thing about Tammy was she tried so hard not to sound Australian, she had purposely affected an accent from Oxford, England. Her well modulated voice sounded a bit tense, but still in control.

Derrick told them first about Amanda and how fond he was of her. Then he told them what had happened with Persephone and how it could mess up his chances with Amanda.

"That bitch!" Tammy's broad, Australian accent came through loud and clear when she was angry. "By God, Holmes, we have to do something!"

"Honey, we can't go off half cocked."

"Derrick, our next run is in a couple days. I'll get that baby tested if I have to do it myself!"

"Get your test done here, buddy. We'll see what we can do when we get home. And don't you worry none. We'll get this mess straight. You just enjoy the hell out of your lady friend."

"Derrick, I'm calling the girls," his sister announced suddenly. "Talk to Holmes if you will, but I'm starting with Sally."

"Bye, sis. Thanks."

She hung up with a click. Derrick sighed, wanting to groan instead.

"Holmes, what am I going to tell Amanda? When she finds out about Persephone and the baby, she's going to castrate me."

"Maybe not castrate. You haven't slept with her yet, that's a good thing. She won't castrate you, maybe break a rib or two."

"You aren't helping."

"Sorry, kid. You know I'd do anything in the world for you, but I can't help you out of this one. I suggest telling her the truth. If she's the woman for you, she'll understand. If not—"

"If not, then Persephone's ruined my life a second time."

"Sorry to tell ya, buddy, but you and your Johnson ruined your life the minute you laid that life leeching bitch. What were you thinking?"

"She was tall, dark haired, dead sexy and Mr. Sparky was hungry. I was also drunk off my ass, your fault as I recall. I met her at your wedding, you bastard."

"I can't help that she worked with Tammy and angled an invite. I'm sorry about that, but you married her."

"Yeah, well the sex was decadent and plentiful."

"Could the kid be yours?"

"I don't know, Holmes. She and I had sex so infrequently towards the end, I can barely remember. I've been gone less than a year, which would mean she was a couple months along when I left. I really doubt it's mine, but you never know. Be just like her to do something like that just because she could screw me over later."

His sister's voice came back on the line. "I talked to Sally. She's going over to Persephone's now. If the little skank wants money from you, she'll be cooperative to a DNA test. If she's just stringing you along, she won't. Get your doctor to order a test tomorrow and we'll fax that to Dr. Withers back home."

"Sally's not gonna be packin', is she?" Holmes sounded worried.

Tammy laughed rather caustically. "Sally doesn't have to be packin' to make people pay attention. She's the aggressive one."

"Oh, and Holmes married the passive-aggressive one, eh?" Derrick couldn't resist a dig.

"Don't be fooled," she slathered on the English charm.

Derrick could picture her batting her big, blue eyes fetchingly. Tammy was the dramatic one, Sally was violent.

"Ye-up," Holmes agreed. "Tammy's the pit bull of the family. Got to cut off her head to get her to unclamp them jaws."

"I'll un-clamp you, Holmes Gregory Lorne, and don't you forget it!"

Laughing loudly, Holmes bid farewell. It hadn't been much advise, but better than none. Derrick's mind had been made up for him long before his conversation with his sister and brother-in-law. Tomorrow, he would have to tell Amanda about Persephone. In the meantime, he was going to take a sick day tomorrow so he could get blind ass drunk.

Calling Mr. Murray, he said he wasn't feeling well and wouldn't be in.

"Have anything to do with the pretty blonde?"

"Indirectly, yeah. I'm not staying the night, if that's what you mean." He sighed heavily, wanting to cry for the first time in his adult life.

"Look, kid, if you need to talk about it. . . . Well, I know I'm an old fart, but I still had my time with the ladies. What's troubling you. I can hear in your voice that something's wrong."

"Remember I told you one reason I was here was to get away from my ex-wife?"

"As I recall, you referred to her as the Evil Hag and the Vulture Bride of Frankenstein."

"Yeah, well turns out the desiccated corpse didn't file the papers. I'm still married to her."

"Awkward."

"Somewhat. Amanda doesn't know about Persephone. I hadn't thought it would be an issue, seeing as how she was an *ex*."

"But she's not."

"Nope, still the current Mrs. Derrick Butler. And another fly in the ointment."

"Don't tell me she's expecting."

"Worse. I was introduced to Derrick Junior, if indeed he's mine."

"DNA is a wonderful thing, kid."

"Yup. So I'm going to buy a case of beer and get progressively drunk while I watch my life go in the toilet."

"Want some advice from an old man who's been in your shoes a couple times?"

"Yeah, I'd love it."

"Tell her the truth. Don't sugar coat it. Tell her why you didn't tell her about the Ex-Wife of Dracula. Who wants to talk about an ex or an ugly divorce? I sure as hell didn't."

"You're divorced?"

"From the original Bride of Frankenstein. She married the Creature from the Black Lagoon, they were miserably happy together until he, wisely, died last year. Thirty-seven years of misery. Glad it was him, not me."

"My brother-in-law offered similar advice, Ruben. I guess it's my only choice. I just hope Amanda understands."

"Maybe not right away, but I saw the way that girl looked at you. There's love brewing in those baby blues. Truth and honesty are very underrated, kid."

"Yeah, so's a tazer to the balls, Rube."

"Enjoy your beer, Derrick. Hammer a few for me, huh? I had to give it up. I developed gout."

Derrick winced, sucking air through his teeth. "I'll drink the first six for you, shall I?"

"Only if it means I get to nail the blonde. Night, kid."

"Night, Rube."

Derrick didn't go out for the beer, he had half a case in the refrigerator already. Popping one open, he put in a DVD and kicked off his shoes. Sucking down his first beer, he got another out, bringing a third with him, and set it on the table. On his next trip to the kitchen, he brought out the box, setting it beside his chair.

He was still drinking after one o'clock when his phone rang.

"Yeah?" He could hardly see straight.

Turning down the Sham-Wow commercial, he listened.

"Derrick?" It was Sam.

"Yeah?"

"You been drinking, buddy?"

"Rather a lot," he admitted. "You?"

"Dude, it's afternoon.

"No, it's one o'clock in the bloody morning. What do you need, Sammy?"

"Sally called me. Apparently Persephone isn't home. I'll have her lawyer contact her and get the information."

"Great. I knew I could count on you."

"Consider this payback for all the times you helped me study and all the papers you wrote for me. In fact, I'll pay for the test myself. Take all the time you want paying me back."

"Oh, that's great! I'll pay it, but pay me back?"

"I'm kidding. About paying it back, I mean."

"Thanks, Sam. You're a good friend and a great lawyer."

"Not sure about the friend part, or the great lawyer part, but thanks. Sleep well. Don't get too drunk."

"Too late."

"Idiot."

"Moron."

He hung up, checking the phone three times to make sure he really had. He staggered to his bedroom, falling on the bed without brushing his teeth or undressing.

CHAPTER SIX

Thursday morning, Maisey Hook dragged Amanda with her to her eight o'clock yoga class. After that, a brisk walk on the beach in forty degree weather, Amanda was ready for a cup of coffee and bagel. Miss Hook didn't have coffee, so Amanda was trying to alleviate her caffeine addiction with a pot of Formosa Oolong tea when her phone rang.

Digging it out of the pocket of her sweat suit, she answered breathlessly.

"Please tell me I dialed the right number," Derrick said feebly.

"Derrick?"

"Shh. The natives are restless, beating their drums in my skull. I feel like the only non-deaf person at a Blue Man Group concert."

"What's wrong?" She spoke more softly.

"I got incredibly drunk last night."

"Why?"

"I'll tell you in a bit. Fancy breakfast? I have absolutely no food in the house and I'm starving."

"I'm dying for a latté. Maisey doesn't believe in coffee and I think this tea is decaf."

"Great. I'm in no condition to drive. Can you get me?"

"If you tell me where you live."

"You know the Captain's Quarters?"

"Yes."

"Top floor, number 819."

"Want to meet me in the parking lot?"

"Yeah. I can do that. Or you can come up and see my place."

"Won't that tempt Mr. Sparky?"

"Love, Mr. Sparky hasn't got the energy to turn on a light bulb. I think your virtue is safe for a bit longer."

"Well, shit. What good is he then?"

Derrick paused. She could almost see him glancing down at his crotch, studying it a moment.

"None, whatsoever. Though after a few Red Eyes, he should be hopping again."

"I'll be over in — how long?"

"Give me thirty minutes so I don't inadvertently commit suicide while I'm shaving."

"Five o'clock shadows are kind of sexy."

"Yeah? I've got the entire clock here, but okay. Make it ten then."

"On my way. I'll call when I get to the parking lot if you aren't down yet."

"God, you're wonderful." He hung up.

Amanda bid farewell to Maisey Hook and headed to Derrick's apartment. Actually, it was a condo and a pricey one at that. Facing the river, to the left of the only existing canal in town, it rose eight stories high. Modest in size to other condos in the area, it was the only one right on the river in the downtown area, making it very exclusive. She wondered how he could possibly afford such an expensive place on a teacher's salary.

He was just stepping off the elevator when she pulled up. He loped over to the car, sliding into the seat in one fluid movement. He was wearing a pair of faded blue jeans and a form fitting Black Sabbath T-shirt that showed off his physique. A tattered jeans jacket completed his grunge era ensemble, accented by a pair of RayBan sunglasses and a heavy shadow on his chin. Amanda thought, despite the hangover, he looked sexy as hell.

She dug the seat belt out for him and drove to a cute coffee shop she'd been wanting to try. It was in an historic home not far from Smokey Jo's and called itself Caffeinated Discs. Instead of being a coffee and bookstore, it sold CD's. Cozy chairs were scattered around in little conversation groups, as well as tall stools at the bar.

Amanda led Derrick in, holding his hand. They walked up to the counter to look at the menu. A tall, handsome man about their age was standing behind the bar wearing an apron. His light brown hair looked like a military cut that was growing out.

"What can I get for you folks this morning?" His soft Georgia accent was almost musical.

"Red Eye," Derrick mumbled.

"That's what ya want or that's what ya got?"

"Both, actually. What's there to eat?"

"I can do bagels or pastries. What do you fancy?"

"Something that doesn't move," Derrick moaned, sitting heavily on the arm of a nearby chair. "Tell the floor to quit that, would you, mate?"

"Aussie boy ain't got a head for drink, huh?" He laughed softly. "I got a hangover remedy that's bang up." He grinned, winking at Amanda.

"Yeah? What's that?" Derrick opened one eye, glancing over the top of his sunglasses.

"Double Red Eye, a cheese danish and a little quality time with the missus."

"Not married to her," Derrick sighed, sliding into the chair. "But that's not a bad suggestion. What do you say, love?"

"We'll see. Okay, a Red Eye for Crocodile Dundee and I'll have a latté grande with lowfat milk, please. And two cinnamon rolls."

"Sure thing. Coming right up. Is he okay?"

"He had a tad too much to drink last night."

"I can see that."

Amanda paid for their food and waited at the counter while the man fixed their drinks. He was a little awkward with the latté, but managed fairly well.

"I'm kinda new at this. My girlfriend owns the place, but she had to run an errand."

"I've been meaning to come in for a long time. Just never had the excuse before."

"Jazzing up Methuselah, huh?"

"Yeah."

"What kind of music do you like? I can throw on a disc or two."

"Got any Portishead? Royksopp? Nine Inch Nails?"

"Boy, is that some variety. Yeah, I've got all three. Which first?"

"Something that won't make me vomit in my Red Eye," Derrick mumbled.

"Non-vomit inducing music coming up." He slipped in a couple of CD's and the mellow, haunting strands of a song by Portishead came on.

"Good choice, mate." Derrick held out his knuckles for the other man to tap.

He walked over to Derrick, tapping his knuckles. Taller than Amanda had realized, she smiled up at him as he introduced himself.

"I'm Kael Thorn."

"I'm Amanda Bitterson. The drunk Aussie bastard is Derrick Butler."

"Oh, there's my girl! Hey, baby! Meet Derrick and Amanda."

A young woman with medium brown hair walked over, hugging Kael around the waist.

She looked incredibly familiar to Amanda, whose face lit up when she saw her.

"Oh, my God! Penny?"

"Mandy? How are you? It's so good to see you!"

The young women hugged, chatting excitedly as Penny showed Amanda her new engagement ring. They talked loudly, making Derrick groan. Amanda moved away from him, taking Penny with her. Kael flopped on the couch across from Derrick.

"So, how many beers did you have?"

"I lost count."

"That's some serious drinking, buddy. Sure you ain't a Marine?"

Derrick laughed quietly, his head bouncing against the back of the overstuffed wing chair. "Not even close. Military life wasn't for me. I can't even obey traffic signs."

Kael laughed, shaking his head. "I did three tours overseas."

"Damn! I admire you, man. I thought about it, I really did. Since I argued rather heatedly with the recruiter, they asked me none too politely to leave. Actually, they threw me out on my bony ass."

"Had you been drinking then too?"

"Somewhat. I remember something about a tattoo as well. Or I could be remembering another time. I don't drink often, but when I do, I overdo. I think I'll quit."

"Been there, man. What's eating at you, brother?" Kael leaned forward, clasping his hands on his knees. "I can see a man in pain, and I don't just mean the head."

"Complications in love," he mumbled.

"You seem pretty chummy."

Kael glanced at the women. They weren't paying any attention to the men, talking animatedly.

"Amanda's not the problem."

"Oh, an ex?"

"Not ex enough. It's complicated."

"I got time. Next rush isn't until eleven."

"I feel a fool telling a stranger my problems."

"We're like bartenders and priests, we don't tell." He laughed dryly. "If I told someone's secrets, they might end up telling mine."

Derrick leaned forward, matching Kael's stance without meaning to. "The ex that isn't ex enough?"

"Yeah."

"Wife," he whispered, pointing to his ring finger.

"And the lovely, luscious Amanda doesn't know?"

Derrick shook his head, then wished he hadn't. "No. We just met a couple days ago and I didn't think it mattered as it was an *ex*-wife."

"Nope, don't seem likely to come up in conversation."

"So now — well, obviously, *she's* gorgeous." He gestured to Amanda with both hands.

"Not tapping it yet, though, right?"

"*No*. That's my only saving grace. Can you imagine?" He didn't have to elaborate.

Both men cringed, instinctively covering their private parts with a wary hand.

"She'd kill you man, after she cut your balls off."

"Yeah. So I drowned my sorrows, so to speak."

"Got it. You're gonna tell her though, right?"

"Yeah. As soon as my brain and mouth can function on the same wavelength."

"Good, cause the only thing worse than not telling her to start with, would be neglecting to tell her now. And tell her before you take her to bed."

"Oh, that's a given! I think she'd pitch me out the window into the river otherwise."

The two women wandered back over to them. Since Derrick had his back to them, Kael put his finger beside his nose to signal their approach.

"You've been talking about us," Penny said, sitting on Kael's lap.

Amanda perched on the arm of Derrick's chair and his hand automatically slipped around her waist. He looked dreadfully embarrassed and took a sip of his coffee to cover his lack of ability to speak.

"Just to say how incredibly beautiful, intelligent and amazing you both are," Kael said with a smile and a kiss.

"Nice save, Kael," Amanda giggled. "Too bad it's not true."

"Are you accusing a United States Marine of lying to a lady?"

"If she's not, I am." Penny kissed his cheek and nibbled his ear.

Closing his eyes, Kael mumbled in her ear before speaking again. "Okay, well, the truth is, we were talking about how beautiful, intelligent and incredibly sexy you both are."

"We haven't seen two such delectable females in one place at the same time in — how long was it?"

"Our entire lifetime. I think that was the phrase we were looking for."

Derrick held out his hand as if Kael had spoken gospel truth. "That's the phrase indeed! God, the man's brilliant!"

"Not very convincing liars are they?" Amanda grinned, leaning over to kiss Derrick. "But for a lie, it's a damn good one."

"I know it's pure fabrication, but I like it," Penny kissed Kael as well, running her fingers up and down his spine, lingering at the small of his back.

Derrick wiped his brow, then rubbed his hands on his pants. "Strewth, I thought they had us there, mate!"

"Can't pull anything over on you two."

"Finish your coffee," Amanda kissed the top of his head.

"It's done. Here's yours."

Amanda sat next to him, sipping her coffee as he played with the hem of her sweater. She leaned against him, playing with his hair. Her breasts were mere inches from his face. He resisted the urge to kiss and fondle them, but it wasn't easy.

"Need another Red Eye?" Kael asked abruptly, nearly dumping Penny off his lap.

Derrick looked up to see another couple walking into the shop.

"Love one," he said. "I feel nearly human again."

"I'll get it, Kael," Penny said as she walked to the counter. "What can I get you folks?" She spoke to the other customers.

"Where's the head?" Derrick asked Kael, sidling up to him.

"I'll show you," Kael said, adjusting his jeans as they walked to the restrooms.

"Better put that thing away, mate. It's dangerous."

"Can't help it. She knows just the right places, you know?"

"Yeah. I have some memory of that — from before my life went to hell."

"Today, take her to the beach or something and tell her. Before anything else, even before lunch. I don't know Amanda, but I know Penny. If they're friends— well, Penny's temper is lethal. She hasn't unloaded on me yet, but her brother's got it twice since I met her a couple months ago."

"Already engaged? You work fast."

"I make up my mind fast. I knew the second I saw her she was gonna be mine."

After a visit to the restroom, they rejoined the ladies. The eleven o'clock rush was starting, so Amanda and Derrick bid farewell.

"Fancy a walk on the beach?" Derrick asked her.

The waves were less than a hundred yards away. It was a sunny day and the urge to walk along the sand, regardless of the chilly wind, was more than he could resist. Growing up next to the ocean back home, he found the Atlantic rather tame in comparison, but the lure of the water was in his blood.

"That would be wonderful. I don't remember the last time I walked the beach just for fun."

Arm in arm, they walked slowly south along the water's edge. Because of the cool weather, only a few die hard health freaks were out. They were passed by joggers and speed walkers, strolling languidly, enjoying the sunshine, wind and salt spray. Derrick was so quiet, Amanda was a little worried that he still felt ill. One look at his face told her he had something on his mind.

"Penny for your thoughts," she whispered.

"Oh, love," he heaved a heavy sigh. "You wouldn't want to pay that much for them."

"What's wrong, Derrick? You've been acting evasive since I spoke to you on the phone."

"That's because what I have to say might just split us apart forever. The idea of losing you, Amanda—It's just too much for me." He looked ready to cry.

Amanda turned to face him, taking his shoulders firmly in both hands. "Talk to me, dammit. Not telling me has me terrified!"

"All right. Come on, let's go sit down." He pointed to the tables scattered around the boardwalk.

They climbed the steep steps and sat at one of the tables that was more or less shielded from the wind by the bathrooms. Huddled together for warmth, he took her hands in his.

"Let me say first, I fully intended to tell you all about this. I didn't expect it to come up quite so quickly, nor in quite the way it did."

"Okay... still in the dark here." She tried to smile.

"I know. There is absolutely no good way to say any of this, so I guess I'll just jump in with both feet and pray." Closing his eyes, he inhaled deeply, exhaling slowly as he clamped his jaw on the emotions building inside him. "About a year and a half ago, I met this girl. Pretty bird, not nearly as pretty as you, mind, but Mr. Sparky liked her."

She giggled feebly, blinking against the cold wind.

"Anyway, we met at this party, hit it off, and spent some quality time together. We dated for awhile, then I asked her to marry me. We were married a month and a half after we met. I thought it was true love. Soon, facets of her personality started to come out. I found out that she was a drug user, didn't have a job and was a serious psycho. I'm not talking just a little whacked when she PMSed, I mean Persephone had psychoses out her well shaped ass. If the drug binges weren't bad enough, she slept with anything she could find; men, women, small farm animals."

Amanda giggled nervously.

"I'm not kidding." He looked so serious, she believed him.

"After I got something very nasty that a physician was fortunately able to clear up with the right medication, I confronted her. I told her I wanted a divorce and I signed my papers the day I left for the states. That was six and a half months ago."

"I see. So you have a psychotic ex-wife. How is this bad? You don't still have that disease do you?"

"No. Clean bill of health. Nothing recurring, I don't break out in running sores."

They both shuddered and not because it was cold.

"The truth is, Amanda, she called me last night after I spoke to you. Seems Persephone, for whatever perverse reason, didn't file her papers. I'm still a married man." He hung his head, wanting to cry or vomit or both.

"Oh!"

Whatever she'd expected, it wasn't this. Derrick's confession took her by surprise and she wasn't able to think straight for several minutes. She felt like a class four hurricane had hit her square in the face. Forcing herself to breathe, she squeezed his fingers.

"Okay," her voice shook as she tried to control her emotions. "You have a psychotic, not so ex-wife. Okay." She patted his hands absently, forcing herself to focus. "Okay. We can deal with this. We can. Did you call a lawyer?"

"That was my next call after speaking to her, yeah." He took her hands, squeezing so tightly they almost hurt. "There's more, Amanda."

She kissed him, lovingly, lingeringly. "Tell me. Just get it all out, Derrick."

"She had a baby recently. She says he's mine."

Amanda's hand flew to her throat. Gasping loudly, she lost the ability to speak for almost a minute. In the meantime, her mind did crazy calisthenics, desperately trying to reestablish her mental and emotional equilibrium.

"Baby?"

"Yeah. Baby. She said she named him after me."

Her only response was a squeak.

"To be honest, I don't think it's mine. I mean, there towards the end, after the doctor thing, I wasn't having sex with her. I was a bit leery, as it were. I'm calling a doctor here to get a DNA test, see if he can really be mine."

"Oh. Oh, Derrick!" She flung herself on him, clinging to his neck, burying her face in his shirt. "Oh, God!" She whispered. "Oh, God!"

Derrick held her, letting her cry. He had no soft words to console her, nothing to help her through this. He was the cause of the problem, he and Mr. Sparky. His hormones had gotten him in a variety of tight situations, from bar fights to near pregnancy misses, but this was by far the worst thing that had ever happened to him.

When she had calmed down a bit, he went to the bathroom and brought out a wad of toilet paper for her to blow her nose and wipe her eyes. Red eyed, with swollen cheeks and a puffy nose, she sniffed and sniveled for several more minutes. Finally, her lips stopped trembling. Squaring her shoulders, she took his hands once more, forcing a smile.

"We can do this." She sounded less confident than she had hoped. "We will get through this together. Come on. Let's go back to the car. I want to make a couple calls, but I don't have the numbers with me."

"You're not mad? I thought you'd be mad."

She hugged him, kissing his cheek. "No, I'm not mad. I've made so many mistakes in my life, who am I to condemn you for yours? At least. . . ."

"At least we hadn't been together yet," he finished what she was thinking.

"Yes. I don't know if I'd have been able to forgive you then."

"Honestly, Amanda, I thought I was no longer married. If I had made love to you, it would never have been intentionally to deceive you. I swear."

"I know, but trying to explain that—well, it would have been harder to accept. And I do accept it. Now it's up to us both to clear it up."

"Why so anxious to help me?" He looked rather curiously at her.

She kissed him deeply. "Because, I'm finally ready for a relationship, but I'm not ready for one with a married man."

"Unless he's married to you, of course."

"Of course".

"God, Amanda, how did I get so lucky?"

"You brought me pizza."

They laughed softly, talking as they walked back to her car. Kael was coming out of the coffee shop with a bag of trash and saw them together. Derrick flashed him a thumbs up. Kael saluted him, blowing a kiss to Amanda.

"He seems like such a nice man," Amanda mused. "Penny says he's amazing—"

"Please don't tell me in what ways he's amazing. You may shatter my fragile, male ego."

"I wasn't going to tell you about *that,* although she says it's the best sex she's ever had." She leaned over, nuzzling his cheek with her cold nose. "I mean in other ways."

"Oh, specifically non-sexual ways."

"Specifically, yes."

"And what did you tell her about me?"

"That you were amazing, in specifically non-sexual ways, as well."

Derrick stopped walking, tugging on her hand until she toppled into his arms. His lips descended, locking against hers as he kissed her. The emotional turmoil he'd been experiencing translated itself into the most incredible kiss he'd given her to date. She could hardly breathe, her brain ceasing to function automatically as they kissed. When he finally let her go, she was flushed and panting, her eyes glittering excitedly. She wanted more, and not just kisses.

Satisfied, Derrick put his arm around her, leading her to the car. She unlocked the doors in a semi-daze, sitting behind the wheel for a moment while she marshaled her thoughts.

"Wow."

"I give you an incredible, earth moving kiss and you say *wow*? There's an understatement for you." He winked, chuckling at her inability to communicate.

"Do you do everything that well?" She started the car, backing out of the parking place.

"*Every* thing." His full lips lingered over the word, fondling and elongating it for several seconds. He brushed her hair behind her right ear, fingers brushing her cheek with tantalizing lightness. "Is it too soon?"

"For what? Lunch? Are you hungry?"

"No, not lunch. Is it too soon to love you? Or am I allowed to know what I want the moment I see it? Because I knew as soon as you opened your door, that I wanted you. Ironically, it took Persephone being unpredictable, to show me that I'm falling in love."

"No," she whispered. "It's not too soon." Blinking back tears, of joy this time, she drove back to her apartment.

Nearly running up the stairs, she used the code to get in her apartment. Derrick followed at a much more sedate pace, standing at the threshold as she rummaged around in her desk. She produced a small book from a locked drawer. It was lavender, pressed with real violets, bound with rough, sheer paper.

Locking her apartment door again, she took his hand, dragging him down the stairs and back to the car. Without talking, she drove to his condo. Once she parked, she waited for him to lead her to his apartment.

"Keep in mind, this isn't my place. I'm borrowing from someone." He opened the door.

The scent of flowers was almost overwhelming as Derrick led her into a virtual paradise. The foyer was covered in glass shelves with bluish tinted grow lights illuminating them. Inside were a variety of plants from all over the world. The entire condo had plants everywhere, all of them lush and healthy. Miniaturized roses graced the dining room table. Every species of flower she could possibly imagine was represented in one of the displays.

There was a gentle rumble of thunder and a soft tune began to play. Amanda laughed as she recognized *Singing in the Rain*. Water sprayed from inside the display cases, watering the plants for a few moments before shutting off.

"How often does that happen?"

"Not often. It depends on the type of plant. Desert plants get very little, rain forest ones get a lot more."

"This place is incredible! Whose is it?"

"It belongs to my mother, but she's in an assisted living facility by the golf course."

"She's not that old, is she? Why?"

"She's quite ill," he said quietly, gazing at the amazing view out the sliding glass doors on the far side of the living room.

"I'm so sorry, Derrick."

"Yeah, well. . . . Life sucks, eh? She's the reason I came here. The doctor wanted to have next of kin to make decisions and suggested we kids be closer. I was the one chosen to come live here, since I'm the only son. And the only one who's single—well, who thought he was single." He shrugged, shaking his head.

"It's beautiful, Derrick. Your mother must be an amazing person."

"Yeah, she is. You'd like one another."

"I'd like to meet her."

"I'd like that too."

"But first," she said, pulling the lavender colored book out of her pocket. "I have some calls to make."

Derrick pointed to a phone on the desk. She flipped to the correct page, running her finger down to a name and number that she wanted. Dialing quickly, she put the book in her pocket.

"Nate? Hi, it's Amanda. I'm fine, thanks. Gabby and the boys? Excellent. Listen, Nate, I need your help. Specifically a friend of mine does. Great! I'll bring him at one." She looked at her watch, it was 12:15. "Okay, see you then. Thanks, Nate." She hung up, turning to Derrick with a happy smile.

"If you need to pee or get something to eat, now's the time. We have to go to Port Orange by one."

"I'm good to go."

"Why couldn't you use your cell?"

"I can't find it. I think it's at Miss Hook's. I didn't want to go in and look for it, or she'd find some way to keep me there and make me take a nap or something. I want to spend every minute I can with you. I need to borrow your bathroom."

He pointed to the hallway to her right. There were bedrooms to the left and right. Ahead of her was a pretty bathroom done in an ocean motif with real fish inset in a tank in the wall.

When she came out, her eyes were glowing. "This place is incredible! How do you keep up with it all?"

"Mum has a crew who come in to clean, tend the fish, check the plants and so on. All I do is make a mess and buy groceries. It's a wonderful arrangement."

"You can show me the rest when we get back. Nate can see us, but only if we're prompt."

They hopped in her car and headed up US-1 to Port Orange. The office of Nathaniel P. Rock, attorney, was on Dunlawton. Amanda pulled into the tiny parking lot moments before one o'clock, having broken nearly every speed limit on the highway. Derrick followed her in. Smiling, she greeted the pretty woman at the desk and walked through a swinging wooden door to a dimly lit hallway. The building smelled of lemon oil and exuded old money.

Amanda tapped on an unmarked door. "It's me," she said, cracking the door.

It swung open and a slightly bald man in his early forties stood up behind his desk.

"Mandy!" He rushed around to hug and kiss her cheek. "And this is your friend who needs my help?"

"Yes. Derrick Butler, my godfather, Nathaniel Rock."

"Pleased to meet you, Mr. Rock."

"Call me Nate. So what's the problem?" He looked from one to the other

Offering them a seat, he took his place behind the desk. The office was done in dark woods and rich reds and greens. It looked like an old English library.

Derrick proceeded to explain to Nate exactly what his problem was. When he had finished, Nate turned to Amanda.

"So, you came to see me why? I don't do divorce."

"I know, Nate. He needs advice though. What's permissible in court as far as a paternity case?"

"Oh! Okay, that I can do. Easy. You get a test done, but you don't want one of those silly, at home things. What you need is a lab that's accredited by AABB, American Association of Blood Banks. There is a specific procedure for taking a sample that's admissible in court."

"I don't have to do anything into a little cup, do I?" Derrick looked a bit worried.

Nathan laughed, tossing his head rather stiffly. "No, no! They do what they call the buccal swab test. They take a thing like a big, sterile Q-tip and rub the inside of your cheek. It's completely painless."

"I thought they had to do a blood test."

"That's old science," Nate replied, waving it off. "The buccal test is just as reliable."

"What about the mom? Do they need to test her too?"

"That works best. Since the mom gave the child half its DNA, they need hers too. Old girlfriend giving you trouble, Derrick?"

"The woman I thought I divorced six months ago, Nate. Not only did she not sign the papers, she had a baby and swears its mine. Even named him after me."

"Have you seen the child?"

"No, he's back home in Australia."

"Ooh. Much harder to deal with — long distance..." He steepled his fingers in front of him, leaning on the desk. "You do have a lawyer back home?"

"Yeah. He's working on it, but Persephone isn't being terribly cooperative."

"Got his number?"

"Yeah." He opened his cellphone and gave Nate the number. Checking the clock, Nate made a note on a phone log. "He's probably sleeping right now, but I'll call him and leave a message for him to call me at home. That will be morning for him. How many hours difference?"

"Fifteen."

"Okay, I'll ask him to call me first thing he walks in the door. We need a consult on this so he can dot the i's and I can cross the t's. Don't worry, young man, if she's lying, we'll get her."

"I'm pretty confident she's lying. She probably planned this before I even filed. If she's had the child already, she knew at the time I told her I wanted a divorce that she was pregnant."What followed was a string of invectives hurled across the ocean at his evil bitch of an not-ex-enough-wife. Nate blanched slightly. Holding up a finger, he placed his call. He got the voice mail for Sam's office.

"Hello, Mr. Hudson. My name is Nathaniel Rock. I'm an attorney here in Florida. I've got your client, Derrick Butler, sitting here in my office and he's come to me for a bit of advice concerning a paternity test." He gave Sam his name again and his number, requesting a call at his soonest opportunity. "I realize this may be a bit hard to coordinate with a fifteen hour difference, so feel free to call me at home tonight." He left his number once more and hung up.

"Piece of cake. You're lucky I love you, Mandy. That call cost a fortune."

"I'll pay you back, Nate, I promise."

"I've got it covered, Nate. Send a bill to this address." Derrick scribbled a name and address on a piece of paper, shoving it across the table to Nate.

Amanda noticed in passing that he was left handed. Why hadn't she seen that before?

The two men shook hands and Nate promised to call Derrick as soon as he heard from Sam.

"And try not to worry, son. It will work out."

"I hope so, sir. I can't have this hanging over my head." He glanced at Amanda.

"No, I don't suppose you can. Derrick, mind if I speak to Amanda for a moment?"

"I'll step out to the waiting room." He kissed Amanda's cheek and walked out, closing the door behind him.

"Want to explain what's going on here?" Nate wasn't quite angry, but he was close.

"I'm not in the habit of explaining my life to you, Nathaniel."

"I'm worried, Mandy. Who is this guy?"

"I met him a few days ago when I was teaching." She decided to leave out the pizza part.

"He helped me when I had trouble with a student at the high school. We got to talking later, had a cup of coffee and found we hit it off."

"Are you sleeping with him?"

"How is that any of your business?"

"It could hurt his case if you two are intimate."

"No. Are you happy? Would you like a lie detector test?"

"No need for an attitude, Mandy. I don't like asking, but for both your sakes, I have to. I don't want you dragged into a nasty divorce if it can be avoided. And this is going to get nasty."

"How do you know?"

He handed her the piece of paper Derrick had written on. She didn't recognize the name or address, but it meant something to Nate.

"So? Who is this?"

"Only one of the most prestigious accountant firms in the state. They don't handle small account holders, Mandy. Your boyfriend is a lot more than he pretends to be. If his wife is after his money, she's going to try very hard to get it, regardless of what it does to anyone else. I don't want your reputation dragged through the mud."

"Thanks, Nate. Don't worry about me. My virtue is still intact."

"Try to keep it that way, okay?"

"Shall I tie my ankles together and chain him to the bedpost?" She shook her head. "Sorry, that sounded different before I said it."

Nate turned red in the face and burst out laughing. "Client/ attorney privilege. It goes no further."

"Thank God! Seriously, we just met. There's an attraction, something we'd like to act on, but I can't — not with a married man."

"Okay, honey. Hey, come by and see us sometime. Bring Derrick. I think Gabby would love to meet him. It's so hard for her to get out these days."

"I will, Nate. Give her a kiss for me, okay?"

"Will do." He kissed her cheek. "I'll call when I know anything."

"Thanks, Nate. I owe you."

"Just a visit."

Derrick was waiting for her in the front room. He and the lady at the desk had exchanged a few polite words, then he wandered around staring at the old photographs on the walls. They were all originals, ranging from early Daguerreotypes, to more modern black and white images. None of them were newer than fifty years old.

Amanda spoke a few minutes to the receptionist. She and Derrick walked out into the bright afternoon sun, blinking rapidly after the dimly lit office.

"What did he want to talk to you about? Me?"

"He's concerned," Amanda said. "He warned me not to get too involved right now. He said if we're lovers, your ex could use that against you." She paused as she unlocked the door. "Just how much are you worth, Derrick?"

"Beg pardon?"

"Ballpark figure. I'm not asking because I want to take it from you. I'm wondering how hard Persephone will fight to get it."

He sighed, adjusting his Ray Bans before replying. "When my mum passes, I'll inherit roughly five hundred and fifty million dollars."

Amanda couldn't breathe. Her hand was on the gearshift to put the car in reverse, but she couldn't move.

"I know," he said calmly. "That's a lot of zeros."

She nodded mutely.

"That's the bulk of the fortune. My folks are rather traditional, I'm afraid. As the only son, I inherit most of their money. My sisters each get a modest sum, about ten million each."

CHAPTER SEVEN

"Modest?" Her voice cracked making her squeak. Clearing her throat, she continued. "You call that modest?"

"In comparison, yeah."

"That's another forty million."

"That's just liquid assets. I can't remember all the other stuff. It's never been all that important."

"Does Persephone know this?"

"Yeah. We were married, after all."

"And if you die, who inherits?"

"I wrote her out of my will when I got that nasty little something. I set it up that if I died before she did, any child I had would inherit."

"Enter Derrick junior."

"Oh, shit. Sneaky bitch, isn't she?"

"Very. Did you tell anyone back home that we'd met?"

"No, not a soul."

"Then she could have had someone following you all this time. Maybe that's why they did the phone calls and the break in."

"Because of me? Do you think?"

"I don't think I've pissed anyone off that much. I mean, I live the life of a nun, Derrick. Literally, down to the celibacy. I go to church, teach religious education, substitute, type term papers and sell stuff on Amazon. I don't think I'm all that controversial. All I did was get in an argument with a smart assed kid at school. Would you get someone to break in and shave a cat for something like that?"

"Can't say I would, no. Then again, I'd not do that anyway, but I get your point."

"It makes more sense than me being the cause, don't you think? If Persephone found out you were seeing me, what would she think?"

"She'd think I was boffing you. No offense, that is how I approached her, after all."

"None taken. I do think we need to call Jasper, don't you?"

"Yeah. Invite him up. In fact, can we buzz by the grocery store? I need food badly."

"Sure. Let me call Maisey and tell her what I'm up to. Can I borrow your phone?"

"Of course. Want me to drive?"

"Sure." She hopped out of the car, letting Derrick take the wheel.

He pulled out of the driveway, heading back to his apartment, while she talked to Miss Hook.

"Tell her you're staying for dinner," he murmured before she hung up.

Nodding, Amanda relayed the message. She hung up and dialed Jasper.

"Hi, Amanda. I didn't expect to hear from you today. How's Muse?"

"I don't know. I haven't had the chance to see him. If the vet called, I didn't get the call. My phone's missing. I think I left it at Miss Hook's."

"Oh, good that I didn't try to call you then. How are things with Derrick?" He was forcing himself to sound cheerful and upbeat.

"Going pretty well. We were wondering if you're free for dinner this evening?"

"I don't have to work. I actually got a day off. *We*?" He hadn't missed that all important pronoun.

"We need your help, Jasper."

"The police department is handling the investigation, Amanda. I can't. . . ."

"This isn't pertaining to that. We'll tell you all about it at dinner."

"Ookay. I'm not doing anything special. I was gonna do pizza and porn."

She giggled, covering her mouth as she laughed.

"You think I'm kidding? Nothing says *love* like melted mozzarella. What time and where am I going?"

She gave him the address and apartment number. "Time?" She looked at Derrick, shrugging helplessly.

"Seven," he replied loudly.

"Seven it is," Jasper said calmly, feeling anything but calm. "So, can I bring anything?"

"A bottle of red wine," Derrick raised his voice to answer after Amanda conveyed the question. "I'm low on alcohol. Mum doesn't drink."

"You got it! I'll see you at seven."

"Thank you, Jasper."

His voice got very quiet, since he suspected Derrick could hear him when he spoke at his normal volume. "Only for you, Amanda."

"See you soon." She concluded the call rather flustered.

She absently handed the phone back to Derrick, her hand trembling slightly before her mouth. Blinking hard, she wiped at her eyes with the heel of her hands.

"You okay?" Derrick's blue eyes held concern.

"Yeah. Fine." Her lip trembled.

"You're not," he said as he swung the car into a parking place.

Shutting off the car, he turned to her, leaning his elbow against the seat. His dark blue eyes gazed at her, his face solemn.

"What's wrong?"

"I've hurt his feelings so much just because I'm with you and not him. Every time I call him or I have a crisis, it's like taking a knife and stabbing him, then turning it in the wound."

"He's tougher than you think, Amanda. If his heart gets broken that easily. . . ."

"You don't know him as well as I do."

"Fair enough, I don't. I like Jasper and I don't want to hurt him anymore than you do. But if his heart is breaking, it isn't our fault. You didn't lead him on, Amanda."

"I feel like I did. I've never had two men interested in me at the same time before. I'm usually lucky to get one."

"Why are you so down on yourself? You're incredible! You're pretty, accomplished, way more intelligent than any other woman I've ever met."

"And there's the problem. Try growing up in a small town like this and being ten times smarter than any guy you meet. Try living in a dysfunctional family where your mother can't bear to look at you and your father left when you were seven, only to come back every couple of years to try to patch it up again. My mother's a drunk, Derrick. My dad is a wonderful, loving, totally spineless man who can't make up his own mind to stay gone."

"Anything else you want to dump on me, or am I safe to come out of the bunker?"

She tried to stay mad, but she laughed somewhat sadly instead. "I'm sorry. I talked to them last night after I spoke to you. That always screws me up for a couple days."

"Well, things being so delightfully normal, that should be easy, eh?" He lifted her chin with his left index finger. "It's going to be all right, Amanda. It will work out." He kissed her nose, smoothing her hair.

"Forgive me for being less than optimistic."

"I've always tried to be an optimist."

"It's easy to be when you have money." She got out of the car, grabbing her purse before heading to the door.

Derrick locked the car, holding the keys so he'd be sure he had them, and trotted after her. Running quickly, he caught up with her as he dodged a bagger with a huge line of shopping carts.

"Sorry, Mister," the kid called after him.

"No worries," he tossed over his shoulder. "Amanda, wait!" He slid to a stop, going slightly past her.

She stopped a few feet in the door. "What?"

Derrick took her elbow, leading her further into the store. "Why are we arguing?"

"I don't know!" She was close to tears.

He grabbed some napkins from the coffee station as they passed. Nodding her thanks, Amanda sniffled, blowing her nose into a napkin.

"I don't want to fight, Amanda."

"Me either." She blotted her streaming eyes. "Why didn't you tell me?" She asked.

"About what?"

"All the—you know—inheritance?"

"Because it hardly seemed important. And talking about it wasn't what I most wanted from this relationship."

"You've got more money than God and it's not *important*?"

"Okay, A. God doesn't need money. And B., you're thinking of J.K. Rowling. I don't have near as much money as she."

"After the first hundred million, what does it matter?"

"Amanda, why are you acting like this?"

"First you didn't mention the fact you're married." Her voice was rising rather rapidly.

"I told you, I thought I was divorced."

"Right. Okay, that didn't seem to be a problem?"

"Don't you have chaps in your past you'd as soon forget?"

She didn't answer, the firm line of her lips answering that one more eloquently than words.

"I didn't tell you because she haunts my nightmares."

"And why didn't you tell me about the money?"

He sighed heavily, moving out of the way of an elderly couple. The old man smiled kindly, the old woman nudged him with her cart.

"If you want to have a conversation, take it outside."

Derrick almost let it pass, but it struck him the wrong way. He followed the old woman who sounded like she was from Up North.

"'Scuse me," he said pleasantly. "Did you speak to me? I was distracted by your cart hitting my ass."

Her husband's smile faded somewhat. The old woman smiled nastily.

"I said to take your conversation out of the way. Other people are trying to shop."

"And some people find it offensive when pretentious old twats like you hit them with a shopping cart. Not that it's my business, maybe you can't see, but there was plenty of room to go round. We're having a crisis here. My fiancée doesn't know which wine to serve with sour pickled bitch. Do you know?" He asked her husband.

The old man's face broke into a grin. "I always thought it went best with a large brandy and a vodka chaser. If it's wine you want, go with red."

"Thanks, mate. Appreciate the advice."

"Want some more?" The old man leaned toward him.

"Yeah, I always like advice from one who's worldly wise."

"Live fast, invest well and die young."

His wife grabbed his jacket, hauling him after her as she scolded him. Shrugging, he trudged after her. Amanda watched the exchange with her mouth hanging open.

"If I ever get sour like that," she gulped. "Just shoot me."

"You won't," he said softly. "I'll keep you sweet." He kissed her.

Derrick's kiss set her on fire, but she wasn't about to let the subject drop and he knew it. Rather than let it escalate, he pulled gently away.

"I didn't tell you because Persephone made it very clear that she was interested in how much money I had that she could spend. She wanted a joint bank account, charge cards, the whole bit. When she spent ten thousand dollars in one day, I gave her a limited card and a monthly allowance that she had to pay her card debt from. It didn't sit well."

"I'd never do that, Derrick."

"I know, love. But think about it from my perspective, we've known each other how long?"

"Three days." She stared at the floor.

"Yeah. If you were me, would you have told?"

She giggled, tossing her long hair. "No. I wouldn't have said a word either."

"So, do you forgive me? I really need your forgiveness, Amanda, or I might shrivel up and turn into that poor old man."

"I forgive you." She kissed him.

"Good. Then let's go shopping. Whatever you want. Go wild! The world is your oyster."

"I hate oysters."

"So do I. That was literary license."

Laughing, Amanda got a cart and they walked together around the grocery store. Derrick pulled different items off the shelves, tossing them into the cart.

"I told you, no food at all in the place. Unless you want to eat out every meal, I need food."

"I've got food at my place."

"Yes, but we aren't at your place, are we? You have no front door."

"And I forgot to contact maintenance." She sighed, shaking her head. "They won't get to it until Monday now. Dammit. Stuck with Maisey until then."

"You could stay with me," he suggested casually.

"And give Mr. Sparky all those naughty ideas?"

He leaned against the shelves, hands in his pockets. "He's already got naughty ideas, love. He's not above temptation. Perhaps not, then." He moved away quickly.

She rushed to catch up, nearly bumping into him when he stopped abruptly. The floral department was an array of brilliant pinks, reds, yellows and oranges. They were having a sale on potted Gerber daisies and mums. His eyes glowed as he walked among the displays.

"They're gorgeous, aren't they?"

"You've got all sorts of exotic plants at home, Derrick. Why something as common as Gerber daisies?"

"Cause the common can be so incredibly beautiful," he whispered, running his fingers along the edge of the shelf. "And you haven't any flowers at home."

"Cause I kill them," she replied in a matter-of-fact tone.

"Then we'll keep them at my place." He picked up a pot of each color, setting them carefully next to her purse on the seat of the buggy.

"My flowers at your place?" She giggled.

"Then you will always have an excuse to come over." He smirked, looking pleased with himself.

"Thank you. They're beautiful."

"But not nearly as pretty as you," he added. "Oh, steak!" He walked to the meat case, completely forgetting the flowers.

"You're like a little kid," she laughed as she followed him. "You've got the attention span of a goldfish."

"For things like shopping, yeah. But I assure you love, I can be very single minded when I want." His hand slipped under her sweater, tugging on her belt loop. "Very single minded indeed." Clearing his throat, he walked a few steps away, leaning over the meat case.

"Ever notice that when you're told you can't have something, you want it that much more?" He spoke to the meat case.

"Yes. It's called the Forbidden Fruit Syndrome."

"Yeah, well...." He eyed her as if she would be something good to eat.

"I'll buy you a bag of apples."

His laugh followed her down the aisle as she wandered to the produce section. He caught up with her a few minutes later holding some steaks, a roast and hamburger meat. He set them in the cart, wiping his hands on the seat of his pants.

"Ew!"

"I'll change when we get home. They were clean though, the fellow just set them out."

"Even so. Blah!"

In the produce section, Derrick picked up a huge container of mixed fruit bananas and stuff for a green salad.

"What do you want for dessert?" He asked her. "I can't fry cheesecake, but you've your pick of anything."

"What would you like?" She asked, diplomatically.

"What I want isn't on the menu." He smirked, eying her hungrily once more.

"I meant food."

"Mandy, I could live off you, drinking in your smiles and kisses, eating your. . . ."

"Okay!" She walked past him. "How about German chocolate cake?"

"You sure? Here's five kinds of cheesecake."

"Key lime pie?"

He wrinkled his nose, shaking his head. "Too tart."

"Ice cream is always good."

"Ice cream is amazing," he agreed, facing the refrigerated cabinets. "Off the hook, totally cool, no pun intended. What flavor? There seem to be roughly six thousand." Hands in his pockets, he eyed the case less enthusiastically.

Amanda reached around him, her hand brushing his thigh, as she pulled out a half gallon of vanilla.

"You're kidding, right? Everything from Moose Tracks to Otter Paws and you're getting vanilla?"

"And toppings," she explained as she walked to a nearby shelf.

Making her selections quickly, she set them in the cart and headed to the checkout. She picked up a couple other items on the way to the register, tagging on the end of a very long line.

"Why this line? It's a mile long. Number five is shorter."

"Number five? That cashier's new, I don't recognize her. It will take awhile."

"What's wrong with four?"

She glanced at it. One couple, two shopping carts, meat and milk separate. They keep kosher, it will take half an hour to bag all that. There's two hundred dollars of groceries there."

"And seven?"

"Who's at lucky number seven?"

The elderly couple they'd met at the front of the store, was waiting the next row down. The old man saw them and saluted. The wife glanced in their general direction, pursing her lips. She tossed her head, sniffing loudly. Derrick smiled. It was the most predatory face Amanda had ever seen.

"What are you thinking?"

"Wishing she were Persephone so I could choke the daylights out of her."

"You're not going to do anything, are you?"

"No. Tempting, but not worth the time." He smiled, kissing her. "I'd far rather spend my time with you."

"Me too," she gave him a peck on the lips.

Their line moved fairly quickly and he had to admit that Amanda had made the best choice. They were out of the store before the nasty old woman, making him very happy.

Back at his apartment, they unloaded the groceries, and she learned his kitchen the have-to way as they put things away. Laughing at her errors, she finally perched on a stool at the bar, watching as he finished the job.

"It pays to be inept. I get out of lots of work that way."

"Eventually, it won't work anymore. I expect you to have the kitchen memorized by the end of the weekend."

"Is that an assignment, Mr. Butler?"

"No, love. It's a request." He sidled up to her, slipping between her legs to stand in front of her. He pulled her toward him, lowering his head to kiss her.

They stayed that way for some time until Derrick couldn't stand it anymore. He was a mere breath from the one thing he wanted more than anything, and he couldn't have it. As delightful as it was to kiss Amanda, not making love to her was killing him. She smelled wonderful and she fit so nicely in his arms. All kinds of lovely, soft, luscious things pressed against him in all the right places. Letting go of her rather suddenly, he flung the door to the refrigerator open, banging it into the wall.

"Did I do something wrong?"

"No. Not that. You do everything incredibly right. That's the problem."

"I'm sorry, Derrick. Even if I were completely ready, you're a married man."

"Yeah, I got that part. Look, Amanda, it's not your fault. None of this is your fault, which makes it that much more frustrating. If I could just *blame* someone other than myself, it would make it so much easier. But I can't. My own stupidity got me into this mess."

"No, Persephone got you into this mess."

"Because I got into Persephone. Don't you see? Mr. Sparky got me in big trouble this time, bigger than anything else I've ever been in."

She came up behind him, tucking her arms under his, holding him about the waist.

"When this is all over, Mr. Sparky can get you out of all that trouble. Surely there are compensations?"

"God, Amanda! You set me on fire." He growled low in his throat as her body pressed against his. "Mr. Sparky is having very nasty thoughts."

"Can't be any nastier than I'm having," she admitted. "How I wish you weren't married."

"Me too. Come on, let's fix dinner so we'll have something to feed our guest when he gets here in an hour."

"Good plan." She looked around the kitchen. "What are we fixing?"

"Steaks, baked potatoes, salad and whatever we got for dessert."

"Ice cream and seven toppings."

"That."

"No sour pickled bitch?"

"Not tonight. I only serve that on Good Friday, it keeps me humble."

Amanda laughed, kissing his cheeks. "I'll prep the salad and set up the potatoes if you marinate the steaks."

* * *

Jasper arrived just over an hour later, walking up to the apartment at 7:05. He knocked on the door and smiled when Amanda opened it.

"You look very at home here," he said, sounding a little disappointed.

He handed her the wine and a bouquet of brightly colored flowers. Kissing her on the cheek, he squeezed her fingers. His eyes held so many different thoughts and emotions, she could hardly stand it. Thanking him for the flowers, she used them as an excuse to go to the kitchen so she wouldn't cry.

Derrick was on the balcony overlooking the river. Jasper joined him out there and together they popped open a couple of beers and watched the river traffic.

"Oops, sheriff's department doing a bust," Jasper said, pointing to a small, fast boat.

"What is it?" Amanda joined them on the balcony.

Derrick put a possessive arm around her, pulling her close. Jasper ignored the gesture, pointing to the craft the sheriff's department had pulled over next to a small island.

"Probably drunk. Could be a drug bust. Lots of weird shit happens on the water. The stories I could tell!"

"You should write a book," Amanda suggested.

"I've thought about it, but I'm semi-illiterate. I can read great, I can't string two words together."

"How do you take your steak, my good friend, Jasper?"

"Medium rare, my good friend, Derrick!"

They slapped five and did a knuckle tap. Amanda continued to watch the boat. Something peculiar was going on down there. Peering at it, she wondered if the men noticed. One of the deputies had gone below while his partner stayed on deck. As she watched, he came back out, but she could swear it wasn't the same man who had gone below. He moved differently and wasn't quite as big.

"Jasper. Jasper!" She hissed, tugging on his arm. "Call someone."

"What? Why?"

"Something's wrong down there. That's not the same man who went down. Hurry!"

Jasper grabbed his phone, dialing the police. Talking fast, he described what was going on, telling them Amanda's observation. He hung up a moment later, taking a greater interest in the activity below.

Moments later, a Coast Guard boat pulled up opposite the sheriff's boat, sandwiching the passenger boat. They couldn't hear the dialogue, but it was obvious the men on the boat weren't interested in compromise. Shots rang out. The deputy on the civilian boat was down and one of the prisoners was bending over him.

Suddenly, the prisoner straightened, aimed at the other deputy, firing at him. He emptied the remainder of the magazine into the officer before one of the Coast Guard shot him. Amanda screamed, horrified by what she saw. Turning away, she buried her face in Jasper's chest, grabbing his shirt hard with both hands.

"Oh, God! Oh, God! Is he dead, Jasper? Is he dead?"

"It's okay. The bad guy's dead."

"The deputy. Is he...?"

"Don't know, Mandy. Shh. I'm so sorry you had to see that."

Derrick felt useless. Distracted by the smell of scorching meat, he went back to the grill. Jasper held Amanda, patting her shoulder, stroking her hair, as she hiccupped and cried. Once or twice, he kissed her hair, rocking her gently.

"I don't suppose any of us feels much like dinner, eh?" Derrick carried the perfectly grilled steaks inside.

"Not a lot," Jasper said softly. "But we need to eat. Come on, Mandy." Brushing her hair from her tear streaked face, he helped her inside.

Amanda sat stiffly on the sofa, staring straight ahead. She hardly blinked or spoke, rather more like a ghost than a breathing human. Both men were concerned, but didn't know what to do for her. The silence of the apartment was broken by the sound of Jasper's phone.

"Yeah, Barry. What?" He listened for a moment, a smile crossing his face. "Really? Damn, that's good news! Yeah, saw the whole thing. I thought for sure he'd bought it. Thanks."

He hung up, smiling and rubbing his hands together. "Good news! The deputy is going to be okay. His vest absorbed the shots. Lucky for the deputy, the bad guy wasn't a very good shot. He's bruised up and took a couple minor hits, but he's okay."

"And the other one? The one who shot him?"

"Hurt, but alive. He's lucky the Coastie wanted to ask him questions. Otherwise, he'd be fish food."

Amanda sighed with relief, the color returning to her face. "Oh, thank God."

Jasper's smile faded slightly as she walked to the kitchen. He didn't mention that the first deputy, the one who had gone below, didn't come out alive. Why tell her that right now? Let her enjoy the fact the others lived. Derrick saw his expression, but a shake of Jasper's head told him not to ask. Instead, they enjoyed their meal, the wine and one another's company. Despite the fact that both men were rivals for her affection, they got along well, finding they had a lot in common.

"You really have four older sisters?" Jasper laughed. "Me too. Did your sisters used to play house and dress you up as the baby?"

Derrick rolled his eyes. "Picture this, yeah? Me, with blond curls nearly to my shoulders. Mum didn't want to cut them off for fear they'd go away." He tossed his long, blond curls. "So I kept them, what can I say? When Mum went out to run errands, she'd leave Sally, the eldest in charge. The girls would put my hair in pigtails and dress me like a little girl. It was years before I got over that!"

"That sounds familiar. Did you get blamed for everything that ever went wrong?"

"Constantly. Didn't matter what it was. They could run out of tampons, and somehow that was my fault."

"Dude, I used to leave the third week of every month and spend it with my old man. You did *not* want to be there!"

"We had a big house. I used to run to the unused west wing and hide. For me, it was the first week of every month, like clockwork."

They clinked beer bottles, laughing as they drained them. Amanda wasn't drinking much, but she kept a glass of wine company for the evening. It made her happy that the two men most important to her were getting along, not fighting over her or competing for her attention. In fact, it bordered on weird that they were bonding so.

"I know you didn't invite me up here to talk about my sisters," Jasper said, leaning forward with his elbows on his knees. "You said on the phone you needed my help with something mysterious."

Amanda glanced at Derrick. He shrugged, turning it over to her. "It's your theory, love. Go ahead."

Taking a deep breath and a gulp of her wine, Amanda told Jasper about Persephone and outlined her theory about wanting Derrick's money. He sat quietly a moment after she'd finished, thinking.

"You're married?" He said to Derrick, trying hard to conceal a smirk. "Oh, this gets better and better."

"Can you help us?" Amanda asked him, her eyes wide.

"What do you want me to do, Mandy? I can't go after some guy because he might know Derrick's wife."

"Can you make the suggestion to someone, whoever's in charge of the case?" Amanda asked him. "I'm not above begging, Jasper." She laid her hands on both of his. "Please?"

The men experienced a pang of remorse and pain when she did that. Both were in full protect mode, they also were romantically interested in the same woman. Amanda had made her preference clear. She obviously wanted Derrick, but Jasper couldn't shut that portion of his heart away. Her blue eyes melted it instead and he found himself going weak.

"I'll see what I can do," he agreed quietly. "On two conditions."

"What? Name it," Derrick said earnestly, leaning forward.

"When this is over, I get a proper kiss from you." He pointed to Amanda. "And you, marry this woman so I won't keep dreaming about her."

Derrick and Amanda exchanged a look, smiling.

"I think we can do that, right?"

She nodded, her eyes sparkling. When she gazed at Jasper, her eyes were full of a different emotion. He was disappointed to see admiration with a big dose of pity. He didn't want her pity, he wanted her love, but he knew he'd never get it now.

Jasper's phone rang again. Looking at it with an exasperated expression, he answered angrily. "Yeah, Buddy? What?" He sat up expectantly. "You're kidding me. Really? Thanks, Bud. I owe you one. Okay, I owe you more than one. Thank you!" Hanging up, he held out both arms as if he were the champion of the world. "How cool is that?"

"What's cool?" Amanda asked him.

"You remember they guy who was watching you outside your apartment the first night I came by?"

"Yes. What about him?"

"He's currently warming a chair at the Coast Guard station. When they ran his prints, his name came up, and it raised a flag with the police department. My name's on the paperwork, so they gave me a courtesy call. My friend Buddy took the call a few minutes ago."

"So what was Trevor Johnson doing on a boat outside my apartment building?" Derrick asked.

"That's what I'm going to go find out. The Coast Guard got the collar, but they asked me to come over and assist in the investigation."

"Nothing like a little professional courtesy," Derrick grinned.

"That and my brother-in-law is commander out there. Nothing like a little nepotism either."

Jasper bid a hasty farewell, promising to call if he found out anything. Kissing Amanda's cheek, he squeezed her hand. "See you," he said softly.

Her smile brightened and she looked less unhappy than she had moments ago. With a heavy, inward sigh, he clasped Derrick's hand and left.

CHAPTER EIGHT

Jasper drove to the Coast Guard station with his windows down, enjoying the crisp, fresh night air against his cheeks. It served the additional purpose of keeping him alert as he'd had just enough wine to give him a slight buzz. He was below the legal limit, but he still didn't want to get stopped.

He turned through the gates surrounding the Coast Guard station, separating it from the state park next to it. He found a place to park in the surprisingly crowded lot and walked up to the front door. He was ushered through to his brother-in-law's office where Duane Stevens met him with a cup of coffee and a slightly stale donut.

"Did I take you away from anything interesting?" He raised an eyebrow. Knowing his wife's brother had a penchant for finding the prettiest ladies around.

"Nope. Dinner with a couple friends, that's all."

"I thought it was date? My mistake."

"Amanda is with Derrick." He didn't bother to hide the disappointment. Duane would figure it out eventually.

"Oh, that kind of friends, huh? Is she pretty?"

"Gorgeous — and vulnerable. What have you got on our boy?"

"Nasty piece of work. How do you know him?"

"He was watching Amanda's the night before someone broke into her apartment. I arrested him, but he got out on bail."

"Surprising. His record says he's habitual."

"I'm still trying to find out how that happened. But you've got him now."

"We've got him and he won't get out of this one. He opened fire on an officer of the law and killed another one down in the hold. He was wearing the guy's jacket and hat when he came back out, carrying his piece."

"Damn! Who *is* this guy?"

Duane tossed a thick file in front of Jasper. "Trevor Johnson. Convicted of armed robbery, 1994. Convicted of assault 1996. Convicted of armed assault and battery 2001. Just to hit the highlights. You name it, if it involves violence, this guy's been there or is involved somehow. His record goes on for ten pages."

"Used to be a cop in Detroit?" Jasper was stunned.

"He was let go for assaulting courtroom officials as well as strong arming the perps. Judge threw the book at him."

"Let me guess, he was one of the ones assaulted?"

Duane nodded. "Our boy Trevor smashed a chair over his head. Judge Harvey didn't take that well."

"Love to know where the security men were."

"Out cold, by all accounts. Fortunately, he didn't get a weapon. No one was killed, but three people were seriously injured."

"So what was he doing on the river at night?"

"He says he was fishing."

"Tell me no one believes him."

"When he wounded one deputy and killed the other? Not likely. He had some rather sophisticated listening equipment on board. We think he was doing surveillance."

"Why would you do that on the river? Never mind, dumb question. Where would he park that wouldn't attract all kinds of attention?"

"Exactly. One of your compatriots would have hauled him in for loitering or whatever it is you land-lubbers do."

"Y'all talked to him yet?"

"Not yet. We've got him in interrogation. I figured we'd let him sit there awhile longer until he gets good and ready to chat. We've plied him with coffee and water, got the room nice and chilly. He should be a bit more mellow and cooperative in a few."

Jasper laughed. "And we get accused of brutality if some douche breaks a nail hitting us in the face with a bedpan."

"Come on down. You might like to listen in."

Jasper followed his brother-in-law to the holding area of the station, nodding to the men and women he knew.

"Slumming, Jas?" One attractive young female ensign asked him.

"Are you kidding?" Duane responded. "This is a step up for him, Mirabelle."

"Thanks, Duane. When I need help making a fool of myself, I'll ask you.

"Just trying to protect my own," Duane mumbled. "I know how you operate, boy. She's a nice kid."

"Yeah, well that kid is twenty-five, jacked and could kick my ass from here to Orlando with one foot. But she's damn hot for a bad ass."

"I thought you were dating Amanda?"

"I'm *interested* in Amanda. She's dating Derrick. If Ensign Bad Ass is available, I've got no commitments. So no helping."

"Never mind," Duane said. "Forget I got involved. In here." He opened the door to what looked like a broom closet. It was equipped with a TV monitor and sound equipment.

"No two way glass?"

"He has no idea we're watching him. The cameras are hidden. The room is bare except for the chair and table. There's not even a clock. He'll be counting the holes in the acoustic tile soon."

Jasper laughed quietly, taking a stool in front of the monitor. A couple minutes later, the arresting officer walked into the room, setting a chair across from Trevor Johnson. Sitting in it, he opened a file folder on the end of the table.

"You've been a bad boy, Trevor." The man's voice was low, lilting with a soft Georgia accent.

Johnson said nothing, frowning as the officer looked up at him. His hands were cuffed behind him, around the body of the straight, rail backed chair. His frown turned to a glare when the officer closed the file, standing abruptly at the end of the table.

"That's Al Oakley," Duane explained to Jasper. "He used to work with the deputy who was killed.

"I wouldn't want to be in Johnson's shoes right now."

Duane held up a finger for silence. Al leaned across the table menacingly.

"You killed a buddy of mine," he explained calmly. "Then you proceeded to shoot another officer in my presence. I take exception to that."

Johnson said nothing.

"I want to know what you were doing on the river tonight, Trevor."

"I was fishing."

"Oh, of course. With no poles or fishing gear, no bait and a hold full of listening and recording equipment. That's how I like to go fishing. More sporting for the fish!" He threw the file on the floor, stomping on it. "Don't pull anymore shit, Trevor! We know what you're doing on that boat."

"I was fishing."

"Got a license?"

"No, I don't got a license."

"Fish and Game won't like that."

"I don't give a damn about Fish and Game. You want to know something, ask me!"

"Okay. Want a coffee? Glass of water?"

"I need to piss."

"Tell me what I want to know, I'll let you go."

"Ask me something, already!" Trevor wanted to come out of the chair, but couldn't. He didn't have enough leverage to rise with the chair at his back.

"Why were you out on the water, Mr. Johnson? And don't tell me you were fishing."

"I got a job," Johnson said in a muted, moping tone. "I got a job to do surveillance on this guy."

"What guy? Does he have a name?"

Johnson shrugged, wincing as the cuffs dug in. "Client didn't give a name. Some guy whose wife thinks he's cheating. I follow him around, take pictures, report his movements."

"But you don't ask a name? You used to be a cop, Mr. Johnson. Don't tell me you couldn't find out his name."

"She says his name ain't important."

"But you looked him up and found out what?"

"He's a teacher at the high school. Name's Butler."

"Why does she want you to follow him?"

"I told you. She thinks he's cheating on her. He's got a real hot piece he's been seeing, he met her at the school. Great tits," he said with a nasty smirk that made Jasper want to go through the wall and slug him.

"Is he having an affair?"

"Not that I can tell. They go for coffee and the grocery store." He shrugged. "Nothing yet, but maybe he's taking his time, finessing her like. He spent one night, maybe. I got picked up by the cops, so I don't know for sure."

"So you've been following him how long?"

"Month or so." He shrugged.

"Do you have a name for the woman who hired you?"

"I'm supposed to call her Mrs. B."

"A first name."

"Something weird, begins with a *P* like persimmon. How do I know? She pays cash."

Jasper looked alarmed. Turning to Duane, his eyes got big. "Persephone's supposed to be in Australia!"

"Where do you meet the Butler woman?"

"Different places. She calls and sets up a place and time. I go with the pictures and recordings I got and she says she takes them to her lawyer."

"Two nights ago, did you break into an apartment on Victoria Street?"

"No. Two nights ago, I was at an A.A. meeting. You can ask my sponsor and the guys who run it. In fact, I talked to the priest afterwards. I'm gonna start helping in the soup kitchen."

"No you're not. You killed a man tonight. The only kitchen you're gonna work in is at the prison."

"That Butler dame, she's the one broke in," he said sullenly. "She said the woman had something of hers and she was gonna get it back."

"She shaved the cat and duct taped him to the hood of her husband's car."

"That's messed up," Johnson said.

"I couldn't agree more."

"About that trip to the head."

"I'll send someone in. Thanks, Mr. Johnson. You continue to cooperate and things will go better for you." He stood, heading for the door.

"I didn't know he was a cop," Johnson said as Oakley put his hand on the door. "The guy I killed, I didn't know."

"I'll be sure to pass that along to his widow," Oakley replied.

"I didn't know." He said again as Oakley opened the door. "I didn't know!" He yelled again.

"Not the brightest crayon in the box, huh?" Duane said to Jasper.

The younger man wasn't listening. His hand hovered over the cellphone in his pocket.

"Persephone is supposed to be in Australia," he said. "I've got to call Derrick."

"Phone won't work back here, you can't get a signal. Come to my office."

Jasper followed Duane. They walked into the hallway just as Trevor Johnson was being escorted to the head. Jasper glared at him. Johnson lunged in his direction.

"You're that cop! The one that arrested me! What're you doing here, cop?"

"Watching you hang yourself, Johnson. That Mrs. Butler, what's she look like?"

"Why should I tell you?"

"Cause it's the only thing keeping you alive at the moment." He flexed his muscles, standing ramrod straight. He towered over Johnson.

"She's a babe. Not as pretty as the new one, but she's hot. Long legs, dark brown hair, violet eyes, cat eye pupils. Nice tits, fake, but sweet."

"Has she got a baby?"

"Her? I don't think. I never seen her with one."

"Thanks." He still wanted to hit the man, but refrained.

From Duane's office, he called Derrick. He told him what Johnson had said. There was silence on the other end.

"Persephone is in Australia."

"Maybe not. Tell me what she looks like. Johnson described her. I don't suppose you've got a picture?"

"Of the Gorgon? Maybe. I'll have to check my stuff."

"So, what's she look like?" Jasper was anxious and agitated.

"Tall, long legs, knockout figure with a pair of tits like—wow." He sucked in his breath sharply, remembering. "Fake as hell, but best looking copies I've ever seen. Dark hair, her eyes are almost purple, they're so blue. Oh, one odd thing. Her pupils are like a cat's."

"I got news for you, buddy, she's here. Your description and Johnson's jibe. If you can track down that picture for a positive ID, that would be great."

"I'll look now. Mum may have some here."

"I'm on my way back over. In the meantime, call your family and call your lawyer back home. And tell Amanda not to leave."

"What? Why?"

"Cause it was Persephone who broke into her apartment."

"You think she's safer here?"

"If she's there, we can watch her back. Besides, you've got the high ground, more defensible position there. Make coffee."

"Will do. And Jasper."

"Yeah?"

"Thanks, dude. You're a good friend."

Before making his calls, Derrick dragged his mother's photo albums out of the cabinet in the living room. He described Persephone to Amanda and started her looking through photos as he made coffee. Phone calls came next. By this time, it was nearly ten PM. in Florida, making it one PM. in Australia.

He called Sam first. He explained the situation and asked for his help. "Can you check and see if she's really had a baby?"

"I don't know, Derrick. I could call her mum."

"Please. Pamela always liked you."

"She liked you too."

"Yeah, but I've got more calls to make. Call me back as soon as you hear anything."

"Will do. Watch your back, buddy."

"Thanks." He hung up and immediately called his sister Sally.

"Derrick? Oh, thank God! I've been trying to reach you for days. Don't you ever answer your phone?"

"I've been out a lot, sis. But my cell—"

"Didn't think about it. I've got Mum's home number memorized. Look, something weird has happened. I went by Persephone's and there's no one there. Her landlord said she moved six weeks ago."

"Was she pregnant? Did he say if he'd seen a child?"

"No. No, he didn't mention it. I didn't think to ask him. Why?"

"If she hasn't had a kid, where did she get the baby I heard on the phone?"

"Oh, I hadn't thought of that. I'll ask around."

"No worries, I've got Sam working that angle. We're looking for a photograph for a positive ID from the guy who was working for her."

"I've got that one from Sally's wedding. She was in the wedding party, remember?"

"Unfortunately. That's how we met."

"Oh, ugh. I'd forgotten. Just how drunk were you that night?"

"Drunk enough to find her attractive."

She laughed unkindly at him. "I used to tell you that your Willy would get you in trouble, Derry."

"Yeah, thanks for the reminder. I need that now." There was a click on the phone. "Oh, that's Sam. I need to go"

He switched over to the other call. "Yes, Sam?"

"Not been pregnant," he said triumphantly. "She was trying to adopt here, but couldn't find anyone stupid enough to give her a baby. You'd have to be as crazy as her to even think that was a good idea."

"Yeah, true. So, no Derrick Junior?"

"Her mum says no way. She had an injury as a kid, her mum doesn't think she could even conceive, let alone carry full term."

"I don't suppose Pam would swear that in court?"

Sam laughed caustically. "With what Persephone's put her through? She's happy to attest to it. In fact, she volunteered! She's on her way over to swear out a statement now."

"Sam, you're a prince! Give Pam a big kiss from me."

"Um, I'd rather not. She might think I was making a pass." He sounded terrified.

"Then thank her for me."

"That I'll do."

Hanging up with a shout, Derrick danced into the living room to tell Amanda the good news. She was sitting happily in the midst of the photo albums flipping pages excitedly. She had found the wedding pictures ages ago and now had an album labeled, "Derrick, birth through four years."

"Weren't you the adorable little boy! Look at those curls. And the big, blue eyes!"

"Where did you find that one?" He made a grab for it.

"No you don't! I want to show you my favorite!" She flipped back a few pages where she had left her finger marking the page.

Derrick groaned, hanging his head. "Oh, you didn't." He banged his head on the table, leaving it there as she laughed and babbled over his photograph.

"But it's so cute!"

It was a picture of Derrick standing ankle deep in mud, covered from head to toes in the red, gooey clay-like slime. He was smeared with muck everywhere but his diaper area, which was clean and spotless. She could see how clean, because he'd whipped off his clay covered diaper moments before the picture was taken, holding it up triumphantly like a war banner.

"Oh, God. I'm never going to live this down, am I?"

"I don't know. I think you were adorable. It makes me curious though."

"I don't go naked into the mud anymore, Amanda."

"No, not that. If you were that well hung as a toddler, what do you look like now?"

Propping his head on his hands, he looked at her feebly. "What?"

"I was saying." She leaned over, laying her cheek on the table. "I wonder what you look like naked."

Gulping, he tried hard to swallow. It was next to impossible because his mouth kept dropping open. "Did you really say—?"

"That I want to see you naked? Yes." She sat up, nodding happily.

"You're full of surprises, Amanda."

"I know." She hopped up, going into the bathroom.

The doorbell rang while he was still digesting the information. Expecting Jasper, he took the album with him intending to put it in a different place. He glanced through the spy hole in the door and saw the broad shouldered police officer standing there. He opened the door and let Jasper in.

"Any luck with that photo?"

"Yeah. I think Mandy found one. If not, my sister has one. She'll e-mail it to me."

He booted up his computer as Jasper picked up the photo album. "These are your sisters?"

"Yeah." Derrick glanced at the picture. "Sally, Tammy, Kim and Bev. Tam's my favorite. She and I always got along well. Sally's too bossy being eldest, and Bev always resented the fact I was born at all. Kim's so quiet, you hardly know she's in the room."

Jasper flipped a few pages, looking at them and the captions while Derrick checked his e-mail. "Ah, here's the one I'm after." He clicked on the file, bringing up a picture.

Amanda walked out of the bathroom a moment later. Persephone's catlike, violet colored eyes filled the screen. She felt as if the other woman glared at her from across the room rather than a picture taken nearly three years ago. A shiver ran along her spine, lodging at the base of her skull, making her want to scratch and claw at it to make it go away.

Neither man knew she was there because she hadn't spoken. She stood in the arch between the living room and the hallway, unmoving.

"Wow," Jasper breathed. "I see now why you were attracted. She's hot!"

"Yeah, in the *I'm going to love you until your skin peels* kind of way. Don't let that pretty exterior fool you like it did me. She's positively lethal."

"In a bold, cosmic, blindingly gorgeous kind of way."

"No, more in the sucks your life out through your dick when she rides you all the way to hell, kind of way. Trust me, brother, she's death on two legs."

"But what legs! Mercy!"

Derrick laughed caustically. "Yeah, that's how she suckered me in, too. Then you get to know her and realize you've married the Bride of Satan. I'd far rather have Amanda. She's beautiful, pure, unsullied. What you see is what you get and, God, what you'll get!" He sucked his breath in sharply, practically licking his lips. "Amazing! I just want this mess solved, Jasper, so I don't have to worry about her anymore. I'm so afraid I'll lose her."

"You won't lose her, buddy. She loves you."

"Can't love somebody that fast, Jas."

"I'm here to say you can. One look at her and I was hooked. I wish there were two of her, or that you were a real dick. Because I'd fight you for her in a heartbeat."

"I'd rather lose a testicle than lose Amanda," Derrick stared at the screen. "There's no comparison, not really. They're both female, but where Persephone poisons, Amanda heals."

"Can we print off a copy and we'll run it up to the station?"

"Sure! Mum has the machine over there." He pointed to the table by the hallway, spotting Amanda. "Hey, love? Been there long?"

Amanda shook her head, stalking to the piles of photo albums. She couldn't look at either of them.

"What's wrong?" Both men were genuinely puzzled by her reaction.

"Is that all women mean to you? If you all treat women like that, how do you expect Persephone to behave?"

"We don't! Didn't you hear what we said about you?" Derrick virtually jumped from his chair to take her in his arms. "Amanda, Persephone is pretty on the outside, but she uses that like the sirens, luring unsuspecting men toward her. When they're good and hooked, she cuts them to emotional ribbons and leaves them for dead."

Jasper excused himself and went to the kitchen for coffee.

"Don't you see? I want you. I don't want anyone but you, because you're as beautiful on the inside as you are on the outside. You'd never do to me what Persephone did. I love you, Mandy. I think I have since the night I brought you pizza."

Derrick's kiss was passionate, controlled, full of love. He expressed everything he wanted to say but couldn't.

"When this is over, I want to marry you, Amanda. More than anything I've ever wanted in my entire life."

"I want that too, Derrick. Really, I do."

"Is that a *yes*?" He held her face in both his hands.

"Was that a proposal?" She grinned, holding the loops of his jeans.

"Maybe not the best one, but yes."

"When this is over, give me a better one and you'll get a better answer."

Jasper cleared his throat, walking out of the kitchen with a cup of coffee, his hand over his face like warding off a glare. "You two done?"

"I've finished mauling her if that's what you mean," Derrick chuckled. "Haven't I, love?"

"Completely. And my clothing is still on."

"Good. I didn't want to walk in on anything." He sat on the couch, his gaze meeting each of theirs in turn. "This picture needs to go to the Coasties so they can show it to Johnson and get a positive ID. We have to be sure."

"Agreed," Derrick nodded.

"I think you should come with me," Jasper said. "I don't think Persephone is stupid enough to come at us tonight."

"Evil, you mean," Derrick said. "She is, though. But if I stay in this place too long, I'll go crazy."

"What could be safer than the Coast Guard station?" Amanda agreed.

"I want Johnson to give a positive ID on you two as well," Jasper admitted once they agreed. "If he really was following and it really was Persephone, maybe he knows what her next move will be."

"I'll grab my jacket," Amanda said softly. She walked to the bedroom to get her coat from the end of the bed.

"Are you sure about going out, Jasper?"

"Not entirely, but we can't stay here like prisoners, Derrick. We'll go to the station, then run by her apartment and pick up her things for the night."

"Good plan," Derrick commented.

Jasper went down first, driving his muscle car up to the elevator entrance on the outside of the building. Derrick brought Amanda out, putting her in the back seat. He crawled in front with Jasper.

"Sweet ride, Jas. Mustang Boss 351!"

"Glad you like her. I got a great deal. Buddy of mine customizes cars."

"Introduce me?"

Jasper chuckled. "Sure. Ed would love to sell a car to you. You could afford an entire fleet."

"I'm driving a hunk of junk right now. It belongs to the guy who's job I've got. I needed wheels and he said I could use it. Piece of crap Pinto with rust holding the bumper on."

"Why drive it then? You can afford better."

"I thought I'd give living on a budget a try. It bites. I'm buying a new car."

Amanda giggled in the back seat. "Men and car talk! I never thought I'd bear witness!"

"Yes, but this car's a classic, love. You have to understand that some cars, like some women, must be put on a pedestal and worshiped."

"Only if I'm driving the car," she said with a smirk.

They got to the Coast Guard station carrying the picture of Persephone that Derrick had printed off for them. Duane arranged for the three of them to meet with Trevor Johnson in one of the interrogation rooms. He escorted the prisoner personally, standing guard with Oakley by the door.

"Hey, it's you!" Trevor said as he walked in. "Hi, Derrick. I'm Trevor." He tried to shake Derrick's hand, but Duane and Oakley stopped him. "Sorry."

"This isn't a social gathering," Duane reminded him.

"Sorry, I've been with you so long, I feel like I know you."

Derrick didn't reply. It filled him with disgust that such a man—a murderer—felt kinship with him any way.

"The guys said you had a picture for me to look at," Trevor said as he took a seat.

He was cuffed and shackled. Oakley fastened his shackles to the table which was bolted to the floor. He wasn't going anywhere.

"Yes." Jasper handed him the photo of Persephone, watching intently for a reaction.

"Where'd you get this picture?" Johnson's eyes were wide. "That's her. She's really your wife?"

"Unfortunately," Derrick mumbled.

"You got sweeter candy right there," Johnson pointed at Amanda. "What'd you want to hook up with a crazy bitch like that for?" He tapped the photograph.

"It was a bad combination of hormones and alcohol."

"Yeah. I don't blame you keeping a close eye on your new babe. She's crazy enough to go after your entire family. Wicked, that's what she is. Crazy and wicked."

"She is that, yeah." Derrick paused. "Oh, God." His face went white. "My family."

"Your family's in Australia," Jasper said, trying to calm him.

"Not all," Derrick whispered. "Mum."

Rising unexpectedly, he grabbed Jasper's keys from the front desk, running to the parking lot for his friend's muscle car. He was in the driver's seat and away before the others could catch up to him. Jasper ran into the parking lot, missing him by seconds.

"Dammit!" He threw his hat on the ground, grinding it under his heel. "Stubborn, Aussie bastard! Duane!" His brother-in-law ran up, panting slightly. "I need wheels, man. Derrick took Beauty."

"Oakley! Get me some keys!" The younger officer ran back inside. "Over here." Duane led them to a spot where several vehicles were parked. "Hop in!" He invited them to sit in the back of a Jeep.

Jasper hopped in first, helping Amanda climb in. Oakley gave her a boost as Duane started up the motor. Handing a jacket to his commanding officer, Oakley hopped into the passenger's seat.

"Where are we going?" Duane asked.

"His mom is in the assisted living facility by the golf course. That's all I know."

"I know the way, Duane. Go like you're heading to Aunt Ruby's, only make a left at the fork, not the right."

"Got it. Hang on!" He peeled out of the parking lot, going far faster than the narrow road was made for.

When they got to the road that ran parallel to the river, he sped up, putting on a flashing light. Traffic slid out of his way, drivers terrified they were going to get a ticket. At the intersection where their road and the one over the bridge intersected, the lights were all red. The bridge was going up, which meant traffic would be stopped for several minutes until that cleared.

Duane picked up a radio microphone. "Bean, get me the drawbridge."

"Yes, sir."

Moments later, he was talking to the controller of the drawbridge.

"Walker Smith here. How can I help you, Commander?"

"I need that bridge down, Smitty."

"I've got six boats lined up to go through, sir."

"It's an emergency, Smitty. You tell those boats they've got to wait. I need to get across that bridge right now."

"Yes, sir!"

As they approached, the bridge started to close once more. Instead of waiting for the gates to rise,

Duane gunned the motor, swinging around them like a madman. Amanda clung to the roll bar with one hand, and Jasper with the other. He had both arms around her, stabilizing himself by propping his long legs on either side of the Jeep. The bridge hadn't quite closed by the time they got to it. Lights flashing, they hit the ramp, suddenly airborne. Landing with a thump, they skidded to their right, then left toward the oncoming traffic.

Terrified motorists gazed in horror as the Jeep careened toward them, swinging wildly as Duane tried to regain control. Nearly sideswiping two cars, he gunned the motor once more, jumping back to his side with a bone grinding thump.

"Sorry about that. Jeeps weren't made for this kind of thing."

"Nothing was made for this kind of thing, Duane!" Jasper gasped. "Not even Beauty!"

Moments later, they turned right onto US-1, heading to the new golf course just north of the mainland Catholic church. Whizzing by the church, Duane skidded to the left turn lane. He was now running a siren with the lights and honking his horn. The red light didn't stop him. He made the turn on two wheels, the Jeep tipping dangerously to the left. It landed with a thud, spinning its tires a moment or two before the tread caught and they jerked forward once more.

The street was dark and narrow, winding like a backwoods trail. Duane didn't slow down, he just put on his high beams as they flew over the railroad tracks, once more airborne. Landing with another teeth shattering bounce, they continued until they saw a sign announcing a fork in the road. Duane swerved left, spinning the wheel wildly as he skidded again, making the turn at around 90. They missed the first entrance to the nursing home, but slowed enough by the second one to turn into the parking lot.

The Boss was parked in the fire lane, surrounded by police officers. Derrick was nowhere in sight. Jasper didn't even wait for Duane to come to a complete stop. He swung out of the Jeep, trotting up to the police officers, showing his badge.

"We were just trying to figure out how your car got here without you, man," one of the officers said.

"We've got a situation," Jasper said without preamble. He explained to his fellow officers what it was.

"Is she armed?"

"I don't know," Jasper admitted. "I'd say it was extremely possible."

"Here's her picture," Oakley said as he walked up.

He handed the folded paper to the man nearest him.

"She doesn't look crazy," the officer said. "She's hot as hell."

"She shaved my cat," Amanda said loudly. "And now she's probably here threatening a helpless, sick woman. Could we dump some hormones and look for the crazy bitch?"

"Will you at least wait out here with one of the guys?" Jasper asked her.

"I don't want to, Jasper. I'm terrified. The only way I feel safe is with you and Derrick."

"The only way I feel like you're safe is if you're not in there." He nodded to the dark nursing home. "Please, Mandy? I'm begging, as a man who cares about you, not to come in."

"Okay." She mumbled. "Okay, I'll stay."

"Thanks." Impulsively, he took the back of her head with one hand, pulling her mouth to his. Kissing her hard on the lips, he sighed, resting his forehead on hers. "For luck. Stay put."

CHAPTER NINE

Amanda nodded, sitting in the back of a squad car to wait for him and Derrick. One officer stayed with her and the cars. The other three went with Jasper and Oakley to find Derrick. Duane sat next to Amanda in the back of the squad car. He tried to be reassuring, but he was worried too.

"So, are you and Jasper dating?"

"No. No, I'm dating Derrick."

"But that kiss—"

"Haven't you ever just wanted to kiss someone you cared about?" Her blue eyes were penetrating.

"Yeah," he admitted. "I have."

"Jasper's a fine man and I really care about him. But I met Derrick first. And, well—"

"No need to explain."

"I feel bad, Duane. He cares for me so much, and I can't return the feelings."

"Don't worry about my brother-in-law, Amanda. He's tough. He'll bounce back. We'll make him our project, shall we? Find him a nice girl?"

She smiled, nodding her head as she stared at her hands. "I'm so worried about him."

"Jasper?"

"Derrick."

In silence, they waited for the scene to play itself out.

* * *

Leaving the Coast Guard station in a blind anger, Derrick grabbed Jasper's keys without thinking. He needed transportation to go to his mother. Never mind that the car wasn't his, Jasper would understand. Any man would feel the same if his sick mother was threatened.

He was fortunate that the bridge was lowered and traffic was light, because he drove like a madman across it, west to US-1 and north to the assisted living facility. Pushing 70, he made the turn onto the narrow country road, barely missing another vehicle. Unfortunately, that vehicle was a police car.

The officer immediately did a U turn, hitting his lights and siren as he gave chase. Derrick didn't stop. He'd pay any ticket he had to if it meant he'd get police officers to the nursing home before Persephone hurt his mother. He had no doubt she was there. He had tried his mother's room a dozen times since leaving the station. Even if she were sleeping, the phone would wake her. She was ill, not deaf. Why hadn't anyone else answered from the switchboard?

Fearing the worst, he sped up. Screeching into the parking lot, he stopped the car in the fire lane and ran inside, leaving the keys in the car. If the cops wanted to tow it, he'd pay Jasper back.

The facility was strangely quiet. Having visited at odd hours, even the middle of the night, he knew that the staff were always active. Even if the clients slept, the nurses and aids did not. No one was at the main nurse's station and he didn't see another soul until he got halfway to his mother's room on the second floor.

A nurse was collapsed in the corridor. She wasn't bleeding, but her breathing was shallow, quick.

Leaning over the check her pulse, Derrick got a whiff of something sickly sweet.

"Shit!" He hissed. Persephone had used chloroform.

He found other nurses and aides scattered around on the floor. Persephone couldn't have used the same method on them all. Worried and curious, he got to his mother's room.

Taped to the door was a huge picture of a baby in a blue cap. Scribbled on it was the legend, "It's a Boy! Meet Derrick Junior." He recognized it as Persephone's hand writing. If he'd had any doubt about her presence before, he didn't now.

Wishing he had a weapon, he crept up to the door, pushing it back. It swung inward silently, only the swish of air heralding its passing. His mother sat in her chair facing the door. She was tied to her chair, beautiful face bruised and pale. Anger filled him, making him want to rush in and untie her. With her eyes, she warned him that Persephone was behind the curtain to his right. He let the door drift all the way open as he searched for a sign of her exact position.

He saw her shoes peeping out from under the curtain. She wore nurse's shoes and scrub pants. He slid the curtain aside, frowning at her. She smiled at him, holding a spray can in one hand. Before he could move back, she lifted and sprayed. He had enough time to cover his mouth and nose with his jacket as he backed up, but he got a partial dose. It was just enough to make him light headed.

Persephone smiled sweetly, her left hand in the front pocket of her scrubs. "Hiya, lover. I brought your son to meet Mummy."

"He's not mine and you know it." He choked, feeling the effects of the spray trying to take hold. Fighting the drug, he kept his distance from her.

"Of course he is, honey. Don't you remember our last, wonderful night together before you left for the States? You said how much you loved me and you couldn't stand to be apart! We made love all night! You were nearly late for the plane."

"Odd, I remember it being more a night of you screeching at me hysterically about how I had no right to leave you. I'd already left you weeks before, filing for divorce."

Persephone laughed hysterically. It was an evil sound. "No, you didn't! We've always been together. So happy!"

"Seph, you're out of your mind. We haven't been happy for ages. I can't stand the sight of you."

"Derry, I know we could work it out if we just tried. We have to stay together for the baby!"

"Show him to me," he said calmly. "Let me see if he's really my son."

"Oh, he's yours, all right," she said angrily. "Can't you hear him screaming? He sounds just like you?"

"Maybe he's hungry, Seph. Have you fed him?"

"He's fine."

"How about I check his diaper. Maybe he's wet."

He moved slowly to the baby carrier with a tiny infant in it. Even from a few feet away, he could smell the feces and sour spit up. There was a diaper bag tossed on the floor by the bed. He stooped to pick it up, watching Persephone as he groped inside the bag. He found wipes, a fresh diaper and a lukewarm bottle. Releasing the baby from the carrier, he cleaned him up and gave him the bottle.

Derrick hoped she wouldn't try to spray him again as he held the baby. If he fell, it could hurt the child. He couldn't defend himself holding the infant, but he couldn't listen to the piteous cries anymore.

"What did you do to the nurses?"

"Drugged their coffee." She giggled inanely, making the hair on his neck rise. "I've been here all night. I came in as a temporary staff member. No one even questioned me."

"How did you get the baby in?"

"It was easy once they were all asleep. I left him in the car until then."

Deciding it was no time to lecture her on that point, he moved close to his mother. He put himself between her and Persephone.

"I bet Mum would like to feed her grandson, wouldn't you, Mum?"

His mother, still sharp on the uptake, nodded, mumbling that she'd love to hold him.

"Can you let her hands free, Seph? She can't hold little Derrick with her hands tied."

"She didn't want to hold him before!"

"Well, she sees I've accepted him. Right, Mum?"

"I want to hold my grandbaby," his mother said softly. "He looks just like you," she said to Persephone.

"No tricks," she said as she walked forward.

She cut the bands holding his mothers hands. After rubbing her wrists a few moments, his mother held out her arms for the baby. She held him close, cooing to him as he drank his bottle. Derrick could see tears in her eyes. Whether for them or the baby, he didn't know. He decided to take a different tactic with Persephone, playing into her fantasy world the best he could. For the sake of his mother and the baby, he hoped he could pull it off.

"You should have told me you were expecting, Seph. I'd never have left you if I'd known."

"I didn't know until you were already gone. And he came so early."

So that was how she was going to explain it. A three month preemie? He wanted to laugh at her but didn't dare.

"You could have called."

"You were coming back. I wanted it to be a surprise."

Right, more like a horrible shock. Derrick tried hard to keep the anger and loathing from his face and voice.

"Well, it would have been quite a surprise."

"See, now we can go home and be a family. Just us three."

"Yes, Seph. Just us three."

"It's pretty late," Mrs. Butler said softly. "Hadn't you better take the baby home? He's tired. He needs to go to bed."

"Oh, bang up idea, Mum. We'll go back to the apartment and he can sleep on the guest bed."

"You're not mad about the baby?" Persephone sounded so plaintive, he almost felt sorry for her.

"No, Seph. Not mad at all. He's a cute little bugger. Where are you parked? I've borrowed a friend's car. I can't carry him home in that. No car seat."

"He's fine in that. It belts right in."

"Okay. I'm sure Jasper wouldn't mind us taking our son home in his car. I've parked out front. We can walk right out and be gone before anyone wakes up." He moved swiftly to the door. "I'll get the car right by the front door and you can carry the baby out."

"No!" Persephone yelled at him. "It doesn't work like that! You're messing it all up!"

"How's it supposed to work, then?"

"You have to carry your son out. So everyone can see he's yours."

"Okay. Let me move the car closer. He can stay here with Mum and you can wait for us in the car, yeah?"

Persephone didn't look like she was going for it at first, but seeing the baby so content in Mrs. Butler's arms, she agreed to walk out with Derrick. He had no way of telling anyone he was coming, so he hoped that the police would understand and not shoot before he explained.

Putting his arm around Persephone, he guided her to the front door. He hoped that at least one police car was there, because he was really worried she was going to do something unpredictable. He had never seen her like this and it scared him far more than her wild, manic fits he was used to.

He saw the flashing blue lights a moment before she did. Screaming, she tore herself out of his arms, drawing a gun she'd had hidden in another pocket. Pointing it at him, she yelled.

"It wasn't supposed to be like this! You tell them. Tell them to go away."

"They aren't here for you, Seph. They're here for me, not you. I was so anxious to see the baby, I stole my friend's car."

"Liar! You're lying! You don't love me. You hate me! You told me you never wanted to see me again. You called me a slut and a whore!"

"I didn't mean it, Persephone. I swear—"

"No more lies. No more. It didn't have to be this way. We were going to be so happy."

"I'll go talk to them. I'll tell them it's all my fault." He inched toward the door.

The gun faltered in her hands, but came up again, calm and steady as he took too big a step. Gesturing with the gun, she made him move away from the door.

"Over there until I decide what to do with you. If you'd just agreed to stay married a little longer, I'd have had your baby. You wouldn't have left me then. You can't leave if there's a baby. You have to stay and fulfill your obligations. You would have loved me if we'd had a baby."

"Persephone, I wouldn't love you if you had an entire fleet of babies."

Derrick was tired of trying to read her moods. If she was going to shoot him, he damn well wished she would, and get it over with. She'd always been moody and difficult, but now she vacillated between a sad child and hostile adult.

"I haven't loved you since you gave me that unspeakable disease that you got by all your whoring around. I did call you a whore and a slut and a cheap circus harpy. You've spread your legs for everyone and everything that walks and slithers on the Earth! Why I married you in the first place, I don't know. My friends and family tried to warn me that I was making a mistake, but I didn't listen. You had me fooled. I was an idiot, but I won't make that mistake again."

"You—bastard! How dare you talk to me like that? The mother of your child!"

"He's not yours or mine and you know it. I don't know who was crazy enough to give you a baby, but you can be sure he's going back once they lock you up."

A flicker of movement behind and to her left caught his attention in the dark lobby. More movement to her right. He didn't let on, just kept her attention focused on him.

"When they finally figure out what's wrong with you, I'll get you help. You need help badly, Seph. I'm sorry that what we had together wasn't enough. I really did care about you at first. I'm over that now."

"It's because of her!" Persephone pointed her gun toward the front of the building.

Derrick hadn't realized that Amanda was there, sitting in full view of the door.

"You want her, not me! She's nothing like me! She can't do the things for you that I can."

"You're right about that," Derrick said. "Amanda is nothing like you. She's better than you in every way, smarter, funnier, prettier and better in bed. She is everything you aren't. And she really *is* having my baby!"

"Noooo!" Persephone ran toward the door, her gun cocked and ready.

As she ran past him, Derrick tackled her, bringing her down with a bone crushing lunge. Her gun went off as he wrestled her for it, firing twice before he got it away from her. He clipped her in the temple, knocking her unconscious. Struggling to rise, he realized his right leg didn't feel quite right. An area of white heat, surrounded by numbing cold and chilling pain caused him to collapse.

From the shadows, Jasper and Oakley dashed forward. Jasper cuffed Persephone as he read her rights to her. Oakley took her gun away from Derrick's limp fingers, helping him to a chair in the lobby.

Suddenly, the place was full of people. Police officers swarmed in, securing the facility. An ambulance pulled up and two EMT's hopped out. Nurses from the staff were coming around, holding their heads as they wondered what had happened.

In all the mayhem and chaos, Amanda fought her way through the door. She stopped just inside, her blue eyes searching until she saw Derrick. Fear turned to relief, then to concern as she noticed he was bleeding from a wound to his thigh. Rushing to his side, she dropped to her knees, anxious to help, but not wanting to hurt him. A paramedic was starting an IV as the other bound gauze around his bared thigh. The leg of his jeans had been cut away from the bullet hole in the cloth. The blue denim was covered in blood.

"Is he okay?" She asked the paramedic.

"He'll need surgery," the man replied. "The bullet's still in his leg. Don't worry, miss. We'll take good care of him. We ready, John?"

"Yeah. Stand back a moment, miss."

They lifted the gurney, turning it so they could trundle it out the door. A moment later, another gurney came down the hall with Derrick's mother on it. She still clutched the baby. A woman police officer took him gently from her, cradling him tenderly before putting him in a car seat.

Amanda approached the frail woman, introducing herself as Derrick's new girlfriend. He had spoken to his mother about her, so she already knew her name and how they had met. Mrs. Butler watched the baby being taken out by a woman in a business suit who cooed and talked to him quietly in all the confusion.

"What will happen to him?" Mrs. Butler asked Amanda, taking her hand.

"I'll ask." She approached the female officer, asking her.

"He'll be taken to child services until we can find out where he's supposed to go. Don't worry about him, ma'am," she said to Derrick's mother. "He'll be fine."

"He isn't really my grandson, is he?" She asked Amanda.

"No, ma'am. But you'd make a wonderful grandmother if he was."

"I knew he wasn't." She seemed so disappointed.

They wheeled her to the same ambulance they were using for Derrick and loaded her inside. Amanda wanted to ride with them, but wasn't allowed. Watching them drive off into the lightening sky, she hugged herself, trying not to cry.

"Hey," Jasper said, hugging her from behind. "I'll take you over. He'll be in surgery anyway. He won't even know if you're there or not."

"Thank you, Jasper. Thank you!" She clung to him, weeping piteously.

"I didn't do anything. My man, Derrick did it all. I just cuffed the harpy. What's too bad is she's probably going to get off."

"How?"

"Crazy as a loon. I've had her Baker Acted. She won't get out of that as easily as an arrest. Come on, let's go get breakfast and then I'll take you by to see your Kiwi boyfriend."

Amanda laughed, hugging him around the waist. He held her close, kissing the top of her head.

"Thanks, Jasper. I'd like that."

As they were leaving, Oakley and Duane came over to the car. Jasper opened the windows, grinning.

"Big time, huh? Who knew?"

"Boy, you get me in more trouble. I was supposed to be home hours ago. Your sister is gonna kill me."

"Tell her it's my fault," Jasper grinned. "She can't touch me, I'm an officer of the law."

They drove to Smokey Jo's restaurant, reminded of their first visit there so short a time ago. Jo was there again, reading her paper. She and Paul greeted them, plying them with coffee until their food was ready.

As they ate, Amanda and Jasper recounted everything that had happened over the last few days. When they were finished, Jasper's phone rang.

"Hello?"

"Hello, young man. This is Miss Maisey Hook. Is Amanda with you?"

"Yes, ma'am. How did you get this number?"

"I found her phone in her room and decided to call. Since she didn't come in last night, I thought she might be with you."

"Um, I'm not dating Amanda, that's Derrick."

"Well, he's not answering his phone. Is she there?"

"Yes, Amanda is here, Miss Hook. One moment."

He handed the phone to her, grinning as she stuck out her tongue.

"What a nice sounding young man," Maisey said. "Are you and he dating?"

"No. I'm with Derrick. Jasper is my friend."

"Well, one can't have too many. I used to see three boys at once when I was your age. I was quite the party girl back then. I was a bit worried when you didn't come in last night. Did you and your young man have a good time?" Her voice implied much about the way she thought Amanda had spent her night.

"Yes, but I spent most of the night with Jasper." She put her hand over the phone, giggling. "And part of it in the back seat of a car with a married man."

"My land, Amanda! You'll ruin your reputation! You should know better than to be seen! Why, when I dated a married man, we always met in an out of the way spot and never more than twice a week. We'd have been caught for sure, otherwise."

"You've lived an exciting life, Maisey. I like my peace and quiet."

"Will you be spending the night out again?"

"Possibly. I'll be stopping to get some things so I can freshen up."

"Of course, dear! Well, I'm glad you had fun. You be careful now. Lots of girls get in trouble when they let a man have his way."

"That's very true. Bye now!"

"Bye, dear!"

"She honestly thinks we're fooling around?"

"Why wouldn't she? Based on what she's done, I'm a nun."

After breakfast, they went by Miss Hook's apartment so Amanda could gather her things and take a shower. Miss Hook kept Jasper entertained while Amanda got dressed and dried her hair. Amanda could only imagine the tales the old woman was weaving and hoped Jasper didn't mind. He was laughing heartily when Amanda came out, carrying a few things in an overnight bag.

"You didn't!"

"I did!"

"You're a naughty little girl, Maisey Hook."

"I am indeed, Jasper. Course that's been a long time ago. But I had my fun! Remember now, no telling Amanda. You'll give her ideas!"

"Oh, then I definitely *should* tell her! I like a woman with ideas."

Kissing Maisey's cheek, he helped Amanda with her coat and laughed all the way to the car.

"That old girl was quite a hot little number back in the day. Wow, if she even did half of what she says she did, she could be in the Guinness Book!"

"Don't tell me, you'll give me ideas."

"Baby, if we were going to my place to fool around, instead of the hospital to see your boyfriend, I'd tell you everything. Damn! I'm gonna need a cold shower."

"You need a girlfriend."

Jasper raised an eyebrow. "Don't remind me, okay? I let the best one get away."

"There's someone out there better for you than I am, Jasper. Someone you can tell all those naughty stories to and she'll act them all out with you."

"Yeah." His eyes and voice got dreamy. "I've been looking so long, Mandy. I really thought when we met... I hoped."

"If I'd met you first, I wouldn't even have looked at Derrick."

"Really?"

"Really. You know what my aunt used to say? You find someone when you stop looking. I never believed her. Then Derrick walked up with the pizza when I'd all but given up. So my advice is, stop looking."

They continued their ride in silence. Jasper dropped her at the entrance while he found a place to park. Amanda walked into the lobby and over to the receptionist's desk. A smiling young woman with dark hair and seven different earrings greeted her.

"Hi. I'm looking for Derrick Butler and his mother. They were brought in from the nursing home about an hour ago?" Amanda asked.

The young woman tapped the computer keyboard, squinting at the screen. Popping it on the side a couple times, she waited for something to appear.

"I'm so sorry. This has been buggy for weeks. I need a new cord. Try to get anyone who can actually do that, though. Ah, here we are." She tapped in a few more commands. "Derrick is in recovery and his mother is in room 412 - A. Do you need directions?"

"Yes. I don't know my way around here at all. It's been years since I was here."

"Not a problem. That's what I do." She handed Amanda a map, picking up a highlighter. She drew the route on the map in pink as she told her where to go. "Got all that?"

"You about need a GPS to get around here, don't you?" Jasper walked up about that time, panting slightly. "I had to park way the hell out in BFE and there's no golf cart out there. I had to hike!"

"Big stud like you can't handle the walk?" The girl grinned up at him, not quite batting her eyelashes.

"Daria?"

"Hi, Jasper. Long time, no see."

"Yeah, since high school. Damn, I suddenly feel really old. How you been?"

She wrinkled her nose. "Lots of duds who used to be studs. You know how it goes."

"Yeah. You look—incredible. I like the hair. You look really, really great."

"Thanks. So, you and your girlfriend are here to see this Derrick guy?"

Jasper laughed. "No, my *friend* Amanda and I are here to see *her* boyfriend, Derrick. He got shot."

"Oh, bummer! Was it bad?"

"Not terrible. Of course, getting shot at all sucks. But it hit him in the thigh. He'll be okay."

"That's good. Do you know the way for sure?" She glanced at Amanda, but her eyes went right back to Jasper.

"Yeah. I'm good. Listen, Jasper. I'm gonna go see Mrs. Butler. Daria, can someone call me when I can see Derrick?"

"Oh, for sure, hon. See that poor woman in the little glass cube over there? She has pagers. They can give you a pager and call you when he's awake."

"Thanks."

"I'll bring up some coffee in a few, okay?" Jasper hugged her, kissing her cheek.

"Take your time," she whispered. "I'm fine." She hugged him, kissing his cheek as well.

"Nice meeting you, Daria. You and Jasper should come over for dinner sometime. Derrick has a great view of the river."

"Thanks," the other woman said with a smile. "I'd like that."

Amanda followed the directions given to her by Daria and found Mrs. Butler's room easily. Tapping on the door, she went inside.

"Hello, dear." Mrs. Butler smiled up at Amanda.

Amanda was struck by how much her son looked like her. They even had the same eyes. It was hard to believe she was only 55, she looked so much older.

"Have you seen him or heard anything yet?"

"No, but I've got a pager. When he wakes up, they'll call me."

"They won't let me go down, I already asked."

"You have to keep up your strength. Derrick wouldn't want you to overdo."

"My children have always been so protective. I've always been frail. They think I don't know I'm dying. How could I not? When my body fails me at every turn?"

Amanda took Mrs. Butler's hand gently in hers. "I hope you're not planning on dying anytime soon." She smiled, trying not to cry. "Because I want you at our wedding. And when we give you a real grandchild, I want to see your face when you hold him for the first time."

"I can't promise, darling. I'll do my best."

"And forget the rest," Amanda intoned, quoting something from the P90X video.

Mrs. Butler smiled weakly, her eyes drifting shut.

"I'll come by later," Amanda said, kissing her cheek.

Moments after she left Mrs. Butler's room, the beeper went off. She found a passing orderly who led her to the post op floor. Dropping her by the nurse's station, he smiled and saluted as he left.

Derrick was pale and sweaty when she got down to his cubicle. The TV was on, but he wasn't watching it. He was surrounded by machinery all of it giving readouts that Amanda didn't understand. She sat next to the bed, taking his hand. His eyes fluttered open and he smiled.

"Hey, love," his accent drew the words out longingly. "How's Mum?"

"She's doing well. She's tired, bruised up, but fine."

"The baby?"

"He'll be okay. They're taking care of him."

"How are you?"

"Better than you, I don't have a hole in my leg."

"Me neither, they sewed it all up. Hop up." He patted the bed. "I can't see you properly that far away."

She sat carefully next to his left leg, not wanting to bump the right. Holding his hand, she felt the tears welling in her eyes. Derrick plucked them from her cheeks with his thumb and forefinger, kissing his knuckle.

"First tears you've shed for me." He grinned weakly. "I hope I never give you reason to shed more."

"Never on purpose." She smiled, her lip trembling. "I'm sorry. I thought I had it under control."

"It was a long night, love. It's no wonder you're tired. You should go back to my place and have a nap."

"I might just do that. Good news, I think Jasper found a lady friend." She proceeded to tell him about meeting Daria.

"Cool. The guy needs to get laid worse than me."

Amanda laughed, kissing his hand. He tugged her to him, kissing her lips instead as the door banged open.

"You two at it again?" Jasper asked as he set down a beverage holder full of coffee.

"You'd think one of you wasn't in the hospital the way you go at it."

"Doctor says I have to be a good boy until the stitches come out. Then all bets are off."

He accepted the coffee with an exclamation of delight. "Did they say I could have this?"

"You're post op, not dead. They didn't say you couldn't. If it kills you, I'll apologize like hell, okay?"

The three of them laughed so loudly the nurse came down to shush them. She gave Jasper the evil eye for bringing in coffee, but didn't take it away.

"You're supposed to spend the night," Jasper told him. "I asked the nurse when I came in. You can go home tomorrow if the doc likes your progress."

"Sucks they cut up my jeans. Did you see how they butchered them?" Derrick sighed. "They were so comfortable, faded just right."

"They were nice," Amanda agreed. "They fit your ass like a glove. You have a great ass, by the way. Mm!" She winked and her eyes glittered over her coffee cup.

"Not what I really wanted to hear," Jasper frowned.

"Why not? Would you feel better if I told you that you've got a great ass too?"

"Why are you looking at another man's ass, Miss Bitterson?" Derrick was mildly annoyed, but not as angry as he was pretending.

"Because I like to look, Mr. Butler. Men as gorgeous as you two, and you don't expect me to take a peek? If you were the only guy with two girls, wouldn't you be looking?"

Derrick and Jasper glanced at one another, straight faced.

"I'd be all over that action," Derrick told Jasper.

"Oh, hell yeah!" Jasper licked his lips.

The surgeon came by to check on Derrick and shortly after that, he was taken to a room. Amanda went with him, Jasper trailing behind. When he saw where they were going, he popped back downstairs to flirt more with Daria.

"What ever will I do with you?" Amanda asked Derrick when they were alone.

"Not enough, I'm afraid. Got this bum leg, you know."

"True, but that hasn't crippled your lips, has it?"

Derrick pulled a strange face, looking as ridiculous as possible. "It's quite possible," he replied, sounding like a bad Quasimodo impersonation.

Her lips on his stopped the antics, making his heart feel like it was trying to stop. A nurse came in a moment later, clucking her tongue.

"I wondered what made your heart monitor go all wonky." She sounded annoyed, but her eyes were twinkling. "Big surprise!"

"You're Australian!" Derrick laughed as the tiny woman wrote down his vital signs, fluffed his pillows and pulled up his sheets.

"That I am. Queensland."

"New South Wales, here."

"Good to hear another civilized accent. This your wife?"

"Not yet. She's incarcerated at the moment for trying to kill me."

"Oi, a gorgeous hunk like you? What's up with that?"

"Bonkers, totally."

"She'd have to be! Here's the thing, love, I'm not really supposed to let you stay the night if you're not family."

"She's my fiancée. Doesn't that count for something?"

"You're engaged and still married? Aren't you the fast worker?"

"Thought I was divorced. Six months ago, I signed, she didn't. So, honest mistake!"

"Well, all right. No fooling around on my floor, you hear?"

"Believe me, you've got me so pumped full of drugs, I don't think I'd be able to. What's your name, by the way?"

"Vicki."

"Lovely. Short for Victoria?"

"The same. And you are?" She glanced pointedly at Amanda.

"Amanda. Thanks for letting me stay, Vicki. I promise he'll behave."

"Only 'til the stitches come out."

"Is he always this frisky?" Vicki asked with a grin.

"Always. He can behave if he has to. He's very grumpy afterwards, though."

Chuckling, Vicki went out to check on her other patients. Moments later, Jasper showed up. His eyes glittered happily. He was fairly bursting with excitement.

"I just got the best phone call in the world!"

They looked at him blankly.

"Okay, you forced it out of me. I heard from your lawyer pal, Sam."

"Why'd he call you and not me?"

"That I don't know. Something about your phone being off. He found out some stuff you might like to know."

They sat forward, listening expectantly.

"First of all, you'll be glad to know you're not a father. Persephone, as you know, has not been pregnant. Her mum swore out a document to the effect that she couldn't conceive or carry a child past three months due to an injury as a child. We're still looking for the real parents of the little guy, but we'll track them down."

This announcement was met by whoops of delight.

"I'm not done. Keep it down. You'll like this even better. It seems, my good friend, Derrick, you're not a married man after all!"

"What? What do you mean?"

"Well, Persephone failed to tell you that when she was vacationing in Mexico six years ago, she got married. They consummated their love, loudly and rather publicly, spent two weeks together and went their separate ways without benefit of the divorce. The husband, when asked, said he didn't remember getting married at all and didn't know the license had even been filed. Apparently they did that while drunk as well. So, as far as the State of Florida and the Territory of Victoria are concerned, you're no longer, nor have you ever been, married. *Mazal tov*!"

"You're serious? That entire thing with Persephone, it never existed?"

"Not a lick. She's got no hold on you legally or financially, my friend. You are free and clear!"

"That's fantastic! Jasper, I want you to be best man when I marry this girl."

"Just let me know where and when. I'll even dig out my tux. Now, I must go. I've promised to take the lovely and unusually frisky Daria out for dinner, drinks and do-tell! I'm hoping for a lot of doin' and not so much tellin', don't ya know."

"I'm happy for you, Jasper. She seems really nice," Amanda said with a smile.

"We dated some in school. Broke up over some stupid misunderstanding. We thought maybe we'd see if the magic was real or a figment of our imaginations. Whatever the case, it'll be fun figuring it out." He shook Derrick's hand, happily clapping him on the back. "Mandy, see me out?"

"Sure." She walked him to the elevator.

"She's not you," he said quietly as they waited for the elevator to arrive. "But she's pretty cool in her own right."

"Who knows, maybe she'll turn out to be better for you than I'd ever be."

"Maybe. I've got to do something before I go. I promise, this is the last time."

Leaning over, he kissed her long, slow and deep, pouring his heart and soul into it. The elevator dinged, the door opening beside them. Amanda's head was spinning. She had to lean against the wall for support.

"That's what you're missing," he said with a sly wink and a grin. "If Derrick can do it better, then you picked the right man. See you later, Mandy."

"See you," she mumbled, not sure her mouth or her legs would ever work right again.

Vicki, who had seen the whole exchange, came over to check on her. "You okay?"

"Yeah, mostly."

"I thought you were with Derrick?"

"I am."

"Then what was all that?"

"That—was Jasper." She had no other explanation for it and Vicki didn't press.

Derrick smiled as she walked in the door, holding out his hands to her. She took them happily, sitting on the bed.

"What did Jasper want?"

"Just to say bye. He'll see us later this week, maybe tomorrow if he gets the chance."

"That was all?"

She didn't want to meet his gaze, afraid he'd see what had happened, reading it in her eyes.

"Yeah. That's all."

Leaning toward him, she pressed her lips against his, kissing him deeply. Her heart fluttered, her arms and legs felt weak and she was glad that Derrick's kiss made her even more wobbly and addle brained then Jasper's.

* * *

Derrick went home the next day as promised. Amanda planned to stay with him. Once he was home, she left for a little while and came back with something in carrier. The something mewed, asking to be let out.

When she opened the door, Muse came out. He looked hopelessly thin in his shaven state, but rubbed against Derrick as happily as ever. Amanda looked inside the carrier.

"Where's your friend?" She asked Muse.

The cat, as if he understood her, went to his carrier, nosing at the door, mewing softly. An answering mew came from inside the carrier.

"He made a friend at the vet's. They were both traumatized and the little one latched onto Muse. He protected her, wasn't that sweet?"

She reached into the carrier, gently pulling out a small, scrawny white cat with blue eyes.

"She's beautiful, Amanda. What did you name her?"

"Aphrodite. I couldn't resist."

Muse hopped into Derrick's lap as he lounged on the couch with Amanda snuggled next to him. Aphrodite leaped prettily into her lap, turned three times and settled into a comfortable mound of white fur.

"Hm, I guess they've marked their territory, eh?" Derrick said with a grin. "Your cat adores me."

"And he hates me. I got Aphrodite for you."

"Well, she likes you more. That's it, love, you'll have to move in with me."

"Do you mean that?" She gazed deeply into his eyes to see if he was kidding.

"Of course, you'll have to marry me, me being a single guy and all."

"I'd like that. Of course I'd like to get to know you better first. You might decide you don't even like me."

"There's not a chance of that. You don't have to answer right away, Amanda. But do me a favor, don't leave me hanging too long."

"I wouldn't want to do that," she whispered. "So I suppose I'll have to tell you *yes* so you'll kiss me."

"That would work."

"Yes," she said with her lips half on his. "Yes."

THE END

Dellani Oakes is a former A.P. English teacher and photo journalist. Now working as a substitute teacher and Mary Kay consultant, she can give skin care & makeup advice, correct grammar, take pictures and write an article while controlling a classroom full of rowdy third graders.

Dellani was making up stories before she could read. Her first really cohesive work began when her older sister started school. Left to entertain herself, she invented an imaginary friend and would regale her mother with tales of Snowy Green and Rainbow School. These stories paved the way for songs and poems in elementary school and short stories in high school and college.

A college theatre major, Dellani took play writing. It became her new love. Scripts being dialog heavy and character driven, this aspect has followed her into her novel writing. She uses verbal exchanges & sparring as a way of revealing both plot and characterization.

Dellani had to set aside her love of writing when she began working as a teacher. Her creative energies were channeled into writing exams to make her students cry—although this wasn't usually intentional. Unfortunately, between that and motherhood, she didn't have time to write.

However, once her youngest son started school in 2001, she was able to write full time. Her first published novel, "Indian Summer", was published in 2008 by Second Wind Publishing. Also from Second Wind, her second novel, "Lone Wolf" makes its debut soon. "Lone Wolf" is the first in her science-fiction series.

When asked recently how she thought of all those stories, she replied: "There are more ideas in my head than I can get written down. I'll have to live forever."

Dellani wrote: "Every second Monday at 4:00 PM Eastern, I host Dellani's Tea Time. I talk to authors & illustrators of children's and young adult's books. On every fourth Wednesday at 1:00 PM Eastern, I host What's Write for Me. On this show, I talk to authors who write for adults. I think it's safe to say that we take ourselves VERY seriously and we aren't allowed to laugh at all. Never ever, ever! She is the author of *Lone Wolf and Indian Summer* and *Ninja Tattoo*. Find her at http://dellanioakes.wordpress.com/ and writersanctuary.blogspot.com

CONTRIBUTORS

Ann Stanmore, author

I retired in 2007, having stayed on at work an extra couple of years. I had an interesting and busy job and now have an interesting and busy retirement. I have several interests which are noted in the Hobbies section. Writing being my main interest at the moment. I am working on a sequel to this first book. I have been asked to write about my working life and not being one to refuse people…

Christoph Fischer, author

Christoph Fischer was born in Germany in 1970 but moved on to the UK in the early 1990s where he is still resident today. *The Luck of The Weissensteiners* is his first published work and concerns a Jewish Family in Slovakia during the 1930s and 1940s. *Sebastian* his second book about a young handicapped man in Vienna in the 1910s was published in May 2013. He has written several other novels which are in the later stages of editing and finalization. Both of his book have received critical acclaim and have entered the indie tribe fiction charts and the Amazon charts for Jewish Fiction.

He is currently on of the Top 1% of reviewers on Goodreads and #1727 reviewer on Amazon.

His recommendations and reviews can be found at http://writerchristophfischer.wordpress.com/ and http://www.christophfischerbooks.com

David Workman, author

David Workman's debut novel, *Absolute Authority,* hit the shelves in early 2012 to roaring acclaim. A native St. Louisan, he was recently named by local television station KMOV as one of St. Louis' Top 5 New Authors. Along with writing novels, David has spent most of his 20-year writing career hammering out advertising and marketing copy for companies large and small, including his current gig as the lead contest specialist for a major athletic shoe company. His second novel, a sequel, is scheduled for a winter 2013 release. Find him on Facebook.

Dellani Oakes, author

Dellani Oakes is a former A.P. English teacher and photo journalist. Now working as a substitute teacher and Mary Kay consultant, she can give skin care & makeup advice, correct grammar, take pictures and write an article while controlling a classroom full of rowdy third graders.

Dellani is the author of *Lone Wolf and Indian Summer* and *Ninja Tattoo.* Find her at http://dellanioakes.wordpress.com/ and writersanctuary.blogspot.com

Diane Dennis, Publicist:

Diane Dennis is President of Inspired Media Communications a multi-media PR agency providing services to authors, speakers, organizations and small businesses. Diane has an extensive media list for pitching clients and has worked with best selling authors and self published authors. Inspired Media also provides social media campaigns, web development and upgrades, collateral materials, and branding. Diane has a background in TV production, Radio production and hosting, and writing for columns, feature articles and is the author of The

Hourglass: How to Live as Time Flies By. Visit her website at http://www.inspiredmc.com

Fran Lewis, Author, reviewer, educator, talk show host, creator of M.J. Magazine

Fran Lewis: Fran worked in the NYC Public Schools as the Reading and Writing Staff Developer for over 36 years. She has three masters Degrees and a PD in Supervision and Administration. Currently, she is a member of Who's Who of America's Teachers and Who's Who of America's Executives from Cambridge. In addition, she is the author of three children's books and a fourth that has just been published on Alzheimer's disease in order to honor her mom and help create more awareness for a cure. The title of my new Alzheimer's book is Memories are Precious: Alzheimer's Journey; Ruth's story and Sharp as a Tack and Scrambled Eggs Which Describes Your Brain? Fran is also the author of Faces Behind the Stones, Bad Choices and M.J. Magazine an E-Magazine dedicated to the memory of her sister Marcia Joyce. She is also a member of Continental's Who's Who of America's Executives and Professionals and the author of 11 titles. She is presently working on creating a second radio show called Chat Time with Fran Lewis on Blog Talk Radio the Red River Network and adding more outstanding shows on the World of Ink Network. Her show Book Discussion is heard all over the world and she has many listeners.

She was the musical director for shows in her school and ran the school's newspaper. Fran writes reviews for authors upon request and for several other sites. You can read some of my reviews on Ezine.comand on ijustfinished.com under the name Gabina. Here is the link to her radio show www.blogtalkradio.com

Karen Vaughan, author

Karen H. Vaugan is a first-time author who enjoys reading and writing. She is a part of Class 1983 at Applewood Heights Secondary School in Mississauga, ON. She is married with one daughter, and four stepchildren. She has two cats at home. She has a warped sense of humor and sees the lighter side of things.

She is the co-author of Dead on Arrival (Julie Faulkner), Daytona Dead, Over Her Dead Body and Dead Comic Standing. Books may be purchased from her website at www.KarenVaughan.info

Kenneth Weene, author

Life itches and torments Kenneth Weene like pesky flies. Annoyed, he picks up a pile of paper to slap at the buzzing and often whacks himself on the head. Each whack is another story. At least having half-blinded himself, he has learned to not wave the pencil about. Ken will, however, write on until the last gray cell has retreated and there are no longer these strange ideas demanding his feeble efforts. So many poems, stories, novels; and more to come.

Learn more about Ken at http://www.kennethweene.com and find Ken's novels in print, e-format, and audio.

Mark Rubenstein

Mark Rubinstein was born in Brooklyn, New York. He dreamed of playing baseball for the Brooklyn Dodgers since his all-time hero was the Dodgers' first baseman Gil Hodges. Rubinstein played high school baseball and ran track. His love of sports led him to read sports fiction, and soon he became a voracious reader, developing an enduring love for all kinds of novels.

He graduated from New York University with a degree in business administration. He then served in the army and ended up as a field medic tending to paratroopers of the 82nd Airborne Division. He was so taken with these experiences that after his discharge, he re-entered NYU as a premed student.

He entered medical school at the State University of New York's Downstate Medical Center. As a medical student, he developed an interest in psychiatry, discovering in that specialty the same thing he realized in reading fiction: every patient has a compelling story to tell. He became a board-certified psychiatrist practicing in New York City.

In addition to running his private practice he developed an interest in forensic psychiatry because the drama and conflict of the cases and courtrooms tapped into his personality style.

He also taught psychiatric residents, interns, psychologists, and social workers at New York Presbyterian Hospital and became a clinical assistant professor at Cornell University's medical school.

Before turning to fiction, Rubinstein coauthored five medical self-help books: *The First Encounter: The Beginnings in Psychotherapy* (Jason Aronson); *The Complete Book of Cosmetic Facial Surgery* (Simon and Schuster); *New Choices: the Latest Options in Treating Breast Cancer* (Dodd Mead); *Heartplan: A Complete Program for Total Fitness of Heart & Mind* (McGraw-Hill), and *The Growing Years: A Guide to Your Child's Emotional Development from Birth to Adolescence* (Atheneum).

Rubinstein lives in Connecticut with his wife and as many dogs as she will allow in the house. He still practices psychiatry and is busily writing more novels. *Mad Dog House*, his first novel, was named a Finalist for the 2012 *ForeWord Reviews* Book of the Year Award (Thriller & Suspense).

Marsha Cook, author

Marsha Casper Cook is the author of eight published books and 11 feature-length screenplays. Her screenplays have been optioned several times and she continues writing screenplays that are multi generation with heart.

Her published works include *Secrets*, a romantic novel about a family in crisis, and *To Life*, a non-fiction biography about being a teenager and surviving the Holocaust. She has also written four books for young children, *Snack Attack, The Magical Leaping Lizard Potion* and the poetry collection *The Busy Bus*. Her brand new book *No Clues No Shoes* is the first of the Emelina Hewitt and her dog Stanley series. She has also published a book version of her romantic-comedy screenplay, *It's Never Too Late*. Her latest work is a sexy contemporary romance series *It's Never Enough* featuring Virginia Templeton, a character from one of her screenplays.

Wanting to help new writers reach their goals, Marsha founded the literary agency Marcus Bryan & Associates INC. in 1996, and achieved signatory status from the Writers Guild Of America (WGA) within two years.

Since early 2010, Marsha has hosted radio shows on Blog Talk Radio as a Red River Writer host and for the last two years she has joined with Host V.S, Grenier as the other half of World Of Ink Network. Her show "*A Good Story Is A Good Story*" is about writing and her other show "*Sizzlin' Hot Romance*" features Romance Authors, Publishers, Bloggers and Reviewers.

Marsha is also the CEO of Michigan Avenue Media Inc. where her team launches books and businesses combining radio interviews and unique social marketing techniques.

Find out more about Marsha:
www.marshacaspercook.com,
Author Services
www.michiganavenuemedia.com
Literary Agency
www.marcusbryan.com,
Radio Shows
www.worldofinknetwork.com
Electronic Distributor
www.marcusmaxwellinc.com

R.J. Ellory, Best selling author

R.J. Ellory is the author of *Three Days in Chicagoland,* which focuses on the brutal murder of a young girl in Chicago in 1956, as told from three different viewpoints: The Sister, The Cop and The Killer. His other books are *Candlemoth, Ghostheart, A Quiet Vendetta, City of Lies, A Quiet Belief in Angels, A Simple Act of Violence, The Anniversary Man, Saints of New York, Bad Signs, A Dark and Broken Heart, The Devil and the River.* Visit his website: www.RJEllory.com

Susan Ross, Children's Book Reviewer

Susan is a former school secretary who worked over twenty years in the New York City Public School System. She is an avid reader and enjoys reading to her three grandchildren. Her main goal is to encourage young children to read many different types of books. Susan's reviews will hopefully encourage parents and young children to read more and choose some of the books that she spotlighted as her best picks in this issue.

Check back at your favorite e-retailer for new editions every other month!

I hope you enjoy reading, and we encourage comments and contributors.

- To be considered for a position as one of MJ Magazine's book reviewers, please contact Fran at riffyone@optonline.net and use **I'd like to be an MJ Magazine book reviewer** as your subject line.
- If you would like to contribute an article, please send the article, a photograph of yourself in .jpg format and a short bio using the subject line **Article for MJ Magazine** to Fran at riffyone@optonline.net (sending a submission does not guarantee it will be run).
- If you would like to have your book reviewed by *MJ Magazine*, please contact Fran (riffyone@optonline.net) for information about eligibility, requirements and mailing information using the subject line **MJ Magazine Book Review Information.**
- Tell us what you think about our first issue, what you'd like to see in subsequent issues, etc. by emailing riffyone@optonline.net with the subject line **Comments for MJ Magazine.**

Until next time …

www.ingramcontent.com/pod-product-compliance
Lightning Source LLC
Chambersburg PA
CBHW082101090726
47910CB00008B/2557
* 9 7 8 1 6 0 4 1 4 7 6 2 9 *